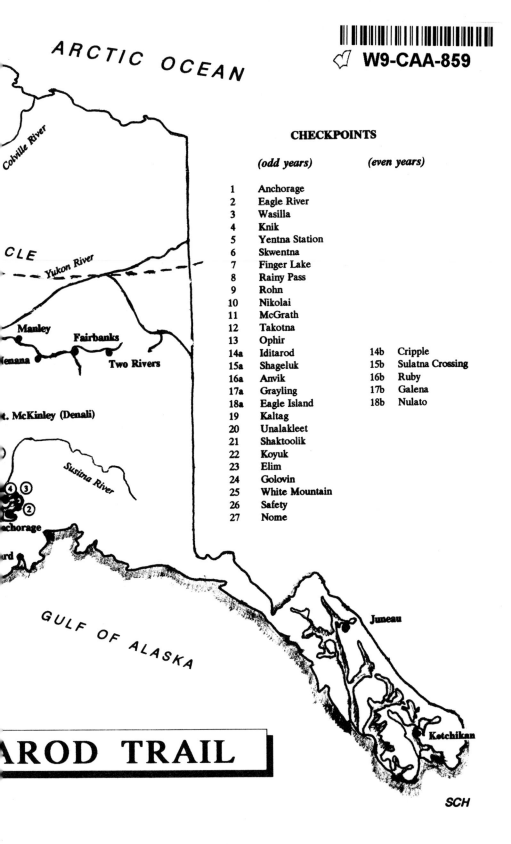

ARCTIC OCEAN

W9-CAA-859

Colville River

CLE

Yukon River

Manley   Fairbanks

Nenana   Two Rivers

Mt. McKinley (Denali)

Susitna River

④ ③
②
Anchorage
Seward

GULF OF ALASKA

Juneau

Ketchikan

AROD TRAIL

SCH

CHECKPOINTS

	(odd years)		(even years)
1	Anchorage		
2	Eagle River		
3	Wasilla		
4	Knik		
5	Yentna Station		
6	Skwentna		
7	Finger Lake		
8	Rainy Pass		
9	Rohn		
10	Nikolai		
11	McGrath		
12	Takotna		
13	Ophir		
14a	Iditarod	14b	Cripple
15a	Shageluk	15b	Sulatna Crossing
16a	Anvik	16b	Ruby
17a	Grayling	17b	Galena
18a	Eagle Island	18b	Nulato
19	Kaltag		
20	Unalakleet		
21	Shaktoolik		
22	Koyuk		
23	Elim		
24	Golovin		
25	White Mountain		
26	Safety		
27	Nome		

Feb. 12, 2018

For Ann Papworth,

Andrew asked me to send this to you. Apparently, it came up in conversation and you expressed interest. So here you are!

I guess we haven't seen you since the 2006 trip we made out West when you graciously hosted your cousin Steve (my beloved husband!), me, James (our older son), and Andrew (your partner in lunches with cousin Isabel Harvey). ↑ And our German Shepherd Sasha Amaroq!

If your schedule permits, you could visit with Hood brothers Jim, my Steve, and David, as well as Andrew, when they are in Logan this spring (May 15) to see John + Nadine. Or you could meet them at Grand Tetons or Yellowstone.

Wishing you many memorable adventures wherever your trails may take you! Dare to Dream!!!

Love, Mary H. Hood

A Fan's Guide

to the

IDITAROD

A Wish for All Iditarod Mushers

To paraphrase sprint musher, dog breeder, and author Jim Welch,
who is now confronting the effects of multiple sclerosis:

May you have enough money in the bank so you don't have to worry about
finances, a lifelong partner so you don't have to keep starting over,
a life work that keeps growing in fulfillment,
and a trail that you can travel forever.

A Fan's Guide
to the
IDITAROD

Mary H. Hood

Alpine
Blue Ribbon Books
Loveland, Colorado

Library of Congress Cataloging-in-Publication Data

Hood, Mary H., 1958-
    A fan's guide to the Iditarod / by Mary H. Hood.
        p.   cm.
    Includes bibliographical references and index.
    ISBN 0-931866-85-5
    1. Iditarod Trail Sled Dog Race, Alaska. 2. Sled dog racing —
    Alaska.   I. Title.
    SF440.15.H66   1996
798'.8—dc20   95-53767
                                                                              CIP

Cover and Interior Design:
    Dianne J. Borneman, Shadow Canyon Graphics, Evergreen, Colorado

Front Cover Photo: *A dog team and musher traverse spectacular Rainy Pass during the 1995 Iditarod. © Jeff Schultz/Alaska Stock Images*

Back Cover Photo: *Iditarod competitor John Patten crests a hill during a training run in Minnesota. © Mary H. Hood*

Frontispiece: *Sled dogs love to find out what's around the next corner. © Mary H. Hood*

Page 81: *Reprinted with the permission of Simon & Schuster Books for Young Readers, an imprint of Simon & Schuster Children's Publishing Division from DOGSONG by Gary Paulsen. Copyright © 1985 Gary Paulsen*

All photos © Mary H. Hood unless otherwise credited

Printed in the United States of America
First Edition
1 2 3 4 5 6 7 8 9

Contents

Acknowledgments

R uth Anne Hood (Momma) accompanied me to Alaska twice. A first-rate research and photographic assistant, she won over many people with her considerable charm. At home, she has been invaluable as the "nit sieve" and "fat police," editing countless versions of the manuscript and proofs. Her penchant for historical detail and sensitive understanding of all aspects of dog mushing have incalculably enriched this book. No one could be a better friend, traveling companion, or editor . . . thanks, Momma.

John Patten, musher and owner of Sawtooth Mountain Sled Works, encouraged me when I first began this project and has provided many important insights. He has also critiqued my manuscript on several occasions, demonstrated equipment, taken me cart training, and made possible the most exhilarating day of dog sledding imaginable.

My parents, David and Esther Hyde, helped care for my sons each time I traveled to Alaska, loaned me their brand-new Nikon N90, and taught me how to turn dreams into reality.

Kathy Niebauer, friend extraordinaire, became a second mother to my sons during the months that I was completing this considerable undertaking. In addition to enabling me to finish on time, she also offered many helpful comments on the text. Thanks to the whole Niebauer clan for their support.

Jeff King, Martin Buser, and DeeDee Jonrowe graciously permitted visits to their dog lots, answered extensive questions, and were extremely cooperative about being photographed. Each musher also reviewed portions of the text for accuracy. (Any errors are the author's.)

Karin Schmidt, DVM, has provided valuable input and been a pleasure to work with.

Profuse thanks to the dozens of mushers who have allowed me to interview them.

I am indebted to each of the sources listed in the bibliography, but especially to the *Iditarod Runner*, the *Anchorage Daily News*, KTUU's Iditarod videos, *Alaska, Mushing, Team & Trail*, and books by Tim Jones, Libby Riddles, Lew Freedman, Gary Paulsen, Nöel Flanders, Jim Welch, and Kenneth Ungermann.

Without the amazing interlibrary-loan service of Hennepin County, Minnesota, I would never have been able to read many of these books. The Columbus Metropolitan Library was also instrumental in assisting my research.

Thanks to Nancy Dressler, Nikon's Midwest tech rep, for her encouragement and advice, and for the loan of cold-weather equipment. Nikon Corporation's 8008 and N90 camera bodies, precision lenses, and SB-25 flash are awe-inspiring technical achievements and a joy to use.

The 1993 race personnel, volunteers, mushers, fans, and local residents extended exceptional friendliness, openness, humility, and assistance to a couple of nosy researchers from "Outside."

Rich Owens, long-time Iditarod volunteer, has introduced me to many wonderful people and been a reliable source for aid and advice.

Thanks to Betty Jo McKinney and Alpine Publications for bringing this book to fruition. Dianne Borneman, of Shadow Canyon Graphics, a discerning editor, also welcomed our input in the editing and layout process, and was instrumental in producing a high-quality final product.

Above all, I am indebted to my husband Steve for his patience, unfailing assistance, expertise, and belief in me. I am also grateful for his typing, computer wizardry, proofreading and editing, computation of race statistics, and creation of all charts, maps, and the index. Without his financial commitment and many hours of caring for our sons, this book could not have been written.

Others who have provided help in many forms are listed here alphabetically: Dr. Gerald Abelsen, DVM; Barratt Best Western, Anchorage; L. L. Bean; Tom Busch, KNOM radio; Joe Cocquyt, Eagle

Pack; Howard Farley; Donna Hawley, ISDRA; Peter Henning; James W. Hood; Alan D. Hyde; Sylvia Hyde Koester; Mike Mathers; Cindy Molburg, *Team & Trail*; David Morris and Dick Westlund, GCI (General Communications, Inc.); Nicki J. Nielsen; Dr. Mary Petersen, DVM; Photography Unlimited, Bellefontaine; Sam Posey; Joanne Potts, ITC; Rae's Harness Shop, Anchorage; Leo Rasmussen; Vi Redington; REI; Marsha Savery, Eddie Bauer; Jeff Schultz; Slide Service, Inc., Columbus; Sally Sonnendecker, Iams; Steger Mukluks; Norm Tibbets, PenAir; Tim White; Wiggy's; Wintergreen Designs; Roxy Wright-Champaine.

Kudos to you all!

"IDITAROD TRAIL"
© Hobo Jim Music/Words and Music by Jim Varsos

Well, way up in Alaska, the state that stands alone,
There's a dog race run from Anchorage into Nome.
And it's a grueling race with a lightning pace
Where the chilly winds do wail,
Beneath the northern lights across the snow and the ice
And it's called the Iditarod Trail.

CHORUS

Well, give me a team and a good lead dog
And a sled that's built so fine,
And let me race those miles to Nome
One thousand forty-nine;
Then when I get back to my home,
Hey, I can tell my tale:
I did I did I did the Iditarod Trail.

Well, the race it won't be easy for the masters of the trail
And some of them will make it and some of them will fail;
But just to run that race takes a tough and hardy breed
And a lot of work done by the dogs that run
Across snow with a whistling speed.

Well, I just pulled out of Safety, I'm on the trail and all alone;
I'm doin' fine and a-pickin' up time and runnin' on into Nome.
There are no sled tracks in front of me and no one on my tail,
I did I did I did the Iditarod Trail.

Dedicated To:

Stephen Carpenter Hood
my beloved and my friend

James Malcolm Hood
my sweet son and research assistant

Andrew Stephen Hood
my undercover Iditarod traveling companion

Sheena Amaroq
everything that a German Shepherd should be

and
to

All of the sled dogs throughout history
who have embodied
endurance - fidelity - intelligence

Founded in part to honor Native serum drivers and to help revive dog mushing in the villages, the Iditarod is celebrated with style in Native settlements along the race route.

Foreword

I met Mary Hood under the big stuffed moosehead in the lobby of the Regal Alaskan Hotel in Anchorage. She told me she was writing a guide to the Iditarod and that she planned to be at several of the checkpoints along the way. The Regal was headquarters for the race in the years I covered it for ABC TV's *Wide World of Sports*, and standing with my back to one of the Regal's blazing fires, I had chatted with many people who said they intended to follow the race and that they would see me along the trail. It was rare that I ever laid eyes on them again. Although the basic facts about the Iditarod are known to millions around the world, the race itself is a lot tougher to follow than most realize, and outside of the competitors themselves, only a handful of people ever see much of the trail.

Mary, however, kept turning up. She was in McGrath at the checkpoint on the Kuskokwim River, enduring a long, moonless night and the -50 degrees of a "severe clear," straining with the rest of us to see the first faint bobbing flicker of an approaching musher's headlamp. She was in Unalakleet, the largest of the Native communities along the trail, jammed into the smoke-filled dining room of Mary Brown's Lodge, swapping rumors with other die-hards lined up for burgers and coffee at the counter. And finally, she was in Nome on Front Street at the burled arch at the finish line, hearing the wail of the distant siren that tells you a musher has reached the outskirts of town.

Mary—who I later found out was four months pregnant—was accompanied by her mother-in-law, Ruth Anne Hood. These two ladies, eager, full of polite questions and nearly invisible beneath the heavy, enveloping layers of their clothes, seemed to have stepped right out of the 19th century, when women were just beginning to leave home to travel the world on grand adventures. And indeed Mary has approached this book with the intensity and thorough diligence of someone recording uncharted territory. "I want to know everything," she told me.

The heft and breadth of this book is proof that Mary found out a great deal. In fact, calling it an Iditarod fan's "guide" is too modest by far because this is truly an all-inclusive, encyclopedic work that will be of value for an audience ranging from those with only a casual interest in the race right up to someone who plans to compete. I can even imagine a rookie lashing a copy to his or her sled!

To me, the book is evidence that the Iditarod is reaching a new level of maturity. When I first went up to Alaska to cover the race in the late 1980s, it was already world famous, an event of mythic proportion—but little hard-core information was available. Most of the people who really knew what was going on were in the race, and once I realized how much strain the dog care and sleeplessness placed on the competitors, it seemed almost immoral to bother them with questions. Mary's book will lead to a much better understanding of the event and provide a factual framework for the authentic heroism which is at the heart of the Iditarod's enduring appeal.

Sam Posey
Sharon, Connecticut
November, 1995

---

* Editor's note: Sam Posey won an Emmy for his coverage of the 1989-1990 Trans-Antarctica [Sled-Dog] Expedition.

Introduction

As a kid growing up in the hills of Northern California, I dreamed of the day I would go to Alaska accompanied by my cherished childhood companion "Sambo," a wonderful and enthusiastic Terrier mix who only left my side as I got on the bus to go to school each morning. By the time I was finally ready to head North, "Sambo" had grown very old and stayed behind.

Now, more than 20 years since coming into this country, I well remember being hunched over a crackling radio as I listened to the live finish of one of the first Iditarod races from the warmth of my small cabin nestled deep in the Alaskan wilderness with a small puppy curled in my lap. With a fledgling team of Huskies outside, Hickory and I decided right then that this was a trip we had to take.

Many tens of thousands of miles have run under our sled runners since then and I realized long ago that Iditarod is more than an event, it is a lifestyle. Bathed in rich history of brave men and braver dogs doing the seemingly impossible. Evolving today to families and communities whose lives revolve around their northern dogs and the wilderness we call home.

For those readers who have tried to follow the race from many locations around the country and the world, much frustration has accompanied the bits and pieces of information that pierce the veil of the national media. This book fills the gaps and bridges those canyons with mushing knowledge. Just how much food does a Husky sled dog eat? Why do the dogs wear booties and what happens when you meet an angry moose? How do the mushers stay warm and where do the dogs get that infectious desire to run? Meet some famous lead dogs and learn the tricks of an informed Iditarod mushing fan.

Mary Hood's *A Fan's Guide to the Iditarod* is exhaustively researched and well organized. It covers the whole adventure, past to present, bringing you as close as you can get without being on the runner tails yourself. Enjoy the book and may all of your trails be hard and fast!

Jeff King
Goose Lake Kennels
Denali Park, Alaska
December, 1995

* Editor's note: Jeff King is the 1993 and 1996 Iditarod champion and also won the Yukon Quest in 1989.

BACKGROUND INFORMATION

A journey of a thousand miles must begin with a single step. In the journey called the Iditarod, that first step and the countless millions that follow it are the steps of dogs, their pawprints tracing a nearly invisible trail across the snowy wilderness of Alaska. Eleven-hundred miles, eleven days, maybe more, this journey lasts. The men and women who race the Iditarod must be full of courage and toughness and know-how. It can be violent for them along this trail: steep ravines coated in ice . . . or maybe at sixty below with howling wind. But it can be quiet, too, and in the stillness of the frozen air, you can listen for the ghosts of the past and the sounds of the great gold-rush days. It is a journey into the twilight of exhaustion when the body slows down and the brain plays tricks. How do you act then when your guard is down? You learn a lot about yourself in this race and that hard-won knowledge comes as one step follows another.

Sam Posey, ABC Wide World of Sports *commentator*

1

Iditarod: What and Why

The Iditarod. The word itself comes from the Indian "Haiditarod," which means "a far distant place." More than just a race, the Iditarod is a dream. A journey. A destination. A life-changing experience.

It's also a multi-million-dollar business. A world-class sporting event. A media blitz. The testing grounds for high-tech racing equipment, scientifically formulated dog food, and ever-improving bloodlines of Iditarod dogs.

The race is run by a core of intensely competitive professionals who seek to secure their share of the purse. The Iditarod, however, may be the only major sporting event in which top contenders regularly sacrifice valuable minutes and even hours to assist an arch-rival who is in trouble, give each other forthright strategic advice, and thereby develop unspoken bonds of camaraderie that transcend the cutthroat atmosphere typical of today's sports.

A complex mix of tradition and cutting edge, the Iditarod is not easily defined. Here are some of the facts:

- It's Alaska's official sled-dog race.
- Congress declared it a national historic trail in 1976.
- The race commemorates the 1925 diphtheria serum run and celebrates the history and spirit of Alaska.

- The mileage is officially given as 1,049 miles (varying year to year, the distance is rounded off to 1,000 miles and Alaska is the forty-ninth state).
- The trail traverses three major geographical divisions—the South Central zone, characterized by dense forests, frozen lakes and bogs, and relatively mild temperatures; the Interior, gained only after crossing the lofty Alaska Range, where temperatures can plummet to -70° F; and finally the Bering Sea coast, renowned for its blizzards and the dangers of sea ice.
- Competitors have entered from fourteen countries and seventeen states.
- Once the mushers leave Knik (63 miles into the race's 1,000+), there are *no roads* to Nome. Access to this untamed wilderness is only possible by plane, snowmobile, foot, or, of course, dog sled!

So, who's crazy enough to do this? Mushers, age eighteen to eighty-six, whose job descriptions include family physician, public defender, ivory carver, bush pilot, carpenter, professional dog musher, trapper, artist, prospector, air-traffic controller, fisherman, novelist, millionaire stockbroker, goat farmer, guidance counselor, and even the "Maytag Man," just to name a few.

It truly is a one-of-a-kind event. In his short story "Dogspirit," award-winning novelist/Iditarod musher Gary Paulsen maintains:

> It is wondrously, gloriously, grandly, magnificently and beautifully senseless and crazy and everyone who does it is altered by it, changed permanently and misses it, misses the dogs and the run for the rest of his or her life and can never look at another horizon, sunrise, snowflake, ocean, sky, dog, tree or blade of grass without thinking of the run and comparing it to other things.

Ask "Why?" and you're likely to get a different answer from every musher. Some view it as a personal challenge, while others seek to make a connection with the past. Dr. Roger Haertel, who completed his first race in 1993, claims that dentistry is easier than running the Iditarod, but somehow not as much fun. Having served as chief pilot of the Iditarod Air Force for many years, Bert Hanson decided to get a ground-level perspective by mushing the trail. Drivers also dedicate their race to causes as diverse as the American Cancer Society, Big Brothers/Big Sisters, Prevention of Child Abuse, and Sobriety.

Of course, there is prize money to be had: $50,000 goes to the first-place finisher, and there are several opportunities along the trail to pick up $500 to $3,500 in awards. Most mushers, however, go into debt just to experience the race—the awesome beauty, the freedom, the discovery of self. There seems to be an almost mystical attraction. So, why do it? Why not? The Iditarod. A far distant place. A journey of discovery. The run.

I'm convinced there is no more noble creature on earth than a good sled dog doing what it loves best. I spend my entire year outside—training, racing, breeding, raising and caring for dogs—in yet unspoiled wilderness. It's all enriched by the joy and purpose they bring me, and exploration of the ancient, mystic bond between man and dog.

Rick Armstrong
Iditarod finisher

2

A Brief History
of Mushing

Aprolonged howl hangs on the air: soulful, melodic, thrilling. Is it the song of a magnificent Timber Wolf or an Alaskan Husky in a musher's dog lot? Ever since wolves crept close to prehistoric man's fire some 10,000 years ago and stayed to become domesticated, dogs and humans have been inseparable partners.

Natives of the arctic regions may have used dogs to pull sleds as long ago as 2,000 B.C. Traditionally, Eskimo dogs hauled transport sleds, led hunting trips, helped bring large game to bay, ran traplines, and guarded the family home.

In the late 1800s and early 1900s, miners, trappers, mail carriers, and explorers relied on dog-team transportation. Sled dogs enabled Robert Peary to reach the North Pole in 1909 and Roald Amundsen to arrive at the South Pole in 1911.

To facilitate travel for gold miners and mail teams, a trail was brushed out and blazed during 1910 and 1911 from Nome through Iditarod to the seaport of Seward (south of present-day Anchorage). Mail and supplies went in, and gold came out. Some of the blaze marks can still be seen on sections of today's Iditarod race route.

With so many dog teams around, it was inevitable that their proud owners would race them. Organized sled-dog racing began in 1908 when the Nome Kennel Club sponsored the first All-Alaska Sweepstakes Race.

A Village Dog stands atop his doghouse on the Bering Sea coast in Unalakleet. The dogs that participated in the 1925 serum run, as well as today's Iditarod dogs, descended from such hardy Native huskies.

The 408-mile race, following the telegraph wires so that regular reports could be sent back, was a round-trip from Nome to Candle. Completing the race in five days, the winner shared in a $10,000 purse, an astronomical sum at that time!

Sled-dog racing spread to Canada and the Lower 48. Major sprint races were held at The Pas, Manitoba (1916); West Yellowstone, Montana (1917); and Laconia, New Hampshire (1922).

By far the most famous race, however, was a race against time and the deadly disease diphtheria. During the winter of 1925, Dr. Curtis Welch discovered that an epidemic of this fatal, highly contagious disease had broken out in the ice-bound village of Nome. The situation was extremely serious because the native Eskimo population had little or no immunity to diseases introduced by outsiders. In 1900, a measles outbreak had decimated the Eskimos, and in 1919 entire villages had succumbed to a flu epidemic. Consequently, an urgent plea for diphtheria serum was transmitted by telegraph.

The life-saving antitoxin was located in Seattle and shipped to Anchorage but would take one month to arrive. Additional units of serum were found in an Anchorage medical storage facility and sent by train to the station at Nenana, located sixty miles west of Fairbanks.

In the 1920s, airplane travel was still primitive. Fairbanks boasted two aircraft, both open cockpit biplanes that had been disassembled and stored for winter. The serum would have to travel by dog sled.

The Northern Commercial Company (NCC) ran the 674-mile mail route from Nenana to Nome. A letter usually arrived within thirty days. The NCC now asked its fastest mail drivers to deliver the serum in fifteen days. The U.S. Post Office also relayed the following message soliciting additional assistance from local mushers: "Request the best musher and team in your section to stand by to receive the serum for Nome starting from Nenana tomorrow." Villages held hurried meetings. The best musher was given the fastest team available, often consisting of dogs borrowed from a number of different owners. In this way, Indian and Eskimo villages provided half of the serum run's drivers (see the map at the end of this chapter).

Meanwhile, in Anchorage the glass vials of diphtheria serum were packed in a cylindrical container that was wrapped in quilting, canvas, and then furs. Each musher was instructed to place the precious cargo near a stove before beginning his leg of the relay in order to avoid freezing the antitoxin.

Anxiously waiting in Nome, Dr. Welch had administered all of the diphtheria serum that he had. The disease had already caused five deaths. Nome's only doctor was now responsible for treating twenty-two confirmed cases and another eighty probable ones.

It was -40° F at 11 P.M. on January 27 when the first driver, "Wild Bill" Shannon, left Nenana, beginning the race to Nome. Each of the twenty drivers participating covered an average distance of thirty miles. Passing Manley Hot Springs and arriving at Tanana, the route followed the Yukon River for nearly 250 miles. Leaving behind the Yukon River settlements of Tanana, Kokrines, Ruby, Galena, Nulato, and Kaltag, the drivers headed west for Unalakleet and up the exposed Bering Sea coast to Shaktoolik.

Two days and six hours after leaving Nenana, the serum was handed to the twelfth musher, Charlie Evans, at Bishop Mountain (eighteen miles west of Galena). When he left there at 5 A.M. on January 30, the temperature registered a dangerous -64° F. Evans had taken the precaution of protecting his dogs' undersides with rabbit-skin covers, but he did not have covers available for two extra dogs that he had borrowed. When these dogs developed severe frostbite on their groins, Evans loaded them into the sled and helped his remaining seven dogs pull it. Tragically, in spite of his heroic efforts, both dogs later died.

In the meantime, Nome had sent racing legend Leonhard Seppala to meet the approaching mushers at the halfway point of Nulato. The forty-eight-year-old Norwegian had won the All-Alaska Sweepstakes three times (and almost every other race in the state). Seppala chose twenty of his best dogs, including his famous twelve-year-old lead dog Togo, a small gray husky. Among the dogs he rejected was a large black dog named Balto, a six-year-old freight hauler. Remember that name.

Having traveled 169 miles, Seppala was surprised to meet Henry Ivanoff on the sea ice near Shaktoolik. The relay teams had made much better time than anyone expected.

Transferring the serum into his sled, Seppala turned around to recross the ice on Norton Sound. Although crossing the ice was riskier, it would cut as much as one day off of his time. As he weighed his options, Seppala thought of his daughter Seigrid, who had earlier been stricken by diphtheria and recovered. Seppala didn't want his friends and their children to go through the ordeal that he had experienced; he would trust in God and his dog team and take to the ice.

As the weather "warmed" to -30° F, Seppala could feel the ice pack shifting. Because of blizzard conditions, he could only see Togo during brief letups and had to rely on his lead dog's skill to bring them safely across. Surveying Norton Sound from shore the following morning, Seppala saw open water where his team had just traveled.

Leonhard Seppala was unaware that the Nome Health Board had dispatched three additional mushers from Nome to complete the relay. Arriving at Golovin, Seppala found Charlie Olson waiting to relieve him. Having carried the serum ninety-one miles, almost twice the distance of any other driver, Seppala had now accomplished his mission.

Charlie Olson braved hurricane-force winds to relay the serum from Golovin to Bluff. Olson, his team, and the sled were repeatedly lifted up and blown off of the trail. Arriving at the Bluff roadhouse, Olson unhitched his entire team and brought all seven dogs inside the

In the 1925 serum run, Leonhard Seppala with his lead dog Togo carried the antitoxin almost twice the distance of any other driver.
Photo used with permission of The Bettmann Archive.

warm cabin so that they could recover from badly frozen groins (which had developed even though Olson had stopped along the trail to put on warm dog blankets); Olson himself was lucky not to lose any of his frostbitten fingers.

After warming the serum, Gunnar Kaasen took over, intending to drive from Bluff to Port Safety, where he would meet Ed Rohn, who was scheduled to complete the race. Balto, Leonhard Seppala's rejected freight dog, was chosen by Gunnar Kaasen to lead his team. Kaasen preferred strength to speed for this job and felt that Seppala underrated the large black dog.

Worried about the increasingly severe weather, the Nome Health Board wired the village of Solomon (located between Bluff and Port Safety), instructing Kaasen to remain there until the worst was over. In the blizzard, however, Kaasen passed Solomon and missed the message.

Two miles past Solomon, a gust of wind flipped the sled. Having righted it and unsnarled the dogs, Kaasen made a quick check to ensure that the serum was secure. Disbelief and then a sickening fear gripped him as he realized that his cargo was missing. Desperately, he began groping through the snow in the dark. If the serum had fallen off somewhere back up the trail before the sled overturned, snow would have blanketed it by now. Mushers had risked their lives to bring this package 642 of the 674 miles to Nome. Would the relay fail now so close to its conclusion? Kaasen's hand finally struck an object, and he shouted with joy as he retrieved the antitoxin and carefully repacked it in the sled.

Exhausted by fighting winds up to eighty miles per hour, Kaasen arrived at Port Safety to find no signal light visible and no relief musher ready to go. Ed Rohn, a sled-dog racer whose team had not lost a race all season, lay sleeping there, believing that Kaasen had been detained at Solomon. Kaasen's subsequent decision to forge on to Nome himself in the interest of time would later spark bitter controversy.

Dr. Curtis Welch heard insistent knocking at 5:30 A.M. on February 2 and braced himself to receive news of another diphtheria victim. He was greeted instead by a rime-coated musher holding the precious package of antitoxin. As Kaasen collapsed into a chair, the doctor unwrapped the layers of fur, canvas, and quilting to find that the glass vials had all frozen solid.

When he had carefully thawed it, Dr. Welch discovered that the serum was still vital. What the mushers had been asked to achieve in fifteen days had been accomplished in five days, seven and one-half hours. There were no more deaths, and the diphtheria quarantine was lifted within nineteen days. One month later, the whole relay was repeated to deliver the additional units of antitoxin that had arrived from Seattle by sea. This second serum run is virtually unknown.

The "Great Race of Mercy" was publicized throughout the United States, and the serum mushers became heroes. For a few moments, a nation jaded by the trivialities of the Roaring Twenties—the brassy music, the latest fashion fads, society-page gossip, news of prohibition and organized crime—focused on the fearless mushers and their teams as they fought their way across the Alaskan wilderness. The press pointed out the irony of men accomplishing with dogs a feat that could not be achieved by man-made means in this age of machines.

When the mission of mercy was successfully completed, the country celebrated. The serum's manufacturers gave Gunnar Kaasen $1,000 for being the musher who delivered the life-saving units to Nome. Kaasen was approached by Hollywood about a film and was

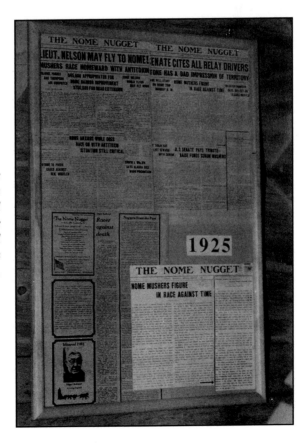

The "Great Race of Mercy" was publicized throughout the United States, and the serum mushers became heroes.

In villages along the serum run route, widow's lamps like this one signified that a team was expected, and welcomed the weary musher to trail's end.

offered lecture tours. A bronze statue of Balto was erected in New York's Central Park. The schoolchildren of Cleveland, Ohio, eventually bought Balto, and he spent his remaining years at the local zoo. Balto continued to be an attraction in Cleveland after his death; he was preserved by a taxidermist and displayed at the Museum of Natural History!

Needless to say, Leonhard Seppala and Ed Rohn were not pleased by the epic notoriety of Kaasen and Balto. Seppala had traveled 260 miles with Togo (including 91 miles carrying the serum) compared to Kaasen's 106 miles led by Balto (53 miles with the serum). Seppala and Rohn accused Kaasen of bypassing the Port Safety trade-off point deliberately so that he could receive all of the glory in Nome.

In fairness to Togo, it should be pointed out that when the Dog Mushers Hall of Fame opened in 1966, Leonhard Seppala and Togo were among the first to be instated. And when he died at age sixteen, Togo was taxidermically mounted and now graces the Iditarod Trail Committee headquarters.

The mushers' heroic deeds had a far greater impact than they ever could have dreamed. Not only was the epidemic in Nome checked, but to a great extent the disease itself was conquered. In the 1920s, there were 210,000 cases of diphtheria and 20,000 resulting deaths *annually* in the United States. Due to the extensive publicity of the serum run, widespread inoculation began. Within a few years, diphtheria had become a minor threat to Americans.

In the years following the serum relay, sprint racing continued to grow in popularity. The first Open North American Sled Dog Race was held in Fairbanks in 1936, and the first sled-dog race to be included in Anchorage's annual Fur Rendezvous winter festival occurred in the late 1930s. These early races are two of the major sprint championships still run today.

Sled dogs have made significant contributions in other areas as well. In World Wars I and II, they hauled supplies, transported wounded men, and rescued airmen shot down in snowy areas. The last official Royal Canadian Mounted Police dog-patrol team served in 1969. And in the United States, the post office did not retire its last dog team in Alaska until the 1970s!

From prehistoric times to this year's Iditarod, dogs and their courageous human companions have been honored. Before each running of the Iditarod Trail Sled Dog Race from 1973 through 1979, there was a two-minute period of silence in memory of Leonhard Seppala. The #1 bib is an honorary one, which was also dedicated to his memory during these years. From 1980 to the present, the Iditarod Trail Committee's board of directors has selected a well-known dog musher or a nonmusher who has contributed to the sport of sled-dog racing and to the Iditarod to be the honorary "number-one" musher or mushers. (A complete list of those who have been so honored can be found in the "Iditarod Award Winners, 1973 to 1996" chapter.)

The following inscription on Balto's statue in Central Park can be generalized to include all sled dogs that have performed bravely and well:

> Dedicated to the indomitable spirit of the sled dogs that relayed antitoxin six hundred miles over rough ice, across treacherous waters, through arctic blizzards from Nenana to the relief of a stricken Nome in the winter of 1925.
> Endurance—fidelity—intelligence

It is not too much of a leap in logic to substitute "serum mushers" for "sled dogs" in the above inscription. The two-minute silence and honorary #1 bib can also be generalized to include *all* of the heroic drivers who participated in both serum runs. Their names are listed below. Each one deserves equal honor.

1. "Wild Bill" Shannon
2. Dan Green
3. Johnny Folger
4. Sam Joseph
5. Titus Nikoli
6. Dave Corning
7. Edgar Kalland
8. Harry Pitka
9. Bill McCarty
10. Edgar Nollner
11. George Nollner
12. Charlie Evans
13. Tommy Patsy
14. "Jackscrew"
15. Victor Anagick
16. Myles Gonangnan
17. Henry Ivanoff
18. Leonhard Seppala
19. Charlie Olson
20. Gunnar Kaasen
21. Ed Rohn
22. Maggie Smoke
    (2nd serum run)

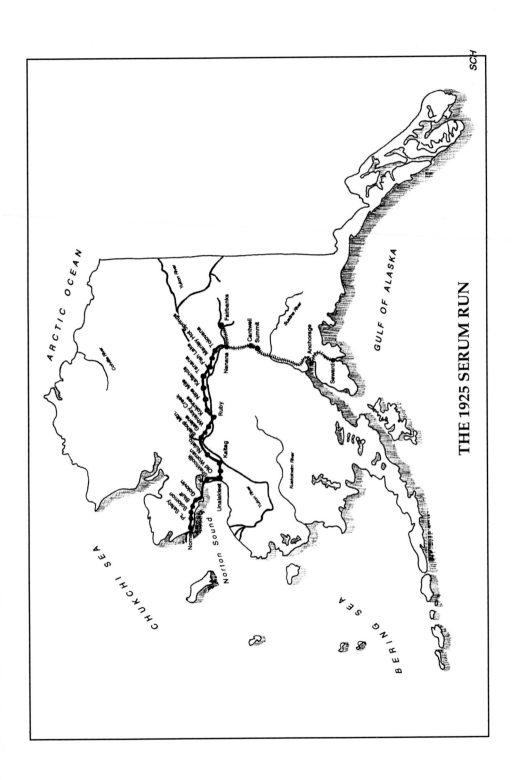

THE 1925 SERUM RUN

This idea of a sled dog race from Anchorage to Nome was a farfetched scheme. It was an adventure that first year. We thought we were racing. But as you look back on it, certainly compared to now, it was a big camping trip.

You never will be able to duplicate the feeling of the first one. Nobody knew what they were doing. Wives and sweethearts were down at the starting line in tears because here we were going off into the wilds, never to be seen again. It was that kind of attitude. . . .

Of course there was no idea of doing it a second time. This was a one-time event. To be part of it was . . . hell's bells, I'd rather have done that than been president of the United States.

Dick Mackey
1978 Iditarod champion
and 7th place finisher in the inaugural 1973 race

3

The Founding Mother and Father

Maybe living so near the Iditarod Trail allowed it to seep into historian Dorothy Page's system by osmosis. Serving as chairperson of the Wasilla-Knik Centennial Committee and secretary of the Aurora Dog Mushers Association, Page worked with local musher Joe Redington, Sr. to organize the first race along the Iditarod Trail in 1967 as part of the one-hundredth anniversary of the purchase of Alaska from Russia. The first race covered a total of 50 miles, spanned two days, and was won by Isaac Okleasik, an Eskimo from Teller. Legendary serum musher Leonhard Seppala was asked to be the honorary race marshal of the 1967 Iditarod debut, but he died before the race. Seppala's wife took his place and scattered his ashes over the trail that he had helped make so famous.

In 1968, there was insufficient snow to hold a race, but in 1969, George Attla, an Athabascan Indian, became the second champion of the forerunner to today's Iditarod. If a little was good, maybe more would be better! Page suggested expanding the race from 50 to 500 miles, from Wasilla to the historic ghost town of Iditarod. Redington and other friends pointed out that mushers would not want to race to Iditarod because there was nothing and no one there. Why not go for broke and race from Anchorage (just south of Wasilla) more than

Dorothy G. Page, the "Mother of the Iditarod," as shown on the Halfway Award, presented each year at either Iditarod or Cripple.

1,000 miles all the way to Nome? That way the event would begin and end where more people could enjoy it, and the race would commemorate the 1925 diphtheria serum run.

Joe Redington, Sr. worried that snow machines were making sled dogs obsolete. His goals in establishing the Iditarod Trail Sled Dog Race were to prevent sled dogs and mushing from becoming things of the past and to foster an appreciation for the importance of dog sledding in Alaska's history. During the years he spent lobbying to launch the 1973 race, he was called the Don Quixote of Alaska by the press. Even the mushers thought that the Last Great Race was an impractical dream. Accustomed to sprint racing, how could their dogs make it all the way to Nome? How could they carry enough dog food for more than 1,000 miles? Where would the purse money come from?

None of these details daunted Redington. He assured the entrants that $50,000 would be waiting for them in Nome, although he hadn't raised the prize money yet. In spite of having trained a dog team for the race, Redington ended up flying food and supplies to the mushers and managed to raise $51,000 in two weeks. Having mortgaged his

Joe Redington, Sr., the "Father of the Iditarod," at his home in Knik. © Jeff Schultz/ Alaska Stock Images.

homestead for $15,000 and sold a small parcel of it for $10,000 to fund the 1967 purse, he wasn't afraid of asking others for a commitment to the race.

Thirty-four dog teams left Anchorage, traveling a trail no one had used for forty-eight years. Fortunately, the 172nd Arctic Light Infantry Brigade, a unit of the U.S. Army, had helped locate and mark the trail in 1972 as part of a cold-weather training exercise. Joe Redington, Sr. and fifty members of the brigade built log tripod trail markers that are still visible today and Howard Farley coordinated efforts from Nome to meet Redington halfway. But to the competitors of the first running, it was all unknown terrain. Only twenty-two teams finished, led by Richard Wilmarth, who arrived triumphantly in Nome after 20 days, 49 minutes, and 41 seconds. The race support consisted of one pilot (Joe Redington, Sr.) and one veterinarian (Air Force Colonel Terry Adkins), in contrast to recent totals of more than twenty-eight pilots and thirty veterinarians.

In 1992, at age seventy-four, Redington completed his eighteenth Iditarod and announced that he planned to pursue other interests. Since then, Redington has led groups of tourists who mush along the trail behind the last of the competitors. Dorothy Page came to the end of her trail in 1989, having seen her local centennial celebration blossom into an international sporting event. Appropriately, her funeral procession was led by dog team. The first running of the Iditarod in 1973 was dedicated to the memory of Leonhard Seppala; the 1990 Iditarod was dedicated to its founding mother, Dorothy Page. In 1991, the Spirit of the Iditarod Award, honoring a person who has demonstrated the ideals of the Iditarod and whose life and guiding philosophy preserve that spirit for future generations, was presented to Joe Redington, Sr. Now celebrating its third decade, the Last Great Race is a testimonial to the spirit of these "impractical" dreamers.

RACE
PREPARATION

Iditarod racers keep a schedule of Olympic athletes to train their animals and then tack on the schedule of a farmer to take care of them.

Martin Buser
Two-time Iditarod champion

4

A Typical Musher's Racing Regime

DAILY CHORES

Twenty-four hours a day, seven days a week, fifty-two weeks a year. Just like parenting—or farming. Taking care of sled dogs is a responsibility that requires serious commitment.

Rising as early as 6 A.M., mushers begin by feeding and watering their dogs. For residents of remote areas, this may mean hauling 100 gallons of water per day over a quarter-mile distance from creek to cabin. Feeding 100 to 150 dogs takes several hours for one person to complete. Cleaning, socializing, and training take many more, so most mushers enlist the aid of their spouse or hire handlers.

Successful racers don't just set down the food and water, then leave. Throughout the whole procedure, they talk to their dogs, calling each one by name and touching them. The dogs also need to be inspected daily for signs of illness or injury. If the musher has basic veterinary training (which is handy if you live 100 or more miles from the nearest vet), she or he may administer vaccinations and conduct physicals as necessary.

Like children, dogs come down with viral infections. Nonmushers usually do not realize that these animals receive the same care and

Twenty-four hours a day, seven days a week, fifty-two weeks a year. Just like parenting—or farming. Taking care of sled dogs is a responsibility that requires serious commitment. Hand-pulled sleds make the job of cleaning up after all those huskies just a little easier.

loving attention as a child with a similar illness. As an extreme example, a dog with pneumonia (which occasionally develops in dogs despite the best care) is kept inside for a month with a vaporizer running next to him. Oral and injectable antibiotics are administered on a strict schedule. The caretaker may even employ chest PT, or chest physical therapy, a technique used to loosen phlegm in the chest of sick children by carefully thumping the lung area.

Dog drivers sometimes ask veterinarians or other canine health specialists to visit their kennels. One recent innovation in veterinary medicine is the use of acupressure. Used for humans as physical therapy, acupressure is preventive, holistic medicine. It is noninvasive and does not require the use of drugs. By exploring all safe avenues of medical care, mushers are constantly seeking to improve the physical and mental well-being of their dogs.

In addition to veterinary care, other daily tasks may include chopping firewood, hunting or fishing in season, gardening, repair and upkeep of equipment, building projects, training, bookkeeping, working at a paying job, and, last but not least, cleaning up after all of those dogs!

Some mushers believe that bringing their dogs inside the house for visits at night on a rotating basis is critical to their success. Others are hesitant to treat their dogs as pets, viewing them instead as outdoor working animals, or have found that huskies become uncomfortably hot inside. Whatever the philosophy, it is unlikely that the weary musher will get to bed much before midnight.

MUSHER PROFILE

What kind of kooks subject themselves to this never-ending abuse? It is difficult to generalize about mushers because they range in age from eighteen to eighty-six, come from far-flung states and nations,

Some mushers believe that bringing their dogs inside the house for visits on a rotating basis is critical to their success.

and have widely divergent views. Several observations can be made, however.

First, caring for sled dogs requires that the musher be a hard worker. Iditarod entrants also tend to have the three "D"s: drive, desire, and determination. Just training for the Iditarod, let alone the dangers of competing in it, demands a willingness to take risks. A catalog of dog driver Gary Paulsen's training injuries includes cracked ribs, a broken leg, a broken wrist, various parts frozen or cut or bitten, and a torn-and-separated kneecap.

Although everyone agrees that the dogs are the real athletes in sled-dog racing, competitive mushers are athletes, too. Four-time champion Susan Butcher explains, "I run every uphill for 1,100 miles and kick one-footed on most of the flats. We all do. Mushers are athletes. I'm not fast—I've got stubby little legs. But they'll go forever."

To get themselves in shape, dog drivers often devise a personal fitness regime. This may involve daily workouts on a Nordic Track® machine, a running program, or other athletic pursuits—in addition to the exercise that they get out in the dog lot. Being in good condition enables the human coach to be a more effective part of the dog team.

While there are exceptions, Iditarod drivers are often loners who prefer the company of their dogs and immediate family in the wilderness to that of other people in established communities.

Finally, most of the individuals who dedicate themselves to winning the Last Great Race don't care what you think about how crazy they are!

LOG HOUSES AND DOGHOUSES

The size and layout of a musher's compound depend upon the location of the operation, the amount of money available to fund it, and whether the musher is a full-time or part-time competitor. An example is Susan Butcher's Trail Breaker Kennels. At the height of her Iditarod career, Butcher's facilities included four one-room log cabins. One was used as an office, living room, and kitchen. A second cabin contained Susan's and her husband David Monson's sleeping quarters. Guests stayed in a third cabin, and handlers occupied the fourth. Dog food was prepared in a wall tent, which also served as a warehouse for dog food and equipment. A shed housed mushing clothes

Susan Butcher and David Monson stand in their dog lot, Trail Breaker Kennels, at the height of Butcher's mushing career in the late 1980s. Their facilities include four one-room log cabins. © Jeff Schultz/Alaska Stock Images.

and miscellaneous items. The layout was completed by a visit to the three-sided outhouse. That's right—no door.

After living in Alaska for eleven years with no electricity, Butcher was brought into the twentieth century by Monson, who installed a satellite dish and three diesel generators. Now she can use a telephone, fax machine, stereo, microwave, and various and sundry wedding presents (toaster oven, corn popper). In 1991, however, Trail Breaker Kennels did not have running water, indoor plumbing, a furnace, or a conventional stove. Butcher and Monson did not want them. The communications network was scheduled to be moved to an office in Fairbanks so that life could return to a quieter pace. As *Sports Illustrated's* Sonja Steptoe observed, "For Susan Butcher, happiness is not having to run out of the outhouse to answer the phone."

Out in the dog lot, each husky that has graduated from the puppy pen gets a private plywood doghouse lined with a warm nest of straw.

(Some mushers use barrels or drums laid on their sides.) Dogs have the range of a five-foot chain, long enough to socialize with their neighbors but short enough to prevent tangling or fighting. Trail Breaker Kennels has about 120 doghouses, which must be dug out and raised after every heavy snow. Puppies stay with their mothers until weaned, then are moved to a large puppy pen that doubles as a secure location for bitches in heat. Each dog participates in training exercises several times a week and is periodically let loose to run and play.

SEASONAL SCHEDULE

In June, mushers (or their proxies) converge on the Iditarod Trail Committee (ITC) headquarters in Wasilla, Alaska, to sign up for the next Iditarod. ITC rules specify that mushers registering on the first day may be among the initial group to draw for starting positions at the prerace banquet. Most competitors prefer to start near the front of the pack so that their dogs are not stressed by a long wait amidst the commotion on Fourth Avenue. Also, the trail is less torn up when they cover it, and there are fewer teams to pass. For this reason, entrants often camp out at headquarters in tents for days in order to be among the first mushers to draw.

Believe it or not, summer in Alaska is sometimes too hot to run sled dogs. When the temperature hits 60° or 70° F, dogs are exercised on a dog walker (sometimes called an exercise wheel), because it requires less energy than cart training. The dogs' leashes are attached to what looks like a giant paddle fan above them, and they proceed to run around in circles for approximately forty-five minutes at a time. This allows the musher to keep the animals fit and to determine which has the smoothest and fastest gait. And for some inexplicable reason, the dogs actually enjoy it.

Jeff King, Iditarod champion in 1993 and 1996, has a breathtaking location near Denali National Park that enables him to employ an alternate summer exercise routine. King paddles a canoe out into the lake for which his Goose Lake Kennels is named, a jewel of water nestled between the bay window of his house and a stand of timber backed by the glorious Alaska Range. His sled dogs are enticed into the water by the calls of their master and by the prospect of chasing waterfowl. Swimming poses no risk of the dogs overheating, and it is a clean, cool, low-impact activity.

Summer is also when puppies are most likely to be born. Even before the pups' eyes are open, the musher picks them up, strokes them gently, calls them by name, and talks to them. Dog breeders call this "socialization"; the object is to get the puppies to trust and love you (and humans in general). After weaning, at about eight weeks of age, the pups are taken on daily walks of one to seven miles. This builds their muscle tone and confidence and enables the trainer to see which pup will go anywhere—through water, across ice, and over obstacles. Usually at least one adult dog accompanies the youngsters on these outings.

Mushers make a point of handling pups' feet frequently, so when ointment and booties need to be applied during a race, none of the canine coursers will be a paw priss. Excellent eating habits are also encouraged early. Pups are given a short time to eat, and then their food is removed. Throughout the day, this process is repeated until the pups learn to eat when it's offered. Eager eating is an essential trait for Iditarod dogs.

When the puppies are six to eight months old, they will be harness-broken and then taken on short (half-mile to one-mile) runs. Mushers take care not to overwork young dogs so that they will always retain their innate love for racing.

In August, serious training begins with each dog going out several times a week for three- to four-mile runs. Until there is adequate snow cover to allow the use of a sled, the dogs are hooked to wheeled carts or ATVs (all-terrain vehicles), which are pulled while left in gear. Yearling dogs are often paired with experienced older racers.

"Training," when used in regard to a sled dog, encompasses two distinct meanings. One aspect of training is conditioning, which is the physical and athletic building up of the dog's body. The other half of training is teaching a dog to do what you want. Cart training early in the season builds up the dog's muscles, gradually toughens the animal, and gets him back into the routine of hard work. It also allows the musher to teach a yearling new commands, while reinforcing the lessons that veterans have already learned. As the length and frequency of runs increase throughout fall and winter, the dog is steadily and carefully brought to peak performance. The trick is to get the entire team into optimal physical condition without driving the dogs so hard that they lose their enthusiasm and attitude.

In a discussion of training techniques in his book *Everything I Know about Training and Racing Sled Dogs*, World Champion George Attla, *the* name in sprint mushing, cautions drivers that "the dog never makes a mistake. He is just a dog, and he does what he does because he is a dog and thinks like a dog. It is you that makes the mistake because you haven't trained him to do what you want him to do when you want him to do it. Or you have misjudged what he is able to do, physically or mentally." A good musher constantly learns from his dogs.

Two-time champion Martin Buser believes in preventive action. In an interview with *Mushing* magazine following his 1992 victory, Buser revealed that "90 percent of my training is positive reinforcement. That's the key. I think there are two schools of training. One is that you wait until the dog screws up, and then you correct it. The other is that you anticipate what's happening, and you correct it before it happens. One of my sayings is that when everything goes right, stop and reinforce that behavior."

Two-time champion Martin Buser, an advocate of positive reinforcement training, listens intently at a prerace mushers' meeting.

Praise is more than just a reward: it is an attitude toward the dogs. Martin Buser has received the coveted Leonhard Seppala Humanitarian Award three times for outstanding care of his dogs.

As the season progresses and the dogs have successfully learned what the trainer wants, occasional instances of willful disobedience will occur. First, the musher must ascertain that the dog in question *does* know what is expected and *is* capable of doing it. Often a dog that *does* know and that *is* capable can be corrected by simply calling his name and repeating the command. Mushers can also emulate wolves and enforce discipline through the appearance of ferocity (a stern "alpha wolf" display). If the dog stubbornly refuses to cooperate, some type of physical correction may be necessary.

Punishable offenses include pulling off of the trail to sniff or to lift a leg, going too slowly, not keeping the tugline tight, disobeying a command (for example, the driver says "Gee," which means "Turn Right," and the dog goes left), being aggressive to humans, or fighting with each other. If repeated efforts to educate the dog and patient positive reinforcement fail, and the musher is certain that the dog understands the command and can perform it, a "spanking" may be administered with a small, flexible object such as a winter mitten or a birch/willow switch.

It is important to note that these methods of correction are not used frequently. A dog may need to be physically corrected only once in his life to get the point across. Typically, however, the sound of the trainer's insistent tone of voice may be enough to solve the problem. Dogs usually know when they are at fault. During cart training, a musher stopped the team to discipline one dog which, in spite of several warnings, would not do his share of the work. As the trainer walked from the four-wheeler up the gangline, every dog in the team stood resting quietly, alert and confident, except for the miscreant. He immediately lay down abjectly as if to say, "I know, *I'm* the one." The musher made a mental note that this dog might not be able to perform up to the standards expected of his racing dogs; perhaps the dog would be sold to a recreational musher and be successful there.

A professional musher must be objective about his or her dogs' capabilities and should remain cool and collected throughout the training process. George Attla advises, "If you want to be a good dog musher, you keep your temper around your dogs. Maybe you couldn't do it in a barroom, but by God, when you are around your dog team, you keep your temper to yourself."

Although corrective actions are occasionally necessary, praise is the key ingredient in a successful musher's training regime. Dogs need to be praised out on the trail for obeying commands and again back at the dog lot after the completion of a run. Drivers do not talk more than necessary while actually training or racing a dog team because the dogs will stop listening to endless chatter. A team will respond positively to enthusiastic, well-timed praise, however. Praise is more than just a reward: it is an attitude toward the dogs. Sled dogs that are raised in an atmosphere of verbal and physical praise learn to trust and love their human partners and are far more likely to achieve their full potential.

As fall turns into winter, training runs are gradually increased until by December the dogs are covering twenty-five to seventy-five miles, four or five days a week. During these runs, the musher is constantly evaluating each dog's performance. Which dog does best in which position? Which dogs run well together as a pair, taking into account their weight, height, and gait? Do some of the dogs run better on the left or right side of the gangline? Which lead dogs hold up against a head wind or side wind, on ice, and near congested areas or other teams? Dog psychology may even determine the selection of pairs. Martin Buser notes, "I have just started learning to put the team together matching subtle personality differences. I used to decide to run dogs together based more on physical matches; now I look more at mental matches."

By observing the dogs' ears, heads, and tails, the trainer learns to recognize when they are slacking off, when they are tired, or when they are under too much pressure. Some mushers take individual dogs on walks to assess their personality or to work out a problem. According to Martin Buser, "If you are a racer, you need to do targeted training. Let's say you have a dog that doesn't like to run on the right side of the gangline. You may have to gear a few training runs for that particular dog, stopping every couple of minutes to put him on the right side of the line and encourage him that it's okay to run on the right. If that is what it takes to make that dog be the best it can possibly be, then you need to do that." This kind of attention to detail can have amazing results. Mushers who pair dogs carefully by size, conformation, build, gait, and attitude may achieve synchrony of pace; that is, the dogs match each other's forward steps, leading off each stride with the same foot. This rhythm cannot be taught, but when it occurs, the team exhibits smoothness, grace, and beauty.

In early winter, Iditarod entrants need to assemble the plethora of food and equipment that will be sent ahead to each checkpoint of the race. To give you an idea of what this involves, Martin Buser ships 3,000 pounds of food and supplies in a total of fifty-six drop bags to race checkpoints.

Serious competitors make special training excursions to parts of Alaska that have a significantly different climate from where they live. Susan Butcher ran her dogs along the Bering Sea coast from Shaktoolik to Nome each February for several years, in order to prepare her team for the renowned coastal blizzards. Rick Swenson covered the second half of the Iditarod Trail, from Ruby to Nome, as a part of his 1990 prerace agenda, and routinely runs a coastal training trip.

Several weeks before the race, the musher selects sixteen dogs to compose what will hopefully become the winning Iditarod team. By now, these dogs have completed at least 2,000 miles of training, including other mid- to long-distance races that are held in January and February. During the few weeks before the Iditarod, the dogs are taken on short, happy "attitude" runs—just long enough to preserve muscle tone and keep their interest up, but short enough to allow them to feel rested before the race.

Twin sisters Miki and Julie Collins, who use their dog team to run a trapline and who also have competed in a variety of sled-dog races, discuss "peakout" versus "burnout" in their book *Dog Driver: A Guide for the Serious Musher*. By the time the trainer has put enough miles on the dogs to condition them properly for the Iditarod, there is a real danger that the whole team will go into a slump or individual dogs will go "sour." To cure a particular dog, the Collins sisters suggest letting the dog rest (a few days off work!), spending extra time with the animal, bringing him inside the house, going for a private walk, playing together, and giving him lots of praise and love. If the whole team has burned out, they need rest, too, but may also benefit from several other restoratives. Often, running a tired team on new trails helps, even if the dogs have to be trucked there. Stopping frequently to give them upbeat pep talks can snap them out of a slump. And a little reverse psychology never hurts. At home and out on the trail, let the dogs rest longer than they want. When they are running, stop before they need the rest. Out of pure contrariness, the whole outfit should soon be screaming to go.

If the dogs have not trained or raced at all in a warm climate (the Alpirod, for instance, is usually run in January through Italy and neighboring countries, where the weather is much milder), the musher may take the team to Anchorage as much as a month before the start to provide adjustment time. Temperatures in the Interior often reach -50° F during late winter, while the temperature in Anchorage on race day may be 45° F, nearly a 100-degree difference!

Whatever the outcome of the Iditarod, spring is the season for rest. Dogs get their exercise on the walker or during short cart/ATV runs several times a week. The musher reflects on the past season, evaluating strengths and weaknesses, and plans ahead for an even more successful program next year.

This is the time to cultivate sponsors, read up on new training techniques, make repairs and improvements around the home and dog lot, and answer fan mail, especially those heartwarming letters from schoolkids. It is also when sled-dog racers make their breeding plans. To some successful mushers, breeding dogs is more important than winning races. Joe Runyan, 1989 Iditarod champion, asserts, "If I make my mark at all, I want to say I did it by helping develop the Alaskan sled dog."

Nature versus nurture is a controversial subject among dog breeders. Some people believe top-notch sled dogs are born that way and a musher is lucky to compete even once in a lifetime with one such dog. Others maintain that superior training of even marginal dogs is more successful than marginal training of superior animals. Susan Butcher claims, "When you've got a pup with the right breeding, the right genetics, you're just an eighth of the way there. It's not just that [some breeders] don't have good sperm and egg. That's not their problem. It's what they're doing with it after it hits the ground. That's the main thing—it's just work. It isn't magic. It's just work and work and work and work and work."

All this work is sometimes made more challenging by Mother Nature. The training season may include extremely cold temperatures (-60° F or lower), record snowfall or a lack thereof, moose charging and injuring the dogs, and even owls attacking the handlers.

As spring slips into summer, the cycle begins again. As you might have guessed, all of this costs a lot of money.

AND HERE'S THE BILL . . .

Estimates of the cost for a musher to enter a team in the Iditarod range from $15,000 on an "economy" budget to more than $50,000 to field a winning team. The accompanying chart, Estimated Iditarod Expenses, shows a breakdown of mushers' costs into "capital investment" (possessions like a truck or dog that are expensive but that are an investment rather than a one-time outlay), "operating costs" (money spent each year just to keep the kennel running), and "race expenses" (the cost of entering one Iditarod—items listed will be used up that year). These figures reflect the cost of operating a fifty-dog kennel. A kennel can be operated more cheaply; these numbers are based upon expenditures of winning teams.

Under "capital investment," only musher-specific costs are itemized. Expenses borne by nonmushers, such as a house mortgage and utility bills, are not given. Because Iditarod competitors do not start from scratch and acquire overnight all of the investments noted here, only the value of thirty dogs has been calculated. Thirty is probably the minimum number of adult sled dogs from which a musher can produce a competitive Iditarod team. Assume that the kennel will breed twenty more huskies, making this a fifty-dog kennel. Also, please note that many of the items categorized as "capital investment" are essential in order to race the Iditarod. Dogs, sleds, sled suits, clothing, miscellaneous gear, dog coats, stove and coolers, and gangline equipment are all reusable and are therefore technically an investment. However, if their cost were amortized over the number of years the musher used them for the race, the "race expenses" total would increase dramatically.

To return to the example of Trail Breaker Kennels, Susan Butcher and David Monson figured that in 1990 it cost $130,000 to fund their breeding and racing operations. Because Trail Breaker Kennels maintains more than one hundred dogs, the totals in the "capital investment" and "operating costs" categories would almost double in order to make a comparison. Adding $88,000 (operating costs times two) and $9,900 (race expenses) results in a total yearly outlay of $97,900. After including a portion of the almost-double investment in a 100-dog kennel (more than $200,000), it is easy to see that Trail Breaker Kennels' costs could easily top $130,000 per year! Their race winnings in 1990 totaled $80,000 ($50,000 from Butcher's Iditarod victory) and they earned an additional $30,000 from dog sales. That's a total income of $110,000. They also receive an undisclosed amount of sponsorship money, but report that even after adding this income, they aren't doing much better than covering expenses.

Of course, Susan Butcher is *not* representative. Musher Paul Sheridan notes, "There are very few people who cover expenses with prize money. You support your hobby with your work." Most sled-dog racers work summer jobs to earn enough money to pay the bills. Libby Riddles, 1985 Iditarod champion, has sewn fur hats during the summer, worked at a fish-processing plant, and been employed by the Bureau of Land Management. Emmitt Peters, the 1975 champion (often called "The Yukon Fox"), is a licensed commercial fisherman. Even four-time champion Susan Butcher was in the red for years before her name became a household word.

If it's this difficult for top-notch competitors to pay the bills, it's no surprise that average mushers are being squeezed out of the Iditarod. Without a major sponsor or sponsors, most dog drivers simply can't afford to enter. As an *Anchorage Daily News* article on the subject observed, "The Iditarod has pretty much become a wilderness race for well-compensated professional mushers, white citizen adventurers

A REPRESENTATIVE FOOD-DROP SHIPMENT

Martin Buser's shipment to Skwentna, consisting of four bags, weighing a total of 124 pounds.

2	1 gallon zippered bags of lamb	} Thinly-sliced ¾″
2	1 gallon zippered bags of beaver	} thick,shaped like a
2	1 gallon zippered bags of beef	} checkbook
2	1 gallon zippered bags of beef byproducts	}Used as a snack or to
4	1 gallon zippered bags of whitefish	}mix with dry food
2	1 gallon zippered bags of Formulinks (fat sausages made by Champaine)	
1	quart corn oil	
4	8 lb. bags of Eagle Pack dog food (equivalent to four meals)	
100	dog boots	
1	set XH black QCR™ runner plastic	
1	audio music tape (prepared by wife Kathy or friends)	
1	spare harness	
1	Carmex™ lip salve	
2	lithium D cell batteries (for headlamp)	
2	AA batteries (for Walkman™)	
2	chemical handwarmers	
2	pairs poly glove liners	
2	pairs chore gloves	
1	pair latex gloves (to apply foot ointment)	
2	garbage bags (for parking place cleanup)	
1	dog-drop cable	
1	Polarfleece™ face mask (velcros to hat)	
1	mailing label (to ship home reusable personal items, such as batteries, music tapes, harnesses)	

People food and drink:

Butterflied shrimp in garlic sauce (boil in bag)	Carrot cake
Angelhair pasta (boil in bag)	Salmon jerky
Tenderloin steak (boil in bag)	Pistachios
Fresh peas/corn/fruit	Cashews
Poppy seed cake	Pecans
Capri Sun™ packaged drinks—1 every 10 miles (90% water, 10% fruit juice)	

ESTIMATED IDITAROD EXPENSES
(Based on a 50-dog kennel)

CAPITAL INVESTMENT

26 sled dogs	52,000
4 lead dogs	32,000
4–wheel–drive pickup with dog box	15,000
3 sleds with bags	4,500
1 high–tech sled suit and accessories	3,000
ATV (All–Terrain Vehicle)	3,000
Doghouses/lot	2,500
Clothing accessories	1,200
(Boots, mittens, snowshoes, headlamps, sleeping bag)	
Miscellaneous gear	800
(Tools, gun, ax, personal items)	
20 dog coats	600
Harnesses	500
Cook stove and coolers	350
Snowhooks, gangline	350

Total	**$115,800**

OPERATING COSTS (Annual)

Dog food	29,000
Kennel operation	10,000
(ATV expenses, license fees, part–time help, maintenance, straw, fuel, etc)	
Veterinary bills	5,000

Total	**$44,000**

RACE EXPENSES

Dog food	3,000
Entry fee	1,750
Airfare (musher, dogs, food drops)	1,200
Dog booties (1,000)	1,000
60 headlamp batteries (lithium)	900
40 new harnesses	560
Food for musher	500
14 sets of runner plastic	420
Foul weather dog clothing	200
38 pairs of chore gloves	105
55 chemical handwarmers	100
Ointment and medications	90
76 AA batteries (for Walkman)	40
15 headlamp bulbs (krypton)	35

Total	**$9,900**

from Alaska who live near populated areas, or dreamers from the Lower 48."

Living off of the road system in Alaska makes a musher's financial outlook even grimmer. Villagers whose kennels are only accessible by air must pay steeper prices for dog food, equipment, and any other supplies flown in to them. They also must come up with airfare to fly their teams, food drops, and themselves to Anchorage for the start and then back to the village after finishing in Nome. (Competitors living on the Anchorage or Nome road system only need to pay airfare *one* way and can truck everything the other time.) Jerry Austin, who has been running the Iditarod since 1976 and resides in the remote village of St. Michael on Norton Sound, estimates that it costs rural mushers an additional $10,000 per year to compete. Akiak resident Mike Williams, a Yup'ik Eskimo, credits the hospitality of Willow-area musher Joe Garnie with enabling him to participate in the 1993 race. By staying with Garnie for a few weeks before the race, Williams could purchase dog food in nearby Anchorage and avoid paying air freight to ship his food drops to the Iditarod Trail Committee.

The financial disadvantages of living in a remote area have a disproportionately large impact on Native Alaskan mushers (Indians and Eskimos). Of the sixty-eight competitors who started the 1993 Iditarod, only three were Native: Mike Williams, Joe Garnie, and Beverly Masek. Even fewer Natives competed in 1994, 1995, and 1996. This is terribly ironic, considering that the Iditarod was founded in large part to honor Native mushers (more than half of the serum run's drivers were Native) and to encourage a revival of sled dogs in the villages.

In its early years, the Iditarod was dominated by legendary Native mushers such as Herbie Nayokpuk, Emmitt Peters, Carl Huntington, and Ken Chase. In 1993, race judge and Native Kotzebue musher Langford Adams contended, "I could show you at least half a dozen Native dog teams sitting at home in the villages who could beat many of the teams that are running this year, but they can't even afford to get to the starting line." A groundswell of support for these Native village teams is occurring, and suggestions for assisting them financially include the creation of scholarships, sponsorship by Native corporations and other bush-community businesses, and stronger leadership on this issue by the Iditarod Trail Committee.

Nevertheless, each year mushers continue to go into debt just to be able to run the Iditarod. Is it worth it? Yes, if just for "the privilege of seeing this land," one competitor explains. That certainly makes it an expensive way to sightsee.

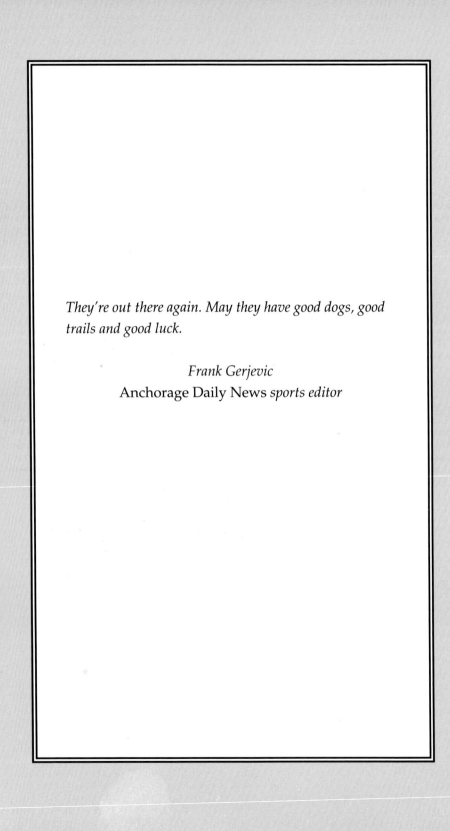

They're out there again. May they have good dogs, good trails and good luck.

Frank Gerjevic
Anchorage Daily News *sports editor*

5

Prerace Details

It's the first week of March—race week in Anchorage—but preparations for this year's Iditarod have been well underway since last November! Trailbreakers begin putting in critical stretches of the trail, such as building up a substantial base of snow through the Farewell Burn, in the fall. Meanwhile, in the race's largest urban areas, Anchorage and Wasilla, plans are proceeding for the start and the restart (the dog teams travel from Anchorage to Eagle River and then, in order to avoid open water on two large rivers, they are trucked from Eagle River to a restart in Wasilla). To give you an idea of the staggering logistics involved in coordinating the Iditarod, here's a partial list of what needs to be organized: permits, police officers, paramedics, animal-control officers, garbage trucks, barricades, fences, signs, banners, sound systems, parking, phones, buses, public relations, press packages, record keeping, volunteer handlers, sled holders, timers, and, of course, seventy-odd mushers complete with their dog trucks, crews, and 1,120 huskies.

Months of preparation are now complete; the Iditarod starts this weekend. Mushers' food drops are being flown to the checkpoints. Each competitor has paid a $1,750 entry fee. And rookies have furnished the ITC with proof that they have successfully completed at least 500 miles of sled-dog racing and have viewed the *Iditarod Rookie Seminar* video. A compulsory meeting is held during the week to help prepare the Iditarod rookies for their first running.

The Iditarod Trail Committee ships straw bales to the checkpoints in order to provide warm, comfortable resting places for the dogs (and here, a volunteer). Mushers use small plastic sleds to tow food-drop bags to their parking spots.

Younger mushers, ages fourteen through eighteen, ran the Junior Iditarod Trail Sled Dog Race last weekend (one week before the main event). Starting at Big Lake, just north of Anchorage, they raced sixty-five miles along the Iditarod Trail to Yentna Station, took a twelve-hour mandatory layover, and returned the next day. As is the case in many sports, mushing often becomes a family affair with child/parent entrants in the two Iditarods.

Two well-known families, the Osmars and the Barrons, exemplify this involvement. Tim Osmar, son of 1984 Iditarod champion Dean Osmar, won the Junior Iditarod in 1982, 1983, and 1984. When he turned eighteen in 1985, Tim entered his first Iditarod, finishing an impressive thirteenth in his rookie year. Since then, he has garnered nine top-ten Iditarod finishes. Most Iditarod insiders believe that it's only a matter of time until Timmy wins the big one. This would make the Osmars the second father/son duo to have won the Iditarod; 1978 champion Dick Mackey was elated to watch his son Rick Mackey finish

Jeff King looks to see what starting-position number he has drawn from an oversize boot at the 1993 prerace mushers' banquet. King went on to win the 1993 race, his first Iditarod championship.

first in 1983. Race watchers also expect to see an unprecedented *four* members of the same family compete in an upcoming Iditarod: John, Laird, Jason, and Will Barron. All three of John's sons have raced the Junior Iditarod; now that youngest son Will has turned eighteen, some year soon a Barron may bask in the glow of victory under Nome's burled arch.

On the Wednesday before the start of the Iditarod, which is traditionally held on the first Saturday in March, veterinarians examine each dog from every team. It takes an experienced vet thirty minutes to an hour to check a sixteen-dog team, listening to the heart rate and breathing pattern as well as inspecting eyes, ears, nose, mouth, paws, skin, joints, and overall condition. Each dog is also weighed and given an electrocardiogram. Occasionally, a dog is pulled; perhaps a heart murmur, a previously undiagnosed tumor, or pregnancy is detected. Because the welfare of the animals is the number-one concern of the mushers and the Iditarod Trail Committee, veterinarians' judgments are final.

Because the welfare of the animals is the number-one concern of the mushers and the Iditarod Trail Committee, each dog is examined by a team of veterinarians before the race.

At a mandatory mushers' meeting on Thursday morning, Iditarod competitors all gather together in one place for the first time since last year's race. This reunion is a big event because the mushers come from homes scattered throughout the state of Alaska, as well as from the Lower 48 and foreign countries. There's a lot of laughter and shop talk as everyone arrives and picks up their "freebies"—perhaps a duffle bag, a pair of boots, or a number of sets of chore gloves—compliments of major sponsors. The meeting begins with a roll call, a veritable who's who of the mushing world. As the hours pass, the drivers sign their commemorative cachets, turn in any required forms, pay their ITC dues if they are not current, and even sing "Happy Birthday" to a surprised fellow competitor. Speeches are given by the ITC executive director, major sponsors, and various race officials. Of greatest interest to the assembly is the discussion of trail conditions and checkpoint amenities by the race manager.

Later in the day, the general public is welcome to attend the mushers' banquet, where each competitor draws his or her starting-position

A DETAILED GEAR LIST FOR THE IDITAROD START
Courtesy of Martin Buser

Dogs
Harnesses
Lines
Sled

Clothing:	Boots, Pants, Jacket, Gloves, Mittens, Hat
	Kept on person in clothing = Carmex™ lip salve, knife, matches, floss, needle, toothbrush and paste, sunglasses, yellow notebook (Buser's "bible," containing reduced photocopies of his drop-bag contents at each checkpoint, and race times from previous years)
On the Sled:	Snub Line (secures sled to hopefully immovable object)
	2 Snowhooks
	Spare Lines
	Drop Cable
	Spare Snaps
In the Sled:	2 Coolers (for preparing and transporting dogs' meals)
	1 Personal Cooler (Buser heats juice packs in hot water, stores them in his cooler, and then drinks them later when they have become lukewarm)
	Cooker, Alcohol, Dog Bowls, Food Dipper
	Snowshoes, Ax, Sleeping Bag, Promotional Material, Veterinary Notebook
	Booties, Blankets, Foot Ointment, Wrist Wraps, Comb
	Spare Harnesses, Great Coat, QCR™ Runner Plastic
	Spare Gangline, Garbage Bags
Personal Bag:	Walkman™, Matches, Face Masks, Gloves, Socks, 10 mm Semi-automatic Gun, Bullets, QCR™ Tool, Music Tapes, Wind Shirt, Wind Pants, Rain Gear, Army Knife, Dickey (with a pouch to store small items), Money, Underwear, Dog First-Aid Kit, Goggles
Dog Food:	4 Ready Meals Eagle Pack, 4 Bags Salmon Snacks, 4 Bags Lamb Snacks, Oil, 2 Bags Charlie Champaine Mix
Headlamp Box:	3 Replacement Lamps, Dozen Bulbs, 2 Battery Packs

number from a boot or hat. Attendance may top 1,300, so tickets need to be purchased well in advance. Because every musher is allowed to speak after drawing a number, and because he or she usually thanks both sponsors and supporters at length, the festivities may last from 6 P.M. until 11 P.M. Many fans take advantage of this opportunity to get autographs and to talk with their race favorites in person.

The number drawn at the banquet is worn on the musher's bib and is also engraved on identification tags that are placed on the collar of each dog in the musher's team. Beginning in 1993, these metal ID tags were supplemented by computer microchips. Developed by American Veterinary Identification Devices (AVID), the microchips were initially designed to reunite lost pets with their owners. The size of a grain of rice, the tiny chip fits into a hypodermic needle. It is injected under the dog's skin on the scruff of the neck and provides permanent identification. A hand-held scanning device searches for and reads the microchip, giving race officials instant identification. This ensures quicker access to the dog's medical history and allows veterinarians to provide better care for dogs that have been dropped at checkpoints throughout the race because they are tired, ill, or simply not running up to the pace of the rest of the team.

The Friday night before the start, a bizarre event occurs: highway crews that have spent all winter working to keep Anchorage clear of snow now deliberately truck snow back onto the streets so that Iditarod teams can use the city's road system for the race's festive start.

Why does the race traditionally begin on the first Saturday in March? The ground underneath the Iditarod Trail is spongy muskeg swamp, which means that it is strictly a winter trail. If the race began earlier in the season, the weather on the Bering Sea coast would be too stormy (it's even worse in January and February than in March), but if the start were delayed until later in March, the weather near the beginning of the trail would be insufferably hot. The first week of March seems to be the best compromise.

Just as the night before Christmas finds children awake with anticipation, the night before "game day" finds most rookies up into the wee hours nervously packing and repacking their sleds and agonizing over every other conceivable Idita-detail. In contrast, pros like DeeDee Jonrowe go to bed at 10 P.M. and sleep until 7:30 A.M., accumulating an enviable nine-and-one-half-hour reserve before beginning a largely sleepless week and a half.

It's race day at last. Mushers line up their trucks on Fourth Avenue

Replacement sleds await mushers at McGrath. After Knik, competitors may only change sleds two times.

in starting order. At 10:00 A.M., team #1 (reserved for this year's honorary musher/s) will be recognized. Following this, the remaining teams will start at two-minute intervals.

Because sled dogs get so excited once they are harnessed, some mushers wait to hook up their team until fifteen minutes before being called. The well-rested dogs leap into the air, pull and twist, yammer and yowl, and generally act completely demented. Drivers leave their "lunatics" (such as harness-biters and gangline-chewers) until last, securing them in place as little as thirty seconds before takeoff. If you doubt whether sled dogs like to race, just watch them being harnessed. Talk about job satisfaction! "Enthusiasm" doesn't begin to describe their attitude; even "zeal" is too weak a word. It takes as many as ten handlers to restrain this raw power, and the musher has to attach a second sled with a second driver (or carry a handler in the sled basket) in order to slow down the crazed dogs for the first part of the race.

5 . . . 4 . . . 3 . . . 2 . . . 1 . . . GO!

In McGrath we have Christmas, New Year's, and Iditarod.

Erin Gerrin
Race checker

6

Volunteers and Staff

Communications expert Jim Johnson flies up for the race from San Jose, California; veterinarians Bob Harwood and Horst Rodenbach arrive from Kansas and Dusseldorf, Germany; and a man simply known as "Speedy" takes a yearly leave from the British Army in order to care for dropped dogs, answer the phones, or do whatever else is needed. The Iditarod is one of the few major competitions in the world of sports still run primarily by volunteers. Not all Iditarod workers travel so far to offer their talents, but each one makes an indispensable contribution. Put simply: no volunteers, no Iditarod.

Five individuals rate special mention for having served each year since the first race in 1973: Vi and Joe Redington, Sr. (Joe is a lifetime member of ITC's board of directors, all of whom donate their time); Joe Delia (Skwentna host and checker); and Audra and Dick Forsgren (checkers at their cabin in Ophir).

The thousand-plus other volunteers who make running the Iditarod possible are its unsung heroes. Kudos and bouquets to each and every one.

TRAILBREAKERS

These hardy souls set out into virtually untouched territory to pack and mark a trail for the mushers. Traveling by snow machines, which often tip over or slide off of the trail, the trailbreaking crews leave wooden stakes topped with orange reflectors or pink surveyor's tape as markers.

Four trailbreakers work two days in advance of the mushers, four more repack the trail just ahead of the front-runners, and three bring up the rear, acting as trail sweeps. This ITC crew of trailbreakers is quick to acknowledge that they could never accomplish their job without the assistance of countless locals. In the Finger Lake area alone, five residents have helped break trail. One of them, Barry Stanley, is credited with whipping the infamous Happy River Hill into fabulous shape for the 1993 race. Stanley set the trail down in a trench so that the snow would provide a sort of guardrail. This was very helpful to the speeding teams, especially on the downhill side of the trail.

The final forty-eight miles of the trail, from Topkok into town, is staked each year by Nome Boy Scout Troop #98. These boys know that this is one of the most critical sections to mark due to the likelihood of dangerous coastal storms and they take pride in doing their job well.

In 1989, Don Burt completed his fourteenth year as an Iditarod volunteer and his sixth year as a trailbreaker. As he sped along on his snow machine near Unalakleet, the toe of one of his boots caught on a stump in the trail and twisted his ankle. Despite his bruised and swollen leg, Burt pressed on to Nome, where he discovered that his ankle was broken. For Burt, trailbreaking took on a whole new meaning.

During the first four days of breaking trail for the 1990 race, perennial volunteer Rich Owens lost seven pounds, even though he was eating 9,000 calories a day. Nobody said that being an Iditarod volunteer is easy.

PILOTS

Called the Iditarod Air Force, a group of some twenty-eight pilots flies more than 1,200 hours and moves more than 90,000 pounds of freight during each year's race. Beginning a week before the start, the pilots fly the mushers' food drops to the checkpoints. During the race, they leapfrog veterinarians, checkers, and race officials along the trail, making sure that each checkpoint is staffed until all of the racers have passed through.

The race start is characterized by crowds, commotion, intense media coverage, and all the trappings of civilization. Iditarod trailbreakers will undertake the arduous task of packing down the trail just ahead of the first dog teams.

To give you an idea of what they are up against, here is an excerpt from the information packet that ITC prepares for the press under the heading of "Pilot Information for Flying the Iditarod Trail":

Rohn Roadhouse - *We would recommend that you NOT land here.* If you do, use extreme caution; the snow becomes hard packed and very slick from the cross winds that usually blow down the canyon. Always try to land uphill (N.E.) if possible. When cross winds become too severe, you can usually land on the river ice to the west of the strip. When parked, get your aircraft as far off the strip as you can. When the cross winds are bad, aircraft are hard to control after touchdown.

Incidentally, Rohn Roadhouse is one of the checkpoints to which the Iditarod Air Force delivers food drops for every musher.

CHECKPOINT OFFICIALS

Some checkpoint volunteers hoist the giant bags containing the mushers' food drops from the planes into their storage locations. Others are assigned to guard these bags. It can make the difference between winning and losing if a musher can't find his or her supply bag. Dogs do not do well if they have to change their highly individualized diet, and the driver may be handicapped by not replacing dead headlamp batteries or having access to other spare parts.

Checkers and their assistants sign in each racer, recording their arrival and departure times. They also inspect for mandatory equipment and relay instructions to the mushers. In the villages along the trail, usually a local person serves as checker, but the ITC has to fly volunteers in to the uninhabited checkpoints.

Because mushers arrive at all times of the day and night and often come in large groups, most checkers have three or four assistants. Iditarod volunteers, like the competitors, do not get much sleep the first few weeks of March.

VETERINARIANS

As many as thirty veterinarians volunteer their expertise at the checkpoints along the trail. Arriving dogs are examined, medicine is administered if necessary, and preventive measures are taken, such as applying ointment to paws that are beginning to look sore.

A volunteer veterinarian who is working with the Iditarod for the first or second year is apprenticed to a more experienced vet. If the newcomer has any question about the best type of treatment, specific medications, or a dog in borderline condition, she or he consults with the mentor. If the mentoring vet is unsure about any situation, the chief veterinarian is in constant contact and can be on the scene quickly by means of a plane designated specifically for this purpose.

If they are concerned about an animal's welfare, these vets have the right to pull the dog out of the race—now, no questions. In the Iditarod, the dogs' well-being is the top priority.

*Karin Schmidt,
Iditarod Chief
Veterinarian,
administers TLC
along with expert
medical care.*

COMMUNICATIONS EXPERTS

For many years, ham-radio operators relayed vital information during the race. The Iditarod Trail Committee passed along requests for supplies and personnel, discussed problems, and reported on mushers' arrival and departure times. Occasionally, mushers used the radio to call home if they needed equipment or just a morale boost.

Hams' work shifts extended to forty-eight hours and the northern lights periodically brought communications to a standstill. The upside of the job, according to a 1990 *Alaska* magazine article, was that they got to know all the dirt—whose dogs were sick, whose girlfriend or boyfriend was impatient in Nome, and who had hot apple pie ready along the trail.

In recent years, however, ham-radio operators have been replaced by VSATs, satphones, and radio telephones. A VSAT (Very Small Aperture Terminal) is a three-and-a-half-foot diameter earth station that receives satellite transmissions. One is flown to the race's uninhabited halfway checkpoint, assembled, and used to enable race personnel to make voice or fax contacts. Race communications sponsor GCI (General Communications, Inc.) allows mushers and locals who have stopped at this checkpoint to call anyone, anywhere in the world, from the earth station. Imagine standing in Cripple, little more than a wide spot on the trail in the middle of the Alaskan wilderness, and being able to call Mom back home in Poughkeepsie! In anticipation of the 1996 Iditarod, GCI has set up a video conference system that will permit mushers to speak to *and see* loved ones who make an appointment to appear at the Regal Alaskan Hotel in Anchorage for this purpose.

Satphones (satellite telephones) are used at other remote locations such as Ophir and Eagle Island. The size of an attaché case, a satphone has a panel that opens to reveal a battery-powered antenna. Either phone or fax calls can be made, but are very expensive per minute. On the other hand, virtually anyone can operate a satphone, and they are easily transported.

Radio telephones link into larger villages' phone systems through VHF frequencies, allowing the use of battery-operated phone and fax. When the range to the nearest village is longer, rural radio can be accessed via UHF. In this case, the operator pushes a button to talk, then releases it to listen.

In established communities, Iditarod personnel have a race-restricted 800 number. Through a combination of the VSAT, satphones, radio telephones and local phone systems, every checkpoint on the Iditarod Trail now has twenty-four-hour phone communication in place, and all except the rural radio setups have fax capability also. Iditarod's hams are fondly remembered, and many now work as communications experts.

VILLAGERS

Along the entire length of the Iditarod Trail, villagers are famous for their warm hospitality. From 1973 to 1991, many locals opened their homes to the mushers (and to assorted volunteers, press, and officials), offering beds on a first-come basis and then floor space for sleeping bags. Competitors were grateful for the opportunity to dry their clothing and their dogs' booties. Usually a pot of stew was simmering on the stove and tables sagged under the lavish spread set out by gracious hosts and hostesses.

During the 1989 race, Joe Runyan arrived first at the Eagle Island checkpoint. After putting down straw for his dogs, then feeding and examining them, he climbed seventy-two snow steps up to Ralph and Helmi Conaster's cabin. The tantalizing aroma of moose stew, blueberry cheesecake, various pies, and cupcakes greeted the weary musher. "This is the high point of the winter," Helmi Conaster explained. It's hardly surprising that Runyan slept soundly after such a grand repast.

Beginning with the 1992 race, ITC enacted the so-called "corralling" rule. This requires all mushers while in the checkpoints to park their teams at designated localized holding areas, rather than in a host family's yard. In addition, mushers at the checkpoints must use accommodations at officially prescribed locations only. Those competitors who desire peace and privacy, however, may still choose to park their teams along the trail, as long as they do not camp within one mile of a checkpoint.

These rules have severely cramped village hospitality. As a result, both villagers and mushers have voiced their disappointment about this arrangement. However, most drivers, though nostalgic about the old days, have been quite pleased at the ways the corralling rule has evened the playing field. Gone are the disparities in sleeping arrangements (a warm bed versus the gym floor), musher meals (a Thanksgiving-like spread versus trail mix), and dog care (hot water waiting at the host family's house for mixing the dogs' food versus filling buckets from a hole in the ice and waiting for it to heat on your stove). Gone, too, are the niggling doubts about whether your competitors are receiving unfair outside assistance. Well-known mushers and trail veterans tended to have more enjoyable checkpoint stays than rookies and relative unknowns. Competitors have also commented that the new system allows them to be less vigilant about arch-rivals sneaking out of town, and it enables faster and more efficient veterinary care.

Village hospitality is not dead, though. As long as it is accessible to everyone, locals may still prepare that famed repast. Offerings are collected at a central location and then taken to a designated Mushers' House, a building that is off limits to everyone except competitors,

Race manager Jack Niggemyer describes his job as "maintaining the Iditarod's spirit of celebrating Alaska, and making all the volunteers happy."

race officials, and a few volunteers. Now every musher has a chance to sample the stews, breads, cakes, and pies of which trail memories are made.

DROPPED-DOG CARETAKERS

At the checkpoints, dropped dogs are cared for by experienced, compassionate volunteers who are under the supervision of race veterinarians. As soon as possible, these dogs are flown to dropped-dog hub checkpoints and from there to facilities at either Eagle River (near Anchorage) or Nome. At Eagle River, the minimum-security inmates and their supervisors at Hiland Mountain and Meadow Creek State Correctional Center care for dogs dropped from the race.

HOTLINE OPERATORS

Volunteers like "Speedy" answer the phones at the Iditarod Race headquarters located in the Regal Alaskan Hotel in Anchorage. The Regal is communications central during the Iditarod. In the foyer, race fans can check the leader board, peruse a huge map of the trail, and select from a wide array of related merchandise sold by volunteers. Down the hall in the information room, the hotline phones ring constantly, and visitors can pick up photocopies of the latest standings and press releases. Large bulletin boards convey weather data and notices to various volunteer groups. The hotline operators work hard to keep current with all of this information so that they can pass it along to their callers. In other private rooms, ITC officials process race data and orchestrate the incredibly intricate race logistics.

During the race, temporary headquarters are also set up at Eagle River and Nome, while ITC's year-round Wasilla base continues to conduct business. These locations provide information to the press as well as to interested individuals. Receiving the standings straight from the race course and relaying them to the public is an exciting and rewarding job.

VOLUNTEER POTPOURRI

At the start and restart, legions of volunteers serve as sled holders, dog handlers, and timers. Others provide crowd control at the easily accessible towns of Anchorage, Eagle River, Wasilla, and Knik. At all but the smallest checkpoints, there is a cook who dishes up sustenance for the vets, pilots, officials, dog caretakers, trailbreakers, and other volunteers. The cook does *not* feed the mushers, the press, or race fans. Keeping tired workers happily fed twenty-four hours a day from a low-budget inventory of ingredients is not an enviable task. Other checkpoint volunteers include clean-up crews and general "gofers." A small but dedicated band of photographers also donate their expertise as they travel the trail.

Who are all of these people? Some are helpful local residents, others are adventure-seeking Alaskans, die-hard fans from the Lower 48 and foreign countries, mushers' spouses, sponsors, and even ITC board members. Anyone can be infected by Iditarod fever.

Jim Kershner is an Iditarod jack-of-all-trades. He completed the race as a musher in 1975 and has also volunteered as a trailbreaker, pilot, checker, ham, race manager, race marshal, race judge, and ITC board member. If he'd just get his Doctor of Veterinary Medicine degree, he'd have covered nearly all the bases!

IDITAROD TRAIL COMMITTEE STAFF

Jack Niggemyer served as race manager from 1987 to 1991 and again from 1994 through 1996. After volunteering as a trailbreaker for the 1989 race, *Alaska* magazine editor Ron Dalby wrote that when Niggemyer resigns, the want ad for his replacement might read as follows:

Help Wanted

RACE MANAGER: Personable, dedicated, budget-minded logistics manager able to work effectively in four distinct cultural environments: Yup'ik, Inupiat, Athabascan and Anglo-Saxon. Must be flexible and patient. Individual hired will manage dozens of airplanes, several hundred tons of supplies and equipment, and 1,500 or more independent-minded volunteers, many working in remote locations. Unflappable sense of humor a major prerequisite. Intense drive and motivation required. Claims of previous experience disregarded; this is the only job of its kind in the world. Contact Executive Director, Iditarod Trail Committee.

But perhaps even more telling is the comment made by Niggemyer in the 1991 *Iditarod Runner Annual*, in which he announced the birth of his second child. He explains that "having two small children around the house prepares me for the Iditarod. I'm all the time being woken up in the middle of the night by people who are whining, smell funny and are impossible to reason with."

In a serious moment, however, Niggemyer confided that he was hospitalized due to stress and exhaustion after two of his eight stints as manager. He is not complaining, though. "I was paid well to worry for everybody," he says. "My job was to maintain the Iditarod's spirit of celebrating Alaska, and to make all the volunteers happy."

It's a toss-up whether being the race manager or the race marshal is less desirable. The position of race marshal is generally held by a musher who has previously run the Iditarod, and it has a one-year tenure. The race marshal's interpretation of the rules in any questionable circumstance is final, and she or he is also responsible for making difficult decisions about whether or not to "freeze" the race or reroute it in case of dangerous climatic or trail conditions. As you can imagine, such rulings are always controversial, and the race marshal is the one who takes the heat.

Working under the race marshal are five race judges. They travel checkpoint to checkpoint and monitor racers' behavior. A citation issued to a musher by a race judge might be for leaving litter at his or her designated parking place or for venturing beyond the prescribed "corral" area (for example, a competitor is found at a local store or bar and has not requested permission to leave the holding area). This may sound petty, but race officials and veterinarians need to be able to locate a musher at a moment's notice if there is any concern about a dog or a team that has been parked and left under the watchful eyes of checkpoint volunteers.

Other Iditarod race personnel include a development director (fund raising), a race director (millions of details), the logistics coordinator (getting everything and everyone to the right place at the right time), a communications coordinator, the start and restart coordinators mentioned in "Prerace Details," and finally a Nome (or finish) coordinator. The board of directors, composed of ten individuals, meets throughout the year to review the race and set policy. The Iditarod's executive director, board president, vice-president, secretary, and treasurer are kept even busier than usual during the month of March.

Thanks to dedicated staff members and tireless volunteers, the Iditarod can continue to be the Last Great Race.

In 1978, Dick Mackey pulled into Nome one second ahead of Rick Swenson. As soon as his lead dogs had crossed the finish line, Mackey collapsed on his sled, exhausted from the hard sprint. Swenson's team continued until his sled passed over the finish line. Who had won? Some said your sled has to cross the line, others claimed that the nose of the first lead dog across the line determines the winner. Race Marshal Myron Gavin was asked to render his decision. Gavin ruled in favor of Mackey, reasoning, "You don't take a picture of the horse's ass."

7

Race Rules

Since its first running in 1973, the Iditarod has developed a lengthy and rather complex set of policies and rules. Basically, they boil down to three simple goals: to protect the welfare of the dogs, to ensure that mushers have adequate equipment to deal with potentially life-threatening arctic conditions, and to provide an "even playing field" for all competitors.

These rules are meant to be guidelines, not commandments written in stone. It is the duty of each year's race marshal to interpret them on a case-by-case basis to the best of his or her ability. In some instances, the spirit, rather than the letter, of the law may take precedence.

OPEN TO INTERPRETATION

The following incidents illustrate the variety of unusual situations that may require interpretation by the race marshal.

During the 1979 race, eighteen-year-old rookie Karl Clauson shipped some laundry home to his mom in Wasilla from the McGrath checkpoint. When a race official checked Clauson's mandatory gear in Anvik, his Iditarod promotional material was discovered to be missing. Each year, the ITC has special mail packets stamped in Anchorage and then again in Nome, commemorating the time when mail was carried

*Only dogs determined to be northern breeds
may now race in the Iditarod. Iditarod dogs often stand
on their houses in order to monitor all goings-on.*

by dog teams; these are later sold as a fund-raising project. Clauson's packet had inadvertently gotten in with his laundry! Because checkers at the points in between had not noticed this omission, the race marshal did not disqualify Clauson. Instead, he had Clauson wait in Anvik until his mandatory mail arrived (which took two days), then allowed him to proceed. The young rookie was the thirty-eighth musher to cross the finish line in Nome.

While taking shelter from a life-threatening storm along the coast during the 1987 Iditarod, Canadian musher Dave Olesen lost one of his snowshoes to the blizzard's blasts. Although arriving at a checkpoint without any one of the mandatory items is grounds for disqualification, the race marshal may make exceptions in the case of accidental or unavoidable loss. In such an instance, the driver is permitted to replace the item at the next checkpoint before checking in. Having weathered the storm, Olesen completed his second Iditarod in twenty-eighth place.

Frank Teasley was not so lucky in 1990. At the halfway point of Cripple, Teasley gave his team an extended rest, trying to overcome his dogs' sickness. (Many dogs were dropped during the 1990 Iditarod due to uncommonly warm weather at the start, or because of ingesting volcanic ash that was erupting from Mount Redoubt.) Race officials decided that too many of Teasley's dogs were ill for him to continue and announced that he was disqualified. Veterinarians emphasized that the team's problems were *not* caused by negligence. A year later, in 1991, Frank Teasley was given the Sterling Achievement Award, which recognizes the most improved musher. Teasley had finished thirty-first in 1988, and nineteenth in 1989, and he had been running in thirty-fifth place when he was disqualified in 1990; he finished the 1991 Iditarod in sixth place.

On the Yentna River near the beginning of the 1991 race, Joe Carpenter's dogs staged a lie-down strike. They lay down and wouldn't get up. For nine hours Carpenter tried everything that he could think of—he fed them, he offered them water, he left them alone to rest, and finally he went up to his leaders and tried pulling them. Nothing worked. In desperation, he accepted a tow from another musher in the hope that once they were moving, the dogs would keep going. But the rules state that one musher may aid another only in an emergency situation. Carpenter's predicament was not considered to be life-threatening; therefore, he was disqualified by the race officials. He did run the Iditarod again in 1993 and was the forty-seventh musher into Nome.

RECENT RULE CHANGES

The Iditarod Trail Committee has made a number of significant revisions in the race rules in the last few years:

- The mandatory layover at White Mountain has been increased from six to eight hours to give the dogs more rest.
- ITC has decided to ship bales of straw to the checkpoints so that all teams, not just those with money, can enjoy its advantages. Straw is warm for dogs to lie on, but it may have an even more important characteristic—it reminds the huskies of home.
- Only dogs determined to be northern breeds may now race in the Iditarod.
- An Animal Care Committee has been created and designated a permanent committee.

- In the event that a dog in a competitor's team dies during the race, the musher will be automatically withdrawn or disqualified unless the death was caused by an external force beyond the musher's control, such as a moose or snow machine.
- An additional eight-hour mandatory layover, to be taken on the Yukon River, has been created.
- The maximum number of dogs with which a musher may start the Iditarod has been reduced from twenty to sixteen, giving the drivers better control in the early miles of the race.
- A veterinary notebook recording each dog's medical condition and any treatment given has been added to the list of mandatory equipment.

ENFORCEMENT OF THE RULES

In the past, one major concern has been that a musher could gain an unfair advantage due to visitation by his or her spouse at the checkpoints. Traveling the trail by bush plane, the spouse could acquire useful information about weather and trail conditions, the status of various competitors, and other helpful tidbits unavailable to the drivers. The "corralling" rule and the strengthening of the "no outside assistance" rule seem to have largely solved this problem. Now spouses are most likely to be seen in Anchorage and Nome, and rarely at points in between. Of course, mushers can "phone home," but that form of communication is available to everyone.

A new twist on this problem that may require enforcement is that some sponsors are sending large delegations of employees to the race. Generally, these enthusiastic supporters merely assist with handling at the start and restart, loading at Eagle River, and celebrating in Nome. Some, however, do fly the trail in private planes and visit with their sponsorees at the checkpoints. This creates the possibility that proprietary information may be passed along.

PROPOSED RULE CHANGES

Competition breeds controversy, and the Iditarod is no exception. As the race matures, problem areas are being identified and possible solutions are being discussed. With the combined efforts of mushers,

The maximum number of dogs permitted at the start of the Iditarod has been reduced from twenty to sixteen. This should make the early going slower and safer. Here, a musher descends infamous Cordova Hill.

volunteers, staff, and friends of the Iditarod, these issues can be satisfactorily resolved.

A Handicapping System?

One proposition has been voted down twice. In 1990 and 1992, a handicapping system was proposed that would have enabled heavier mushers to start the race with more dogs than their lighter-weight counterparts. For instance, a 190-pound musher could start the race with the maximum number of dogs permitted (now sixteen), while a 110-pound musher would start with four to six fewer dogs (perhaps ten or twelve). The proponents of the handicapping system argued that lighter-weight racers have an unfair advantage; those opposed noted that any such advantage disappears when the smaller mushers have to maneuver a heavy sled around an obstacle or up a hill.

Rookie Entry Requirements

An important safety issue is the amount of experience that rookie mushers should be required to have. Since 1993, rookies need to show that they have successfully completed 500 miles (in contrast to a previous minimum of 200) in an Iditarod-sanctioned race. Critics feel that this is not the best approach and that it would be preferable to require two to three years of mushing experience, rather than a specific number of miles run. And perhaps an entry requirement stipulating an amount of time spent mushing should also specify that a substantial amount of it have been spent in *competitive* mushing, because the demands of racing are quite different from those of recreational mushing.

The Pro/Am Phoenix

Periodically, someone suggests that the race should be divided into two separate divisions—one for professional mushers and one for amateurs. An entrant would only compete against those running in his or her division, which would help to equalize the playing field.

Realistically speaking, as it exists now, there are two separate Iditarod Trail Sled Dog Races. One occurs at the front of the pack, among those competitors who seek to finish "in the money," that is, in the top twenty positions. The other Iditarod is run by a middle group who seek to finish respectably, and by the so-called "tourists" or "campers," those mushers at the back of the pack whose goal is simply to survive and finish the race.

The challenge now facing the Iditarod is how to preserve its mystique and allure by accommodating the "dreamers" while protecting the dogs, volunteers, and race officials from inexperienced entrants and those lacking an appropriate level of commitment to dog mushing. Hopefully, a solution can be found that will safeguard the well-being of the dogs and race support and still satisfy those whose goal is to enjoy the run and finish the race, as well as those who wish to win it.

A Home-Stay Program

Anchorage Daily News sportswriter Lew Freedman has another suggestion for the ITC. Why not create a home-stay program, he asks, so that mushers could have a chance to stay in local residents' homes at the checkpoints? This would enable the competitors to get to know the villagers and vice-versa. If the details of such a program could be arranged so that it were fair, and drivers as well as their teams were easily accessible to race officials and vets, many would welcome a return to the renowned hospitality of bygone years.

IDITAROD
DOGS

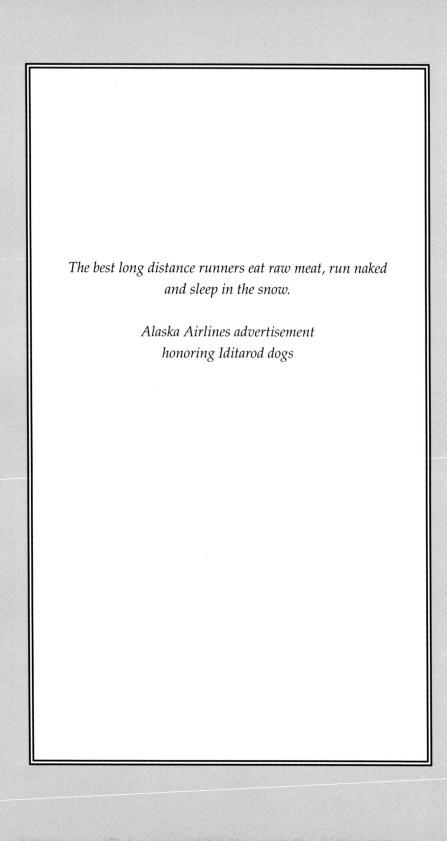

The best long distance runners eat raw meat, run naked
and sleep in the snow.

Alaska Airlines advertisement
honoring Iditarod dogs

8

Canine Competitors

How can they do it? Iditarod dogs pull a load of 300 to 500 pounds, including the contents of the sled and the weight of the musher. The average musher starts with sixteen dogs, which means that each dog pulls about twenty to thirty pounds. Because the dogs are usually pulling the sled over frictionless snow and ice, this is not an excessive expectation.

The distance the dogs cover during the timed portion of the race (from Wasilla to Nome) rounds to 1,150 miles and the record speed for completing this mileage is 9 days, 2 hours, 42 minutes, and 19 seconds (set by Doug Swingley in 1995). This means that the fastest dogs average 127 miles per day. To say that these dogs really fly is only a slight exaggeration.

BREEDS

The desire and ability to pull is a genetic trait that has been present in arctic dogs for thousands of years. The Iditarod dog (usually called an Alaskan Husky) is a mixture of several arctic breeds, most notably the Alaskan Malamute, the Siberian Husky, and the Village Dog (with a little Samoyed, hound, and retriever added to the blend).

These breeds all have several characteristics in common: a double-layered coat, composed of a long, coarse outer coat and a virtually

71

waterproof, dense, oily inner coat that enables them to survive at -60° to -70° F; large, flat "snowshoe" feet that have a protective cushion of hair between the toes; tough, thick pads; and a bushy tail that can be curled over the nose while sleeping to warm the air they breathe. Another interesting adaptation that makes them especially well-suited to arctic climates is that the dogs' circulation puts their feet first; therefore, unlike their human partners, getting frostbite on their extremities is not a matter of great concern.

Alaskan Malamutes are named for the Malmuit Eskimos of the Kotzebue area. They are good freight dogs—large and tough, but slow. They average 75 to 100 pounds. This AKC breed is recognizable by its wedge-shaped ears set on the side of the skull, by its brown eyes, and by its curled, plumelike tail.

The Chukchi Eskimos of northeastern Asia bred Siberian Huskies—small, fast dogs, but still tough enough to run long distances. In 1908, a Russian trader brought the first Siberian Huskies to Alaska. The next year, Fox Maule Ramsay, a Nome miner, traveled to Siberia and shipped sixty back home with him. He won first, second, and fourth places in the 1910 All-Alaska Sweepstakes with teams composed of these dogs.

Leonhard Seppala used Siberians to win the All-Alaska Sweepstakes in 1915, 1916, and 1917, and to participate in the 1925 serum run. He later popularized the breed by competing with them in the racing circuit on the east coast of the United States.

The Siberian Husky, also an AKC breed, is distinguished by its erect, high-set ears and its blue or brown eyes (sometimes one of

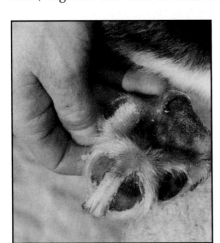

Sled dogs have a protective cushion of hair between their toes.

*A bushy tail can be curled over the nose to warm the air that
a sled dog breathes.*

each). Typically, Siberians weigh thirty-five to sixty pounds. (For
many years, skeptical Alaskans—accustomed to seeing heftier dogs
race—called Seppala's dogs "Siberian rats" or "those little plume-
tailed rats.")

The Village Dogs raised in small Indian and Eskimo settlements
traditionally have been a mixture of whatever was available: Alaskan
Malamutes, Siberian Huskies, wolves, hounds, bird dogs, and strays.
As long as they were fast and tough, it didn't matter what was in
them. Breeders such as Isaac Okleasik, George Attla, Don Honea, Herbie Nayokpuk, Emmitt Peters, and Joe Garnie have increased the
daunting reputation of these Native dogs.

Although the mixed-blood Iditarod dog can weigh anywhere from
thirty to seventy-five pounds, mushers generally believe that a forty-
to-fifty-pound dog is optimum. Top breeders aim to produce dogs
with good feet, a healthy appetite, speed, endurance, drive, a good
coat (if it's too shaggy, it will ball with ice, but if it's too thin, the dog
will get cold), and a good attitude.

Occasionally, you will see purebred Siberian Huskies, Alaskan
Malamutes, or German Shepherd mixes racing in the Iditarod or other
mid- to long-distance races, but they are definitely the exception. The
unassuming Alaskan Husky deserves to be honored with the title of
Iditarod dog.

POSITION IN THE TEAM

Dogs in an Iditarod team run in one of four positions: lead, the first dog or pair of dogs; swing, the pair immediately behind the leaders; team, all of the other dogs except the last two; and wheel, the dogs that run just in front of the sled. The sex of a sled dog does not determine speed, strength, or aptitude. Dogs of either sex are chosen because they are endowed with certain abilities. Although each position requires specific skills, most mushers change the placement of their dogs during training and racing to reduce fatigue and boredom.

Lead Dogs

A musher has no reins or other means of direct control over the dog team except a foot brake, which sometimes slows them down, and a snowhook, which is used as an anchor to secure a team at rest. Instead, the driver gives voice commands to the leaders to start, turn, change speed, or stop the team. The lead dogs are a team's brains and its steering wheel.

The job of a lead dog is to keep the gangline tight and the other dogs moving, to run faster than his or her teammates, and to find and stay on the trail even if bad weather has obliterated it. Good lead dogs use their feet to feel through a snow-covered trail for the firm, well-packed surface below. They also use their powerful noses to detect the scent of any preceding teams and employ their keen sense of hearing to find village checkpoints.

Above-average intelligence is also a prerequisite. In fact, most mushers speak of their leaders as having a sort of sixth sense. They have an uncanny ability to find hidden dangers such as weak ice or open water, to sense the direction of shelter, and to remember years later the details of trails they have traveled.

Lead dogs should also have a special desire to please and be confident enough to face challenging situations like crossing a creek bed filled with rushing water or running across a cattle guard or a narrow bridge. They should not be distracted by other dog teams or by the many surprises waiting along the trail.

Perhaps you can remember your mother or a teacher lecturing you about having "an attitude." Maybe you'll be a lead dog in your next life! A good leader *should* take on an attitude. She or he should demand respect and be accepted by the rest of the team as trail boss. Overly aggressive behavior or fighting is not tolerated, however.

Finally, because they function as the team's steering wheel, lead dogs must respond well to basic commands. A special subset of lead dogs, called command leaders, are particularly adept at this and are valued accordingly. (In contrast to a command leader, a trail leader excels at finding and staying on the trail but may not take commands very well.)

Command leaders are put up front when accurate steering is essential—for example, when crossing numerous other trails or when passing through villages. These amazing animals understand the following commands:

Line Out: Stretch the team straight out from the sled (used when hooking up or unhooking dogs)

All Right, Let's Go, OK, a soft kissing noise or a low whistle (used to sneak away from competitors): Start running (No, mushers do not say "Mush")

Hike or Get Up: Run faster

On By or Straight Ahead: Go straight past a distraction (another trail, team, or people)

Gee: Turn right

Haw: Turn left

Come Gee: Turn the sled around 180 degrees by going to the right (and do it without tangling the lines)

Come Haw: Turn the sled around 180 degrees by going to the left

Easy: Slow down

Whoa: Stop

Obviously, it takes a lot of time and energy to train command leaders. Most mushers consider themselves lucky to have any. Iditarod competitors will usually have three or four command leaders, but top drivers may start the race with as many as twelve of their dogs able to take commands. A well-trained command leader can sell for $5,000 to $10,000.

Commands are not always given by voice. To celebrate the U.S. Bicentennial, Joe Redington, Sr. hooked together 200 sled dogs at one time and towed a tour bus as part of the festivities. Because his lead dog could not have heard a voice from that distance, ever-resourceful Redington rigged a walkie-talkie at the front of the gargantuan team. At the appropriate moment, Redington gave the starting signal to his lead dog Feets over the airwaves.

*Spencer Thew finished the 1993 Iditarod running this team
of purebred Siberian Huskies.*

Karin Schmidt, Iditarod chief veterinarian in recent years, used an alternate technique when she ran the 1989 Iditarod. Emery, her two-and-one-half-year-old lead dog, did not take verbal commands well, but Schmidt had discovered that if she touched the brake, he would look back at her for directions. She would then give Emery a hand signal, canine sign language if you will, indicating what she wanted. When asked if this slowed down the team, Schmidt asserted, "That was our way of communicating. You learn to work with what you have, bringing out each individual dog's strong points."

No lead dog, even a command leader, is perfect. Like knights of long ago searching for the Holy Grail, mushers continue to seek for that once-in-a-lifetime all-around leader. But even the best have flaws. Some lead dogs don't like to run into the wind, others hate working their way through dense forests. Some can't keep the lines tight, while still others tangle the team on turns. This is one reason why drivers move dogs around in the team, using certain ones at specific times to best advantage.

Lead dogs that come close to being ideal achieve legendary stature. One such dog is five-time-champion Rick Swenson's amazing Andy. During the 1982 race, the front-runners got caught in a terrible storm only forty miles from the finish line. For seven miles below Topkok Hills along the beach to Nome, various mushers tried running their team in front to see whose lead dog would be able to plow through the tremendous side winds, which were gusting up to eighty miles per hour! Jerry Austin, Emmitt Peters, and Susan Butcher all took turns, but to little avail. Finally, Rick Swenson put his Andy up front, and he successfully led the others through the storm.

Swing Dogs

The dogs that run immediately behind the lead dog or dogs are called swing dogs. If the musher is lucky, they will also be command leaders. Their job is to keep the team on the trail by turning it around corners in a wide arc, thus preventing dogs from jumping off of the trail into deep snow.

Team Dogs

The unsung canine heroes are the team dogs, who act as its heart or motor. They have the power and stamina to get the job of pulling done. In a very competitive team, they may also be command leaders. If possible, team dogs are allowed to run lead, swing, or wheel, giving them a break from the boring grunt work that they are so well-suited to do.

Wheel Dogs

If the leaders are the brains of a team, the wheel dogs (or wheelers) are its brawn. Usually the largest dogs on the team, the wheelers provide the first burst of power when the command to start is given, breaking the sled loose and building up momentum.

They are also responsible for keeping the sled on the trail by guiding it around obstacles and steering it through curves. When the rest of the team has crested a hill and slacked off momentarily, the wheelers are left with the task of dragging the sled the last few feet over the rise.

Wheelers have to be confident dogs because the sled is constantly bouncing behind them. Bold and brawny, these canines seem to enjoy their challenging position.

Leaders given the command "Line Out" will stretch the gangline straight out from the sled so that other dogs can be hooked up for a run.

SPEED AND POWER

A competitive dog will be able to trot at ten miles per hour, lope at fourteen miles per hour, and maintain an average speed of eleven miles per hour (on a good trail) over the nearly 1,200 miles of the Iditarod. In a 1992 *Road & Track* April Fools' article, Sam Posey road-tested one of 1989 champion Joe Runyan's dog teams. The huskies accelerated from zero to twenty-five miles per hour in 6.3 seconds. Posey noted that the "top speed of 28 mph is reached very quickly, and the sensation is that you're going more like 60."

A number of improvements in recent years have enabled mushers to run at a faster pace. The clothing that drivers wear is more breathable and thus dries faster, eliminating time previously spent hanging wet apparel on a line over the fire to dry. Refined training and breeding programs have increased the speed of the canine athletes. And the reduction to sixteen dogs has actually decreased the amount of time spent on dog care because there are four fewer dogs to straw, feed, massage, examine, and otherwise tend to.

In a postrace interview, 1995 champion Doug Swingley pointed out that although he set a record pace, his dogs received more rest than in previous years because they were covering the distance between checkpoints faster due to improvements in their training. Swingley feels strongly that it is the humans who are the limiting factor—Iditarod dogs' abilities are as yet untapped.

SUPERIOR ENDURANCE ATHLETES

Dr. Arleigh Reynolds of the Cornell University College of Veterinary Medicine has researched the question, "What makes the dog superior to humans in its ability to perform sprinting and endurance events?" He has concluded that a dog's metabolism is better at converting energy fuel into muscular work for several reasons. One is that dogs can metabolize fat as a fuel better than humans. In fact, canine athletes can tolerate a diet of up to 60 percent of calories from fat—twice what is recommended for people. In addition, dogs use less glycogen, a starchy substance, the depletion of which is thought to cause fatigue. Canine systems also do a better job of providing oxygen to muscle cells and removing wastes from these cells. Finally, Reynolds notes that a "four-legged gait is more efficient than a two-legged gait and does not seem to increase the cost of running." It's no wonder then that Iditarod huskies are able to sprint into Nome, heads down, lines taut, tails waving, with "smiles" of satisfaction on their faces.

DOG TALES

Anecdotes illustrating sled dogs' uncanny intelligence proliferate among mushers.

During the 1979 race, Ron Brinker was mushing his team up the Yukon River into a strong head wind. To give himself shelter, Brinker would periodically duck down behind the sled bag. On one such occasion, Brinker's lead dog Rabbit looked back and couldn't see his master. Rabbit stopped the team and curved back around to the sled, where he found Brinker huddled down out of the wind. After ascertaining that his master was okay, Rabbit turned the team back onto the trail and resumed running, all without any commands. He was just checking things out.

Newbery Honor Book medalist and Iditarod competitor Gary Paulsen believes that he owes his life to his dogs, as he explains in the short story "Dogspirit":

> On a long training run in Alaska I went too far and while the dogs had rested each time they stopped I had not, taking time to cook for them, so that when they ran again I stood on the sled without sleep, again and again for twenty-nine hours. Somewhere in the mountains not too far from Mt. McKinley we stopped so that I could rub ointment in their feet. It was to be a short stop, a few minutes, but as I kneeled on my haunches and took my gloves off to rub the ointment between the toes of a big black and white dog named Fonzie, my eyes closed and would not open.
>
> Just in that way. I could *not* open them. The exhaustion was so deep, so complete that my head fell until my chin was on my chest and my hands fell into the snow at my sides and I was asleep.
>
> I do not know how long I slept that way. Hours at least. When my eyes opened it was close to dark and it was snowing heavily and I would have been in trouble—would have frozen that way, my hands bare and in the snow—would have perhaps ended there except that I was packed all around with dogs. They had moved in around me, all of them, packed and tangled in a great ball of snarled ganglines and sleeping forms so that my hands and legs, up to my chest were covered with them, kept warm by them and it is easy to say that it just happened, that they did not mean to keep me warm, that they simply pulled into a ball to ride the storm out and I was lucky enough to be in the middle. But the closeness was there, their breath was there, their heat was there and the reality—the love of them—was and is more important than explanation.

Inexperienced drivers quickly learn to trust their dogs' instincts. When she was first learning to mush, back in 1977, Susan Butcher was out in the Wrangell Mountains, fifty miles away from the nearest person, on a training run. As the team crossed a frozen river on a trail that they had been traveling all winter, Butcher's lead dog Tekla disobeyed her order to turn left, instead heading to the right, away from the trail. Butcher was puzzled and annoyed but let Tekla go. Just as they pulled to the side, the entire trail collapsed into the river. Her lead dog's enlightened disobedience probably saved Susan Butcher's life. Most mushers can tell a similar tale.

CANINE COMMUNICATION

At times, dogs' ability to communicate with their human partners seems nearly mystical. In *Dogsong*, a work of fiction about a disenchanted Eskimo boy who seeks to integrate his people's past into his modern lifestyle, Gary Paulsen describes young Russel's eventual success running a dog team: "He drove them with his mind. . . . he was the leader and the leader was him." At the conclusion of his long journey of discovery, Russel sings his song:

Come, see my dogs.
    Out before me they go.
    Out before me they curve
    in the long line out
    before me
    they go, I go, we go. They are me.

Rational explanations can be attempted. Dogs can "intuit" what the musher wants because they have experienced the same situation before in their training. Dogs can tune in to the musher's attitude and temperament by reading physical and verbal clues that the driver may not realize are being given.

On a winter night, a trainer stayed out later than he had planned and ended up driving his team home in the dark without a headlamp. Traveling along a country road, the driver peered into the blackness trying to locate a small side trail that turned off of the main track. Dogs are generally reluctant to take a sharp turn from a larger route to a smaller one, especially if it means leaving open countryside for a narrow, wooded corridor; therefore, the musher wanted to find the path in time to give the command to turn onto it. Just as the driver thought that they must be nearing it, his lead dog veered into the woods, taking the offshoot without being commanded to do so. Did the lead dog read the musher's mind? Probably not. This leader had

Tim Osmar enters early checkpoint Eagle River towing a second sled. The two dogs directly in front of a sled are called "wheel dogs" or "wheelers."

often taken the side trail in question on last year's runs. He was familiar with it. If the musher had been concentrating on getting home quickly down the main road, the leader might still have taken the turn out of habit.

Despite these logical explanations, most mushers have periodically had the feeling that "we are really clicking today." John Patten had such an experience during his rookie run in the 1988 Iditarod. His dog team was braving seventy-mile-per-hour winds climbing up the hill nicknamed "McKinley" past the Elim checkpoint. Having trained in Minnesota, the dogs were not familiar with such severe weather conditions and were spooked by the roaring wind. Lacking experience, they sought security from Patten. "The dogs were completely tuned in to me," Patten remembers. "They were listening so carefully that they heard the slightest signal, and immediately obeyed every 'Gee' or 'Haw'. Due to the strange conditions, I drove them to my will. It was intensely satisfying." Sometimes life does imitate fiction.

Two-time champion Martin Buser feels a physical connection with his dogs as well. "I hold onto the handlebar and my fingers extend through the sled, through the gangline, and into each dog. The connection is more than physical. We're one unit. The oneness that you have with the team is what I call the 'Spirit of the Iditarod'. That high is why we do it."

Doug Swingley, 1995 champion, believes that dogs' mental telepathy also transfers through the gangline from the leaders back to him. Elmer, Swingley's three-year-old leader, sees "things" on the trail, especially on boring sections such as traveling up the Yukon River. The team will be running along smoothly when suddenly Elmer jerks the sled forward, chasing something not visible to anyone else—a snowflake, perhaps, or a shaft of light? The whole team breaks into a lope chasing Elmer, figuring that something exciting must be going on, even if they are secretly wondering what it is. All of this energy gets transferred directly into the towline and flows back to Swingley, who gets psyched up along with the rest of the team each time eccentric Elmer activates his afterburners.

WHAT'S IN A NAME?

How do mushers name their dogs? Many breeders name litters thematically to make it easier to remember their dogs' relationships. Names of sled-dog litters have fallen into such diverse categories as Russian novelists, Olympic athletes, stars of *The Tonight Show,* brands of crackers, and even types of rocks.

Minnesota musher John Patten was so impressed by the film *Dances with Wolves* that he named a whole litter after its characters. Littermates included Dances With Wolves, Stands With A Fist, Two Socks, Smiles A Lot, Kicking Bird, and Wind In His Hair.

Breeders can reel off the names of any given dog's parents and grandparents, so don't ask a musher genealogical questions unless you have a long time to listen to the ensuing recitation.

SONGS AND SILENCE

One other aspect of Iditarod dogs needs to be mentioned: their beauty. Alaskan Huskies have an amazing repertoire of songs. Mushers note that their dogs sing "Pick me! Pick me!" songs when teams are being selected, and "Don't leave me" songs when other teams are pulling away. "Death songs" are sung when in the presence of a dead or dying animal, and "I'm so gorgeous/handsome—come mate with me" songs reverberate throughout the dog lot during breeding season.

Alaskan Huskies have an amazing repertoire of songs. Most beautiful of all, though, may be their wolflike howl—that haunting, resonant wail which evokes images of wilderness and stirs dormant memories of prehistoric times.

Most beautiful of all, though, may be their wolflike howl—that haunting, resonant wail which evokes images of wilderness and stirs dormant memories of prehistoric times.

Less known is the wonder of their silence. Knowles Dougherty, an Austin, Minnesota, publisher, had what he describes as a "peak life experience" while attending the 1991 John Beargrease Sled Dog Marathon (a 500-mile race) in Duluth. Dougherty had founded an alternative high school in the Boston area in 1969; having since relocated to the Midwest, he came to the 1991 Beargrease to see four-time Iditarod champion Susan Butcher, his school's most famous graduate. Standing in eight inches of snow on a starlit night, Dougherty was waiting about a quarter of a mile up the trail from the finish line for Butcher to pass by.

At 4:35 A.M., an official posted along the trail near Dougherty yelled down to the finish area that the first musher, Terry Adkins, was approaching. Dougherty describes his experience:

> We could see this light [Adkins' headlamp] bobbing in the woods and then the silhouette of the dogs. Very soon Adkins' team and his sled and Adkins came by us and we couldn't hear the dogs at all. No rustling. No jingling. No nothing.
>
> In fact, when he went by, for a second I thought, "Maybe he didn't really go by, maybe it just looked like he went by." It was like somebody had turned off the sound. That was just electrifying to me. It was one of the peak experiences of my whole life. I had the feeling that we were out in the middle of the wilderness and here was somebody coming by like a worker would have done 100 years ago taking supplies from Anchorage to the outposts in Alaska.

When Butcher drove by about twenty minutes later, Dougherty experienced the same thing—the eerie sensation of a dog team racing past in silence. It's a moment that he'll never forget.

In silence and in song, the Iditarod dog leaves a legacy of beauty and wonderment.

Challenge is the Iditarod's spine, and history is its soul, but love of dogs and mushing will always be its heart.

Tony Dawson
Field editor, Alaska magazine
and Iditarod veterinarian

9

Welfare of
the Animals

No one is more concerned about the humane treatment of sled
dogs than the mushers, volunteers, and officials connected with
the race. Without the dogs, there could be no Iditarod. They are its
lifeblood and are treated accordingly. The goal of everyone connected
with the Iditarod is to take every possible precaution to preserve the
mystique and magic of the Last Great Race.

PRECAUTIONS

In "Prerace Details" the mandatory examination of each dog in every
team by a group of veterinarians was discussed. This usually occurs
the Wednesday before the start. At this time, mushers must provide
proof that their dogs are properly vaccinated. Any dog not 100 percent ready to race may be prevented from starting.

Although formerly blood samples were taken at this prerace
screening, now most veterinarians agree that urine testing is a much
more reliable method of screening for prohibited drugs. Therefore, an
extensive urine-testing program has been implemented. In Anchorage, statistically random samples are collected from dogs in selected
teams. Teams can be tested at any point throughout the race, and near

the end of the Iditarod (perhaps in White Mountain, although the exact location is not revealed in advance), teams are randomly sampled again. Finally, mandatory urine testing of the top twenty finishing teams occurs in Nome. All Iditarod drug testing is performed by a professional, independent team—a completely separate entity from the volunteer veterinarians.

Every dropped dog and a statistically random sample of 100 finishing dogs is also given a CPK diagnostic test, which studies the impact of the race on the muscular system of the dog.

In 1991, a group of veterinarians founded the International Sled Dog Veterinary Medical Association (ISDVMA). According to the group's inaugural newsletter, *Vet Check*, "Our objectives focus on animal welfare, education of race participants, drug testing, and permanent identification of the racing animal. In addition we plan to actively promote research into the sled dog and encourage co-operation between racing organizations." This effort is one indication of how important the issue of the dogs' safety is thought to be.

Many of the rules are specifically designed to protect the dogs. Any tired, ill, or injured dog removed from a team on the trail must be carried in the sled to keep the animal comfortable and safe. Giving drugs to the animals to improve their performance artificially or to mask symptoms of illness or fatigue is strictly forbidden.

While on the trail, mushers use several protective devices to ensure that their dogs stay healthy and happy. One mandatory item is the dog bootie. Dog booties look like anklet socks. They are two pocket-shaped pieces of fabric sewn together to make a pouch which is then slipped over the dog's paw. Many types of fabric have been used, including canvas, nylon, and soft leather, but professionals now favor polypropylene or fleece materials.

Booties are fastened by a strip of Velcro® or elastic sewn into the top of the fabric. It is important to secure each bootie carefully. If it's too tight, the dog's circulation is restricted, and if it's too loose, the protective sock is flipped off.

This footwear is used primarily to protect the dogs' paws from ice, which abrades their pads, and from snow, which can cause an injury if allowed to ball up between the toes. Booties are not worn at all times—only if specific weather conditions warrant them (a melting and refreezing of the trail, for instance). As soon as a musher arrives at a checkpoint and gets the team settled on straw, each dog's booties are removed. Booties with holes are discarded because they cause

*Dog booties
are mandatory
equipment. Slipped
over a dog's paw like
an anklet sock, the
bootie fastens at the
top by a strip of
Velcro®.*

more trouble than no footwear at all. Because they are not waterproof, booties are usually taken off just prior to running through overflow and are then put back on afterward. There are not a lot of convenient places to dry dog booties along the Iditarod Trail, so this is one way that mushers preserve their supply. Individual dogs may be more prone to foot problems than others. Although the rules only mandate carrying 128 booties, most competitors will use more than 1,000.

As you might imagine, putting a bootie on each paw of sixteen dogs is a time-consuming task. Lavon Barve, 1994 Yukon Quest champion, quips, "There isn't a musher who hasn't wished for some device like a car wash where you could drive through and have it put booties on your dogs." Unfortunately, the conscientious mushers have to do it the old-fashioned way—one foot at a time.

Another preventive measure used on dogs' feet is the application of various topical ointments that help to protect their feet. One ointment used by mushers contains zinc oxide. This ointment may be rubbed onto a healthy foot to keep it soft and dry. If a dog has picked

Terry Adkins' 1993 dog team started in style, wearing bandannas and booties.

up an ice ball and is beginning to get a sore foot, this ointment will promote healing. You may be familiar with zinc oxide from using Desitin® on a baby's diaper rash, or perhaps you have seen this white ointment protecting an athlete's nose from sunburn.

A second type of ointment is made with a Povidone-iodine base (or sometimes with a Furacin base). Like the zinc oxide, this formulation may be used as a preventive, but it is also an antiseptic. A dog with a crack or split on his paw would be treated with this ointment. Betadine®, which you may have used to prevent a cut or scrape from becoming infected, contains Povidone-iodine.

The third major kind of ointment is an anti-inflammatory containing less than one percent of a corticosteroid. Useful for reducing swelling or inflammation, this compound should *not* be applied to any open wound, such as a split or crack, because steroids can interfere with the healing process. Cortaid® is a common hydrocortisone cream that you may have put on itchy skin to reduce the irritating inflammation. The ointment that mushers use for their dogs has a different active ingredient from Cortaid®, but it's the same basic principle.

Each veterinarian and each musher has his or her own preferences (and secrets) for mixing up foot ointments, but these are three of the most common ones. There are even tricks to applying ointment. Five-time champion Rick Swenson prefers to warm the ointment slightly and to apply it with a paintbrush. He believes that this enables the medication to make better contact with the dog's foot and promotes faster absorption. At checkpoints and rest stops along the trail, mushers can frequently be seen applying these ointments to each of the dogs in their team.

One reason why mushers are so careful about their dogs' feet is that a minor problem not treated promptly could become a major one. A split, nick, or crack in a dog's pad is usually no more dangerous than a hangnail on your finger. If ignored, however, a treatable foot problem could turn into an elbow or shoulder injury, which would result in discomfort for the dog and necessitate his removal from the race. Consequently, drivers are ever alert for the first telltale signs of trouble. If the musher sees any blood on the snow, for instance, she or he will quickly

Veterinarians examine dogs in the shelter of Dodge Lodges like this one, provided by one of the race's sponsors.

determine on which side of the gangline it appears, whether it is coming from the front, middle, or back of the team, and finally which individual dog has a problem. If the dog has merely nicked his tongue dipping down for a mouthful of snow, action may not be necessary. However, if a dog's foot is bleeding, an immediate stop will probably be made for an application of ointment and a protective bootie.

A second item of clothing that some drivers pack for their animals is a flank protector. (Remember—Charlie Evans used this during the severe cold on his leg of the serum run.) This is a belly warmer for dogs that have less fur on their abdomens (especially for males that do not have sufficient fur to protect their genitals from freezing) and for females whose coat may not have grown back completely after raising a litter of puppies.

Mushers also carry dog coats to keep their canines comfortable. These are especially useful in the tempestuous weather that often characterizes the end of the race along the Bering Sea coast.

As mentioned, procedures are in place during the Iditarod to provide for dropping dogs if it is not advisable for them to continue. Mushers may leave tired, ill, or injured dogs at a checkpoint, where they receive care from veterinarians and volunteers until they can be flown out to other facilities. If race veterinarians deem that any dog is not fit to race, they can overrule the wishes of a competitor and keep the dog at the checkpoint.

Education is often the best precaution. With that in mind, a group of top-notch mushers (including authorities like Butcher, Champaine, King, Schmidt, and Shields) formed Mush with PRIDE (Providing Responsible Information on a Dog's Environment). This organization is dedicated to enhancing the care and treatment of sled dogs, promoting public understanding of mushing, and welcoming and assisting new members. PRIDE publishes *Sled Dog Care Guidelines,* which covers subjects such as dog housing, feeding and watering, exercise and training, and basic health care.

TENDER LOVING CARE

Sled-dog racers have a special relationship with their dogs. This is true for any musher, whether recreational or professional, but no one is more famous for using TLC than four-time Iditarod champion Susan Butcher. Before setting out to make a journey by dog team

One of Susan Butcher's dogs snoozes comfortably in a nest of straw.

across Alaska, novice musher and Scottish novelist Alastair Scott spoke with Butcher at her Eureka home. When he asked if she would tell him her secret, Butcher grinned and replied immediately:

> Sure. . . . I've always had a way with animals. It was birth-given. I know the power of a dog's mind and can harness that power. I know how to shape a dog's attitude. I take my dogs running and swimming with me in summer. They come into the cabin, we play a lot, we have fun and I reckon we've developed a special bond. All my dogs love to race.

Butcher's dogs not only love to race, they love their mistress. The feeling is definitely mutual. After losing the trail and running twenty miles through rough conditions during the 1982 race, Butcher's lead dog Tekla began to limp and had to ride in the sled to the next checkpoint. Tying Tekla under a tree to await a flight home, Butcher had tears rolling down her cheeks. Together they had learned how to mush when she moved to Alaska in 1975; together they had first encountered moose, caribou, and wolves. Tekla had led Butcher's team when she and Joe Redington, Sr. became the first to reach the summit of 20,320-foot Denali (also known as Mount McKinley) by sled-dog team. Butcher claims that Tekla not only saved her life on several occasions, but could read her mind as well. Dropping this dog from the race felt like abandoning a best friend.

Tekla, in addition to twenty or thirty other retired dogs, occasionally would go on training runs with puppies and yearlings. Butcher explains, "If I had sold them [her retired dogs] in their last year of racing I could have gotten two, three, four thousand apiece for them. But there's no way I would. They deserve a retirement here. I'm their life, just like they're mine." At the age of fifteen, Tekla died in the summer of 1990. Commenting on her loss, Butcher said, "You know it's coming, but I was all broken up."

Love and trust are the main ingredients in Butcher's strategy. She has maintained all along that given the choice, she would rather lose a race than lose her dogs' trust. She demonstrates that raising sled dogs as if they were pets can certainly be a successful formula for winning the Iditarod.

DISQUALIFICATION AND BANISHMENT

In any competitive sport, there are people who resort to unethical means to gain an advantage. Iditarod participants are a cross-section of the general population and inevitably will include some drivers with less consideration for their animals than the mushers who consistently win.

Near the beginning of the 1992 race, the *Anchorage Daily News* reported that two well-known Iditarod mushers were warned that they needed to pay more attention to their animals. The warning was issued after veterinarians in Skwentna observed that the mushers had neglected to remove their dogs' booties and had not spread straw for their teams before going inside to tend to their own needs. In the Iditarod, the dogs come first.

Rule 16 states: "There will be no cruel or inhumane treatment of dogs. Cruel or inhumane treatment involves any action or inaction which causes preventable pain or suffering to a dog." Penalties for violating this rule range from disqualification from that year's race to being banished for life from running the Iditarod.

Iditarod rules also require that a necropsy, a technical term for an autopsy, be performed on any dog that dies during the race. This applies whether the dog's death was due to accidental causes, an undiagnosed medical problem, or for no apparent reason. The Iditarod Trail Committee investigates thoroughly the death of any dog and provides an immediate and full press release giving the details. A race rule specifies that in the event that a dog in a competitor's team dies during the race, the musher will be automatically withdrawn or disqualified unless the death was caused by an external force beyond the musher's control, such as a moose or snow machine.

The Iditarod Trail Committee will not tolerate any abusive behavior. There is no room for compromise when the integrity of the Iditarod and the welfare of its dogs are at stake.

A MUSHER'S GEAR

My hands tightened into a death grip on the handlebar as it became all too clear that I was taking off alone on a vehicle with a throttle stuck open and without a steering wheel.

Galen Rowell
Nature photographer, describing his
first experience mushing a team of dogs.

We're just a bunch of weirdos looking at the south end of dogs going north.

Jack Niggemyer
Iditarod Race Manager

10

Harnesses, Lines, and Sleds

HARNESSES AND LINES

They say that the best way to learn something is by doing it. So to clarify how a team is hitched to the sled, you are going to take one dog through the entire process of being hooked up. Before starting, you need to know these four terms:

harness: a device that a dog wears, through which his pulling power is transferred to the lines leading back to the sled
gangline (or towline): the main line that runs forward from the sled down the center of the dog team
neckline: a line connecting the dog's collar to the gangline
tugline (also called a tug or backline): a line fastening the back of the dog's harness to the gangline

Traditionally, all of this gear was made of leather or hide, which dogs found irresistible to eat. If you have a dog who enjoys chewing rawhide, or perhaps your shoes, you can believe this. Now the materials of choice are polyethylene, polypropylene, nylon, and kevlar. Determined chewers can still make short work of the most modern equipment, however.

Harnesses

When hooking up their team, many mushers prefer to start with a quiet dog. If all of the dogs have been trained to remain fairly calm during this process, the driver may attach the leader(s) first and work back toward the wheelers (or vice versa). Because the way in which leaders are connected to the gangline differs slightly from the rest of the team, for this demonstration a reliable team dog will be selected.

Sled dogs wear a flat collar, usually made of nylon, with a large ring on it. The harness that you are about to slip over this collar is called a cross-backed (sometimes written X-backed) racing harness. It's made of a lightweight, one-inch-wide nylon-webbed material that lies close to the dog's body. The harness is padded where it fits around the dog's shoulders and forelegs to prevent cutting or chafing.

The ultralight harness is a recent innovation. Made from closed-cell foam padding encased by ripstop nylon, these new harnesses weigh half as much as traditional models but cost about 33 percent more. The primary advantages are their light weight and the fact that they do not absorb moisture, enabling them to keep drier. Their major drawback is that they wear out sooner than other harnesses.

Most harnesses come outfitted with reflective tape to provide night visibility. Racing harnesses and lines come in many vivid colors (bright red, yellow, and blue, for example, and even fluorescent pink, lime, and orange). Colored ropes serve a practical purpose as well. Some mushers use a different color for each type of line so that when they are untangling their team, they can easily distinguish the necklines from the tuglines from the gangline.

Ready? To begin, stand over the dog, straddling him with his waist held securely between your knees. This gives you both hands free to slip the padded neck opening of the harness over the dog's head. Slowly ease each front leg through a side loop. Now pull the dog's collar up through the neck opening until it is clear of the harness. Sled dogs do *not* pull against their collars, nor are their collars in any way attached to the harness.

Looking at the dog from the front at eye level, his harness resembles a "Y", with his head in between the forks of the "Y" and the stem of the letter running under his belly. From above, the harness makes a diamond or double-diamond pattern as it runs down the dog's back, ending in a loop at the base of his tail. This loop is where the lines connect that transfer all of the dog's power to the sled.

The design of the harness places the effort of pulling onto the dog's shoulders and chest. Each dog must be carefully measured and fitted so that his harness will be comfortable. One size does not fit all sled dogs. Often, mushers color-code their harnesses by size so that all small harnesses are red, medium harnesses are blue, and large harnesses are yellow, for instance. A dog with an unusual build would have a custom harness, however. If the competitor's budget permits, each dog might have his own individual harness, even if he could wear a standard size.

Iditarod dogs wear their harnesses throughout the entire race with several exceptions. Mushers usually remove them while the dogs rest at the longest stops. Harnesses are also removed if they become wet or frozen so that they do not irritate the dog's skin. Notorious harness-chewers will have theirs taken off at every extended rest stop, however.

Necklines

Now that you have the first dog in harness, you can hook him to the gangline. It is advisable to clip the dog's neckline on first. That way, if his harness slips out of your hand while you are trying to fasten the tugline, he can't run off.

The neckline is a short length (twelve to sixteen inches) of one-sixteenth- to one-quarter-inch-diameter rope. Necklines are made of smaller diameter rope and are fitted with smaller snaps so that they *will* be breakable. If a dog ends up going the wrong way around a tree or other obstacle, the neckline should break before the dog becomes injured. Nylon is the toughest rope and is the most resistant to chewing, but mushers often use poly ropes for various lines. The advantage of poly ropes is that they can be braided together (necklines and tuglines can be woven into the gangline), and they resist knotting better than nylon.

Holding the dog securely, snap one end of the neckline to the ring on his collar; the other end of the neckline is already affixed to the gangline. The dog is now standing on one side of the long gangline with his neckline coming straight out from it at a ninety-degree angle.

The purpose of the neckline is to keep the dog facing forward and to prevent him from running wide or becoming tangled with obstacles. Iditarod dogs do *not* pull against their necklines.

Tuglines

Because the dog is secured by his neckline, you can now clip on the tugline. Made of one-quarter- to three-eighths-inch-diameter rope, the tugline is thirty-six to forty-eight inches long. One end of it branches off the gangline at a forty-five-degree angle, like one leg of a "V". The

A view from the sled showing the gangline, tuglines, and necklines.
© David C. Hyde

other end has a heavy snap that attaches to the loop on the dog's harness near the base of his tail.

Occasionally, you will still see a toggle connecting the dog's harness to the tugline instead of a snap. Traditionally, Native mushers used ivory or wood to make toggles, but now plastic is a more likely material. A toggle is a solid circular or rectangular shape attached to the loop on the dog's harness. It is then slipped through a rope loop on the end of the tugline. When the tugline rope is cinched tight, the toggle cannot slip out of it. The advantages of toggles over snaps are that they do not freeze shut, they can be operated wearing gloves, and they are less expensive. The only major disadvantage is that snaps are usually quicker to use. Toggles may be unjustly discriminated against merely because they *look* old-fashioned. In Iditarod racing, as in many sports, high-tech is *in*.

If snaps are used, they are generally made of brass. Brass snaps are stronger than plated metal ones and are less likely to break in extremely cold conditions. If they do become frozen, you can open them by blowing or rubbing on them.

The dog is now fastened to the gangline in two places: his neckline runs straight across to the gangline (to keep him going in the right direction and out of trouble), and his tugline runs from the end of his harness back to the gangline at an angle. All of the dog's pulling power is transferred through the tugline.

A slightly different arrangement is sometimes used for the wheel dogs. Instead of the wheelers' tuglines angling back and connecting to the gangline, a few innovative mushers have begun connecting the wheel dogs' tugs directly to the sled runners. This gives the wheelers a straightforward pull and, consequently, more leverage with which to maneuver the sled. When utilizing this setup, Iditarod champion Jeff King adds an extra section of rope from his sled's bridle to a point on the gangline past his wheelers' necklines, which then allows him to add or subtract sections from the gangline.

The tugline enables a musher to tell if any of the dogs are slacking off. A clever dog can take a break from pulling but keep just enough pressure on the tugline to make it appear that he's still working. Dogs that pull all of the time, even when they are tired, are called "honest" dogs. Everyone loves an honest dog.

Gangline

The gangline is the heaviest rope, usually three-eighths to one-half inch in diameter. It is composed of a number of sections so that by adding or subtracting lengths, mushers can run whatever number of dogs they wish. During training, mushers often use poly or nylon rope ganglines, but Iditarod rules require that competitors must either have a cable-core gangline or carry cable tie-out lines for each dog. This rule ensures that dogs will not be able to chew themselves loose if for some reason a large number of teams end up in one area for a long period of time. Many Iditarod drivers choose a hollow poly rope gangline with a cable core that comes in two-dog sections with a loop at each end. Because necklines and tuglines cannot be braided into a cable gangline, they are snapped to these loops.

Serious competitors are now experimenting with kevlar cable-core ganglines. Kevlar lines are stronger than poly or nylon ones, which make them a good choice for training young pups that are likely to chew on their lines. The downside to kevlar lines is that they are expensive, they tend to kink, and they absorb moisture, thus becoming heavy. The search for the ultimate gangline material continues.

The end of the gangline connects to a bridle that extends forward from the front of the sled. A heavy snap or carabiner (a "D"-shaped metal ring having a threaded lock that is used by mountain climbers and usually called a "biner"—pronounced "beaner") attaches the gangline to a reinforced rope loop or to a sturdy metal ring on the bridle. (Occasionally, a shock-ring bungee is inserted between the gangline and the bridle. See the upcoming "Bridle" section.)

Mushers also use a safety line, an extra line that runs off of the gangline, connecting to a point behind the main ring or loop on the bridle. If the gangline snap (or carabiner) does not close completely and later works loose, or if it breaks, the safety line keeps the team secured to the sled. This little twelve- to fourteen-inch line can save a driver a long walk in search of his or her team. If you are familiar with towing a trailer, think of the safety line as the safety chains that provide a backup in case the hitch comes undone.

You can now go up and down the gangline hooking on the rest of the dogs. Iditarod competitors use a gang hitch, which means that two dogs run directly across from each other, one on either side of the gangline. Each pair's necklines join the main line at the same place, and their tuglines angle back to a common connecting point as well.

The leaders require a slightly different setup. Because the front of the gangline ends where the lead dogs' tuglines branch off from it, you cannot fasten their necklines to the gangline. Instead, a pair of leaders will have a single piece of rope with a snap at each end running from the collar of one dog to the collar of the other. This simply keeps them side by side. A single lead dog is run with both tuglines attached to his harness and no neckline.

If the leaders have been trained to obey the command "Line Out," you may want to hook them up as soon as possible so that they can hold the gangline tight while you get everyone else in place. Some mushers feel that this places undue pressure on the leaders and prefer to wait until last to hook them up. If the team is inexperienced, if the team is not likely to hold still, or if it is unable to be given the "Line Out" command, you can anchor the dogs to a sturdy post or a heavy concrete block. A chain from the stationary object clips to the front of the gangline or to the lead dog's collar, depending on the musher's preference. No matter how you line them out, be sure to save any infamous chewers or jumpers until last.

It would take about half an hour to harness and hook up a team of sixteen sled dogs if you were a professional and if you were lucky. (If you were in a hurry, you'd have the dogs' harnesses already on them and could then have them ready to go in about fifteen minutes.)

HARNESSES AND LINES

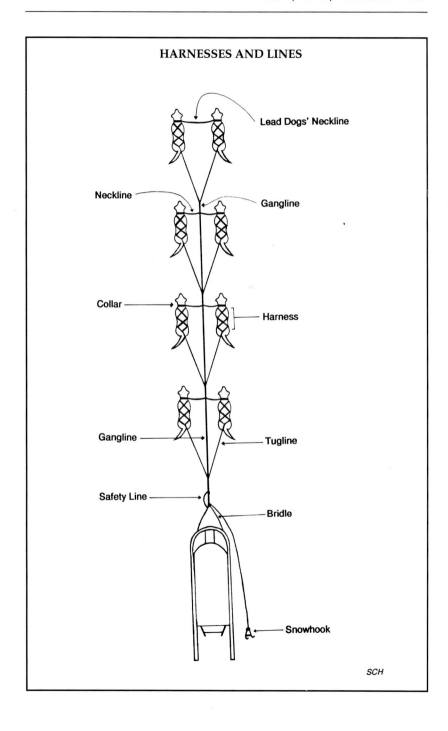

Lead Dogs' Neckline

Neckline

Gangline

Collar

Harness

Gangline

Tugline

Safety Line

Bridle

Snowhook

SCH

The author "test drives" a beautiful basket sled that awaits its owner at the McGrath checkpoint.
© Ruth Anne Hood

"Lucky" means not having any major tangles or any dogs biting through their lines. If the overly enthusiastic dogs jump over their necklines or the gangline, or somehow get snarled with their neighbors, you may have to unhook and rehook the entire team. Bad tangles can result in serious dog fights or unplanned matings! This is the stuff of mushers' nightmares.

You can now jump on the sled's runners, pull out the snowhook, and shout "All Right" to the anxious coursers. It's a long way from your vantage point behind the sled to the lead dogs—more than forty feet from you to them. You may have some surprises in store for you, especially around the curves, as you ride on down the trail. Enjoy the run!

SLEDS

Because trees are scarce in northern Alaska, Eskimos had to exercise ingenuity in selecting sled-building materials. Driftwood, bones, and even ivory were used. Frozen mud and water were smeared on top of the ivory or bone runners to form a layer of smooth, frictionless ice where the sled came into contact with the ground. In a pinch, sled runners could be fashioned by soaking strips of hide in water, bending them into place, and allowing them to freeze solid.

Early freight sleds weighed as much as 300 pounds empty and stretched out fourteen feet from front to back. Today's ultralight racing sleds have evolved from these functional giants.

Dedicated craftsmen still handmake traditional Eskimo-style racing sleds. A beautifully crafted sled is a work of art. Purists use no nuts, bolts, screws, or nails. The sled's framework is constructed from ash, birch, hickory, or maple that is steam-bent into place. Rawhide strips (called "babiche") lash the wood together at mortise and tenon joints, for instance, where the upright supports meet the runners. This construction (opposed to the cheaper, more conventional, bolted sled) provides much greater flexibility, allowing the sled to "give" on rough trails instead of shattering.

Most lightweight racing sleds (also called basket sleds or sprint sleds) are built utilizing time-honored techniques in combination with modern materials. Instead of babiche, heavy nylon cord may be used. Bolted joints may be added to provide extra strength. The least expensive basket sleds use screws as fasteners, with no rawhide reinforcement.

Basket sled.

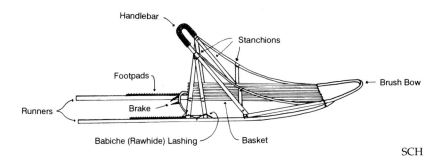

Handlebar

Stanchions

Footpads

Brush Bow

Runners

Brake

Babiche (Rawhide) Lashing

Basket

SCH

Well-built racing sleds will be light, strong, and flexible. Usually about eight feet long, they weigh approximately twenty-five to forty pounds empty.

Following a description of each of the components of this traditional sled, a second, newer type of Iditarod sled, called a racing toboggan, will be examined. Many Iditarod competitors leave Anchorage driving a toboggan and switch to some type of basket sled for the second half of the race.

Runners

Basically, a sled is a frame built on two runners, which enable it to travel over snow without sinking. Modern-day models have wood runners covered with plastic or steel strips, rather than a coating of mud or ice. Steel-covered runners do not mar easily, but in very cold weather, snow sticks to them. Runners with a plastic overlay are nearly frictionless, gliding over the snow smoothly and quickly. Unfortunately, plastic becomes scratched and gouged and needs to be replaced during a long race like the Iditarod.

Polyethylene plastic is the material of choice for sled runners. One type, called XH black, is a high-density polyethylene. The XH plastic is fairly soft and has the feel of a waxed cross-country ski. It is preferred for its low resistance but is not durable and may need to be changed three to five times during the Iditarod.

If the driver knows that a particular section of the route is bare and rough, she or he may carry a second kind of runner better suited to these conditions. UH yellow (or Orange V) is an ultrahigh-molecular-weight (UHMW) polyethylene. It is less slick but more durable. On bare ground, a musher might not make it from one checkpoint to the next without having to change the softer, near-frictionless XH runners. This is when UH yellow runners prove their worth.

How can drivers afford to spend time changing runner plastic during the race? In the early 1980s, engineer/designer Tim White patented the Quick Change Runner (QCR™) system. A curved metal rail is bolted to the sled's wooden runners; grooves on the plastic runner shoe fit into tongues on the metal rails. The musher merely removes one bolt at the front of each runner, slides off the worn plastic shoe, and slips on a new one. Voila! Ready for action.

White's newest innovation is the use of 7000 series high-strength aircraft aluminum for the QCR™ metal rails. These aluminum runners are virtually indestructible, yet maintain their flexibility. They also offer greater versatility in attaching the runner system to the frame of the sled.

Extending approximately three feet behind the sled, runners resemble skis on which the driver stands.

Extending approximately three feet behind the sled, the runners resemble skis on which the driver stands. This is in contrast to early freight sleds, whose runners did not extend back behind the basket area for the musher to stand on; nor did these sleds have a handlebar for him to grasp. The driver was out in front of the dog team on snowshoes breaking the trail! Most contemporary sled runners come equipped with footpads to provide a nonskid surface. A twelve- to twenty-two-inch length of synthetic plastic with a herringbone pattern of treads is bolted to the top of the runner. Although the treads on these footpads don't completely solve the problem of mushers slipping on icy or snow-covered runners, every little bit helps.

Stanchions

Stanchions are vertical pieces of wood that rise up from the runners and form the framework upon which the rest of the sled is built. Depending on the sled's design, it may have one, two, or three stanchions. As mentioned, they may either be bolted at connecting points or lashed together with nylon cord or babiche (or bolted *and* lashed).

Brush Bow

An arrowhead-shaped brush bow (rhymes with "go") extends forward from the front of the sled, acting as a bumper. Because it receives the brunt of the damage in a collision, the brush bow must be very strong. Drivers traditionally reinforced a wooden brush bow by wrapping on a strip of wet rawhide which was then laced into place. When the rawhide dried, it strengthened the structure tremendously. Duct tape or nylon cord have also been used. Recently, heavy plastic brush bows have become common on Iditarod sleds.

If a count of the total number of brush bows broken during the history of the Iditarod were available, it would be staggering. The Farewell Burn alone (a dense forest that burned down in a 1977 wildfire, leaving thousands of charred stumps along the trail) shatters many mushers' sleds and dreams every year and has probably kept several sled builders in business.

Handlebar

The handlebar is the highest point on the sled. It is an inverted "U" that the driver grasps and uses to steer. It is also sometimes called the

The brush bow and bridle assembly.

drive bow, the driving bow, the steering bow, and the handle bow—take your pick.

Like the brush bow, the drive bow used to consist of wood wrapped with rawhide, nylon, or tape to increase its strength. Even today's plastic handlebars are usually wrapped with materials as diverse as hockey tape and halibut fishing line to provide a better grip.

By shifting his or her weight to one side and twisting the handlebar, the musher can put the runners on their edges. This enables the sled to make sharp turns in the same way that skiers maneuver quickly by tilting their skis.

During the Iditarod, the most important function of the handlebar may be propping up the limp bodies of trail-weary drivers. Many a musher has slept soundly while slumped over the drive bow. In fact, some competitors who know that they have a habit of falling asleep will tie themselves to the handlebar so that when they do *doze* off, they don't *fall* off! It's not unusual for a good lead dog to bring a sled into a checkpoint with the musher doubled over the handlebar. The dog team suddenly comes to a stop, and the surprised (somewhat rested) driver awakens to the sound of the checker's voice.

Basket

The basket is *not* a container (that's the sled bag); it is merely a wooden framework mounted four to six inches above the runners. Composed of slats, the basket runs lengthwise from the drive bow toward the brush bow. A sled may have a full or a half basket, depending on how far forward the slats extend.

Providing the floor for the sled bag, the basket is used to carry the musher's gear and to transport dogs when necessary. It can even support the weight of passengers if desired.

Brake

On a traditional sled, one long brace runs down the center of the sled, beginning at the middle of the brush bow, passing under the slats of the basket, and ending at the back of the sled. The brake consists of a two-to-three-foot-long board attached underneath this center brace so that it protrudes behind the basket between the driver's feet. A steel claw is bolted on the end of the brake board with two or three metal prongs facing downward (the points are at a ninety-degree angle to the board). When the musher steps on the brake, the steel claw drags through the snow, slowing the sled. A long spring holds it up out of the way while not in use.

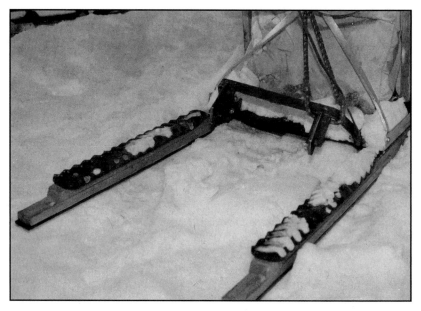

The U-shaped bar brake is now favored.

Most contemporary sleds, however, are equipped with a U-shaped bar brake (having integral prongs) that is affixed directly to the runners. Carbide points on the prongs assure greater durability.

Unlike the brake in your car, a sled's brake does not really stop a dog team. It is more of a signal to the dogs which, along with the command "Whoa," will hopefully bring them to a halt.

Taking a wild ride with the brake firmly depressed is a common occurrence for mushers. Maybe the team has sighted caribou or ptarmigan on the trail ahead and is in hot pursuit. Or perhaps it's the driver's first experience with the raw power of a dog team.

Alastair Scott, an adventurer/writer/photographer hailing from Scotland, decided to mush more than 800 miles across Alaska. The fact that he had never handled a dog team did not faze Scott a bit. He simply went to Joee Redington (son of Joe Redington, Sr.) for lessons.

In his book *Tracks Across Alaska: A Dog Sled Journey*, Scott recounts his memorable initiation to mushing:

> Frantic to be off, the dogs were straining at the traces, yipping and cavorting so high they almost flipped. With my feet on the

runners, one hand tight on the handlebars, I bent down and pulled up the snowhook. . . . the sled jolted with a violence that surprised me, and we were off.

Joee had impressed on me not to use the claw brake unless in an emergency, as it dug up the trail and ruined the surface. My senses might have been partially numbed by shock but one thing was obvious: I had embarked on one long emergency. I was standing on this brake with all my weight as we descended Joee's steep drive.

* * * * * *

The trail became bumpy. Half the time we seemed to be airborne. The dogs were on their own, I was merely useless ballast waiting to be ejected. Down a bank, up a bank, over a bridge, across a road, through a wood: they went as they pleased. As they twisted this way and that I was wrenched from side to side, clinging on only because falling off appeared marginally more painful. . . .

After a mile we swung round a loop and returned. I delivered the team back safely—at least, they delivered me back, with only two cuts, a torn jacket and a large assortment of bruises.

And yet, I hadn't let go. I had stayed on. There were no teethmarks on the handlebars—though perhaps this was where I had gone wrong.

Joee had followed me on the ATV, watching from a distance. He was waiting for me when I got back. . . .

"You did great. I'm *real* proud of you."

I beamed. I felt pretty proud of myself too.

"*Great!*" he enthused. "Maybe next week we'll try it with more than three dogs, OK?"

Bridle

The bridle is the means by which the pulling power of the dogs is transferred to the sled. Consisting of a length of heavy rope or cable, the bridle looks like a "V": the open ends of the letter connect to the front stanchions, the midpart runs under the brush bow, and the point extends out in front of the sled, ending in a reinforced rope loop or a metal ring. The gangline is clipped to this ring or loop. In addition to the gangline, a safety line is fastened to the bridle, as well as the snowhook.

Under certain circumstances, mushers will add a type of shock absorber, called a shock ring or an SIP (sudden impact protector), into

Above: *The rope attached to a snowhook should be just long enough to allow a musher to pick up the hook and pull it over the back of the sled bag to stow it there.* Below: *A snowhook and a snubline help keep a dog team anchored.*

their gangline hookup. The shock ring is a heavy-duty aircraft bungee encased in a plastic tube that may help reduce the impact of a sudden stop on a dog team. It may be used during cart training, in conjunction with a cable (less stretchable) gangline, or near the beginning of a race when the dogs are supercharged and more prone to sudden jolts. A "D"-shaped locking carabiner on either end of the shock ring enables it to be inserted between the gangline and the bridle.

Sled Bag

Made of heavy canvas or nylon, the sled bag rests on the basket within the framework of the sled, and is held on by a series of Velcro® fasteners, tab buckles, and lashing grommets. All of the musher's mandatory and optional gear is stowed in this bag, and dogs are carried in it when they are tired, sick, or injured. The way in which the sled bag is loaded can have a significant impact on the sled's maneuverability; therefore, drivers experiment with different configurations until they discover one that is successful for them.

If the sled bag is big enough, the driver may crawl into it to take refuge from a storm. Protected by arctic clothing and cocooned in a warm sleeping bag, the musher can zip up the sled bag and burrow down for the duration. Encamped on the trail in a raging blizzard, it's the next best thing to a shelter cabin!

Snowhook

Resembling a giant double fishhook without barbs, the snowhook anchors the team when stopped. One end of a heavy rope snaps to the bridle and runs the length of the sled until it reaches about even with the handlebar. The snowhook is tied to the other end. This rope should be just long enough to allow the musher to pick up the snowhook and pull it over the back of the sled bag in order to stow it there. Alternate methods of storing the hook are to secure it on a crosspiece spanning the handlebar with a bungee cord or to place it in a leather holster that hangs from this same crosspiece. The driver must be able to grab the hook quickly in order to make an emergency stop, but the snowhook should be fastened firmly so that it does not endanger the musher. One unfortunate competitor required five stitches near his eye because the snowhook flew loose and hit him when he rolled his sled.

As soon as the team comes to a stop, the musher plants the snowhook. Usually, it is positioned on the outside of the runners to one

Above: *Martin Buser models his basket sled. As he mushes, Buser often helps the team by pushing off with a ski pole.* Below: *Buser demonstrates his racing toboggan. The basket of a toboggan usually sits directly on the runners.*

Above: *A basket sled viewed from the front.* Below: *Viewing a toboggan from the front, you see a piece of plastic curving up from the snow to the brush bow. The wheelers' tuglines attach directly to the runners on this sled.*

Jeff King exhibits his hybrid basket sled that telescopes from the length of a toboggan to the size of a sprint sled. This feature allows King to use one sled throughout the entire Iditarod, thus saving him the cost of shipping several sleds to various checkpoints.

Iditarod toboggan.

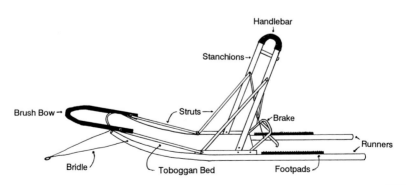

SCH

side of the sled, although it can also be placed between the runners. To embed the hook, the driver pushes it into the snow as far as possible, then steps on it while urging the team forward slightly to ensure that it is firmly set. As Nöel Flanders points out in her book *The Joy of Racing Sled Dogs*, it's no fun to discover that the snowhook hadn't quite caught when you are up among the team untangling the lines and suddenly you get flattened by your own sled as it comes barreling by.

Runaway sleds are such a big problem that some drivers carry two snowhooks to increase their margin of safety. One hook (or a rope called a snubline) may be secured to a tree or other immovable object. Sometimes mushers will even lay a sled on its side to further discourage a restless team. In hard snow or ice, getting the hook *out* may be the problem, but given their druthers, most drivers would rather fight a stubborn snowhook than chase an exuberant dog team.

Racing Toboggans

In 1974, Iditarod rookie Tim White unveiled his prototype toboggan, finishing the race respectably in twentieth place. Four years later, Rick Swenson popularized White's refined design when he drove a toboggan to a second-place finish. Since then, the racing toboggan has become an Iditarod institution.

These sleds, a modern design, tend to be larger and sturdier than the traditional basket types. The basket of a racing toboggan is composed of one long piece of plastic that is bolted directly to the tops of the runners and extends from the handlebar to the brush bow. This basket design gives the toboggan a lower center of gravity, making it less likely to tip over. When it does roll, however, it rights itself quickly.

On a racing toboggan, the runners are shorter where the driver stands, but the basket is longer. As a result, the overall length is still about the same as that of a traditional sled. The sled bag is usually larger, however, which is an asset in bad weather because the musher has more room to climb in for shelter. It also allows more gear to be carried. The weight of an empty toboggan ranges from twenty-seven to fifty pounds.

The easiest way to tell these sleds apart is to eye the sled bag. If there is a gap between the runners and the bag, it's probably a basket sled; if the bag rests directly on the runners, it's a toboggan. From the front, you can also look for a piece of plastic curving up from the snow to the brush bow, which is another distinguishing feature of the toboggan.

Many mushers have installed bicycle seats on their sleds so that they can ride lower and reduce wind resistance. When not in use, the seat folds up and out of the way. Jim Oehlschlaeger shows how his is used.

Other Innovative Sled Designs

Since his 1993 victory, technical innovator Jeff King has designed, built, and successfully raced a hybrid basket sled. Because this sled telescopes to whatever size he needs, the cost of shipping out several types of sleds is eliminated. A specially designed sled bag expands to fit the largest setting and folds out of the way when the sled is compressed. King appreciates the sled's strength and versatility and also the ease with which it can be fixed.

Other technological advances include the trend toward laminating wood for the framework of the sled, which is thought to strengthen it significantly; the lamination of carbon-fiber-reinforced material instead of wood; and the use of a foam core inside laminated runners.

Customizing Your Ride

Sleds are as unique as their owners. Each driver has preferences about every aspect of the sled—its design, construction, and outfitting. Some mushers even build their own.

Swiss-born Martin Buser installed a bicycle seat just behind the handlebar on his sled so that he could sit down comfortably while reducing wind resistance (drivers sometimes kneel on the runners to minimize drag—a real knee killer!). This bicycle-seat feature has become so popular that sled designer Dennis Baker has patented the Restor®, a custom-made lightweight seat mounted on a hollow aluminum tube. When the musher stands up, spring-loaded legs force the seat forward and out of the way. During the 1993 Iditarod, front-runners Rick Swenson, Martin Buser, and Jeff King all traveled up the Yukon River in comfort sitting on their bicycle seats. Swenson sat facing backward, because, as he explains, "the scenery is prettier behind you."

Veteran musher Terry Adkins, who has a history of back trouble, modified his sled by positioning a mountain-bike-style handlebar at a comfortable height in lieu of a drive bow. Adkins has also experimented with a fabric basket that replaces the wooden slats on his sled. Like a trampoline, it is much lighter in weight.

Since 1992, Iditarod rules have specified that no racer may use more than two sleds after Knik. This is a big change from previous years, when it seemed that the top competitors were changing sleds at every other checkpoint. Most mushers continue to choose a larger, sturdier toboggan for the early going, but the question of when to switch sleds and what size to select has now become a critical strategic issue. A small sled can be dangerous in the infamous coastal weather experienced near the end of the race. The weight-versus-safety dilemma is a true test of drivers' judgment and luck.

Despite this restriction, future Iditarod champions will continue to buy, build, and test-drive traditional and ultramodern sled designs of all sizes, searching for a good fit and a winning edge. If you've ever cherished a car, you can understand how mushers feel about a well-built, finely honed racing sled: it's a thing of beauty and a joy to drive.

Anyone can climb a mountain, or run a marathon. The Iditarod is a true test of your mettle! Attitudes change when the mercury drops and the wind begins to blow and you are hundreds of miles from your destination. There is little on earth that can match the inner pride of succeeding in a battle with Mother Nature one more time.

Stan Smith
Iditarod finisher

11

Clothing

KEEP WARM OR DIE

In a television commercial aired during coverage of the Iditarod, one of the race's major sponsors used to state that its products were field-tested in the Alaskan wilderness "by the most unforgiving judge of all." Alaska's weather certainly is unforgiving. If you're going out, you'd better get it right the first time or there may not be a second!

Before examining the details of the type and construction of Iditarod clothing, look at what it's up against. The temperature doesn't have to fall below zero to be dangerous. At about 32° F, the freezing point, mushers often get frost nip. The damp cold leaves a firm, white, chilled spot on the skin. If the area is rewarmed quickly, frost nip will not be damaging.

Frostbite is more serious. The body's extremities (nose, ears, fingers, toes) are the most vulnerable. Explorers cite the "30-30-30" rule: at -30° F with winds of thirty miles per hour, human flesh freezes solid in thirty seconds. The affected skin turns cold, hard, and white.

Note: In this chapter, the author is not endorsing any specific manufacturer, fabric, or type of clothing—she is merely describing representative wardrobes successfully worn by prominent Iditarod drivers.

Although frostbite is painful initially, once an area has frozen, the victim will not be able to feel anything at all. If the tissue is rewarmed immediately, it can be saved; otherwise, gangrene may set in and amputation may be necessary.

The most deadly danger, however, is hypothermia, which can occur when the air temperature is as high as 50° F *above* zero. Hypothermia is the lowering of a person's body temperature to an unsafe level as a result of becoming wet, chilled by wind, and/or being exposed to extreme cold. Dehydration is also a major cause of hypothermia. Early symptoms include chilling, violent shivering, slow or slurred speech, memory lapses, irrational behavior, and stiffening of the body. All of this takes place while a person's normal body temperature of 98.6° F is dropping to about 95° F.

Becoming soaked with perspiration from working too hard in arctic clothing is a grave danger. To avoid this, mushers often drop the top half of their sled suit down, as Jeff King has done here.

At a body temperature of 95° F, the victim begins to fumble, loses use of the hands, and may stumble or fall. Below 90° F, the heartbeat and breathing become irregular, and an overwhelming feeling of exhaustion and drowsiness occurs. Soon the person becomes unconscious. Cardiopulmonary functions may cease below a body temperature of 85° F. Hypothermia is usually fatal if a victim's temperature reaches 78° F or lower.

A victim of hypothermia should not be rewarmed until there is no further danger of refreezing. As a Nome medic put it succinctly, "Freeze, thaw, freeze means guaranteed amputation." The best way to rewarm damaged tissue is now thought to be in a 100° F bath for about thirty minutes. Another medical axiom admonishes that "hypothermic patients should not be considered dead until they are *warm* and dead."

Becoming wet and being exposed to wind both speed heat loss. As those who participate in water sports know, air temperature isn't everything. Fishermen quote a "50-50-50 Law of Survival": when the water temperature is 50° F, a person has a 50 percent chance of surviving for fifty minutes.

On the Iditarod Trail, becoming soaked with perspiration from working too hard in arctic clothing is one of the gravest dangers. Skin dampened by perspiration loses heat twenty-six times faster than dry skin. To combat this, drivers often remove several layers, sometimes stripping down to short sleeves while performing heavy chores.

TRADITIONAL ARCTIC DRESS

Native Alaskans developed what many consider to be the ideal clothing system. A combination of animal skins and furs, their garments were effective at temperatures as low as -100° F. The skin side of their dress provided an excellent shield against the wind, while the fur side proved to be very efficient at holding in heat.

Many arctic animals have hollow hair, with each hair containing an insulating layer of air. In addition, the hair is often wider at the tip than at the base, thus trapping another layer of air between the surface of the animal's skin and the tips of its hairs. As a result, the furs of arctic animals are excellent insulators.

Natives often wore two layers of fur clothing: the inner one lay with the soft leather against their skin and the hair side out, and the outer layer faced hair side in. Clothing was made without zippers or buttons to prevent the entrance of deadly cold. The fit was loose, facilitating movement and enabling water to evaporate. Drawstrings on the legs, wrists, waist, and neck permitted venting of the clothing so that sweat did not accumulate.

Many Iditarod competitors still use traditional arctic materials as components of their boots, gloves, hats, and parkas.

HOW MUSHERS DRESS FOR SUCCESS

Each musher's clothing needs and tastes are different, but most wear a combination of the following items.

Underwear

The inner layers of clothing should wick moisture caused by perspiration away from the skin, while retaining their insulating capabilities. Personal preference dictates the material chosen for long underwear. Polypropylene and silk are popular choices.

Shirts and Pants

These insulating layers retain body heat, keeping the competitors warm and cozy. There is a wide range of styles (turtleneck or crew, pullover or button-front, vest or sleeved), and favorite materials include wool, polypropylene, Thermax®, and fleece. Several insulating garments are usually worn under the final outer layers.

Parkas, Bibs, Sled Suits, and Ponchos

Outer shells make the insulating underlayers more efficient by protecting them from wind and moisture. Usually some type of insulation is incorporated into these weatherproof garments. In addition to being waterproof, windproof, and warm, they should also be lightweight, tear-resistant, relatively breathable, and comfortable.

Parkas may be the traditional Native skin-and-fur pullover or may be filled with goose down with a waterproof outer layer. Most Iditarod competitors' parkas, however, are insulated with a synthetic material, such as Thinsulate®, that will not absorb water. They are then protected by an outer shell made from a nylon laminate, such as Gore-Tex®. Parkas generally have large inner and outer pockets, freeze-resistant zippers protected by storm flaps, wrist cuffs to keep in heat, and an oversize hood with a fur ruff. In addition, they are often thigh length to provide extra protection from the severe cold.

Under their parkas, many mushers wear bibs, a pair of insulated pants with shoulder straps, and an overall-like chest covering. If you live in the northern half of the United States, you may have seen snowmobilers wearing bibs. They are very warm, even if you do feel like you have on a sleeping bag that has been slit up the middle and you look like the Michelin Man. Bibs feature freeze-resistant zippers along each leg, allowing boots to be put on and taken off easily; adjustable shoulder straps; an ample chest pocket; and, of course, an operable fly.

Reminiscent of Indy 500 racing apparel, high-tech sled suits are worn by top Iditarod competitors. A musher may have several such outfits of varying weights and construction. These suits are a one-piece jumpsuit that can be opened to the waist and dropped down (supported by built-in suspenders) while doing hard work, thus avoiding overheating. They are characterized by bright colors, sponsor logos, and huge fur ruffs on the hoods. The fur from northern animals such as wolverines or coyotes will not frost or freeze even in the most severe weather; this helps save the mushers' faces from frostbite.

A lightweight rain poncho or wind suit (a lightly lined anorak and pants) may also be carried for use as outerwear in specific conditions.

Socks

Some mushers wear only one pair of heavy polypropylene socks inside a set of well-fitted lined boots. Others prefer thick wool socks or a combination of thin and thick socks. The important thing is to change socks as soon as they become damp in order to avoid getting frostbite!

Boots

The shoepac is a common type of Iditarod footwear. Rubber up to the ankle and leather above, the standard shoepac laces up the front and comes with removable wool-felt liners that add warmth but can be changed when wet. Liners and socks should be changed at least twice a day. One rookie who neglected to do so had so much moisture condense in his boots that the liners froze to the boots and the whole business had to be cut from his feet in order to save them. Newer models have water-repellant nylon uppers, Thinsulate® insulation, and moisture-wicking polypropylene, poly-felt, or fleece liners. Another advanced feature is the use of Radian-Tex®, a space-age, foil-like material that reflects warmth back toward the foot. A good pair of shoepacs can keep feet comfortable down to -85° F.

A second type of boot has a very vocal following. Called "bunny boots" because of their oversize profile, these vapor-barrier boots are made of double-layered white rubber with an insulating air pocket between the layers. Developed by the U.S. Army for cold-weather operations, they are very effective in extreme conditions, but the rubber prevents air circulation and can result in damp, smelly, and uncomfortable feet if the boots are worn too long. Mushers wearing bunny boots should change socks three times a day, dry their feet, and rub cream into them each time. A heavy cream such as Eucerin® Dry Skin Care Creme will protect the face, hands, and feet from developing splits or cracks.

Like shoepacs, bunny boots also lace up the shins. Devotees note that if overflow (water lying on the surface of a frozen river or lake) pours into their boots, shoepacs are useless until the liners are dried, while bunny boots can simply be emptied of water and worn sockless. Similarly, if a musher's bunny boots are freezing cold when they

These modern mukluks have rubberized leather soles, waterproof synthetic uppers, leather lacing, and wool-felt liners. Like their Native predecessors, they help keep an individual's feet warm and dry, and are very comfortable.
© Stephen C. Hood

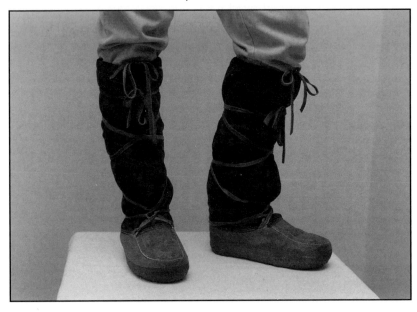

are ready to be put back on, the resourceful driver may simply pour hot water into the boots to prewarm them. Bunny-boot fans are willing to put up with stinky, wrinkled feet in exchange for the increased protection from frostbite provided by the all-rubber construction.

Eskimos and Indians traditionally wore mukluks, a knee-high boot made with hard sealskin soles and caribou fur or moosehide uppers. The boot was constructed without zippers or other openings, was lined with grass, and was fitted to the wearer by adjusting rawhide ties that wrapped around the outside from the ankle up to the knee. It often included a drawstring at the top. These mukluks provide good protection in very cold, dry snow, but in wet conditions, water will soak through.

Mukluk-style boots made by a variety of companies are often seen on the Iditarod Trail. The soles may be rubber-coated leather, and the uppers may be treated leather, treated oxford cloth, or a waterproof synthetic fabric. Wool-felt or poly-felt liners are used. Because these boots are so tall and their construction allows great flexibility (hence better circulation), their advocates claim that they are warmer and more water-resistant than shoepacs.

Eclectic mushers resolve this debate by carrying all three types of footwear with them—one on their feet that suits current conditions, and two in the sled bag for future use.

Gloves and Mittens

In the *Iditarod Rookie Seminar* video, required viewing for all aspiring entrants, survival savvy Joe Redington, Sr. points out that you can still walk on frozen feet, but once your hands freeze, you won't be able to put on mittens, don additional layers of clothing, or build a life-saving fire. Keeping your hands warm and functional at all times is absolutely critical.

Generally a three- or four-layer system of gloves and mittens is used to keep mushers' hands warm. Several liner gloves made of silk or polypropylene may be worn, with a wool glove or chore glove over them. When it's cold, these three layers are covered with overmitts (made from fur or synthetic open-cell foam), which look like hugely overblown oven mitts. These enormous mittens have a gauntlet extending past the elbow. They are attached by long strings (sometimes called "idiot strings") to a mitten harness, which looks like a yoke worn across the shoulders on top of the parka or sled suit. When doing detail work with their hands, mushers can simply drop the mittens at their side; if the weather warms up, the mitts can be thrown over the shoulders to dangle behind. Drivers need to balance their need for warmth against their need to keep a firm grip on the handlebar—or should discipline themselves to wrap an arm around the drive bow if their overmitts are too unwieldy. "Warm hands/loose team" is not a successful equation.

Fingerless gloves and cotton chore gloves (worn with poly or silk liners) usually appear in Iditarod wardrobes. One other specialized glove is also carried. Surgical gloves (with a liner for warmth) allow mushers to apply ointment to dogs' feet without getting it on their usual gloves.

Headgear

Believe it or not, wearing a hat warms up your hands and feet! The brain requires heat and oxygen to function, which means that even when the body is trying to conserve heat, the brain must be supplied with blood. The blood vessels that supply the head and neck do not constrict and therefore radiate heat constantly. As a result, as much as 50 percent of a person's body heat may be lost through the head and neck. Warm headgear reduces this heat loss, thus allowing more warmth to be sent to other "lower-priority" body parts. Mushers who are dissatisfied with the insulation of their boots and mittens might be better off upgrading their headgear.

To protect their face, competitors often wear a fleece face mask, which may velcro onto their hat. A snug-fitting fleece or poly cap is often worn under another hat and/or the parka ruff. A neck gaiter (a wide band rather like a giant turtleneck) extends protection downward and can be pulled up over the chin and/or nose.

Like modern-day cowboys, a musher's hat may be his or her trademark. As long as it is warm and weatherproof, the stylistic possibilities are endless. Hats range from what looks like a baseball cap with earflaps (called a "bomber" or "yazoo" hat) to awe-inspiring furs, with every conceivable design in between. There's the high-tech sponsorlogo look, the plaid outdoorsman style, the Russian fur-trader image, and the arctic-expedition-in-the-frozen-north motif. Nome's favorite son, Iditarod musher Matt Desalernos, is widely known as "Matt the Hat" because of his distinctive fluorescent orange cap. It is also important for a headlamp to fit above the brim (if there is one), centered in front of the hat; this provides the driver with night vision.

Headgear is rounded out by a pair of sunglasses, often with leather eye protectors along the sides, and glacier goggles. Snow blindness in the bright white, open expanses of Alaska has been respected as a real threat ever since the first Native dweller fashioned a cup-shaped piece of wood with narrow slits as protective eyewear.

Jewelry . . . Best Left at Home

Those who have worked in hazardous occupations or with dangerous machinery know that it's prudent to remove any type of jewelry that could become snagged or caught while working. The multitude of lines and rigging involved in running a dog team create many opportunities to become ensnared. Mushers should also consider the risks posed by extreme weather. Dog drivers often injure their hands—a good reason to leave rings at home. Injured hands swell, and a ring can restrict circulation so severely that it has to be cut from the finger.

PUTTING IT ALL TOGETHER

The Traditional Layered Approach

Top competitors with good sponsors can develop a clothing system in which individual garments complement each other, thus reducing the number of layers.

DeeDee Jonrowe's gear, for instance, is supplied by catalog and retail-clothing merchant Eddie Bauer. In extremely cold weather she might wear this combination of clothing:

- underwear
- silk long underwear top and bottom
- poly liner and wool-blend socks
- windproof fleece long-sleeved shirt and slacks
- heavyweight sled suit with ruff
- goose down parka (only for *severe* cold)
- silk glove liner/poly glove liner/beaver mitts with a pocket for a chemical handwarmer
- windproof fleece neck gaiter
- modified mukluks

Jonrowe also carries a down vest with her. Goose down is one of the best insulators available. When the down is fluffed, motionless air is trapped, and the wearer enjoys the same warmth that protects birds from extreme cold. Down has a serious drawback, however. Unlike wool, fleece, or synthetic insulation, wet goose down is essentially

DeeDee Jonrowe's parka is made with special zippers and snaps that will not fracture or pack with ice. A ventilation system (reminiscent of the drawstrings on traditional Eskimo clothing) allows for temperature control. This parka is warm, lightweight, easy to slip on and off, and has conveniently placed customized pockets.

useless. Water pushes out the trapped air, and water is not a good insulator. Jonrowe prefers down because of its light weight—she finds wearing heavier fabrics continually to be tiring. Down also saves on room and weight in the sled bag. Her down parka and vest are kept dry in a waterproof stuffsack.

Top mushers like Jonrowe have several weights of suits. Her wind suit is lightweight, made with ripstop nylon; her two-piece sled suit is medium weight; her heavier-weight jumpsuits are insulated with waterproof synthetics; and her heavy down parka has a Gore-Tex® laminate shell.

Jonrowe's sled suits and parka are made with special zippers and snaps that will not fracture or pack with ice. A ventilation system is maintained by a separate set of snaps and zippers, reminiscent of the drawstrings on traditional Eskimo clothing. The sled suits and parka are lightweight, easy to slip on and off, and have customized pockets placed conveniently for Jonrowe. At the end of each year's race, her main suits are shipped back to Bauer for cleaning, updating, and revising.

Jonrowe emphasizes that individual musher's needs dictate clothing preferences and requirements and points out that to stay warm, she needs to wear more clothing than most of her fellow competitors. In fact, they enjoy giving her a lot of heat about being so cold!

Mushers' sled suits are highly individualized: Jonrowe's designs tend to have high fashion flair (her most recent ones are purple, turquoise, and black accented with a copyrighted motif of her famous lead dog Johnny's face). Susan Butcher's signature suit is a vibrant red with Purina Pro Plan patches on the shoulders and back, and Rick Swenson wears fluorescent pink with the Iams "Eukanuba" logo and pawprint emblazoned in black down the sleeves and legs. Just because they're battling the elements in the backwoods doesn't mean that mushers' wardrobes won't dazzle you.

A Monolithic System

Northern Outfitters is well-known for its monolithic or single-layer clothing system, which was "developed with the goal of finding better ways to avoid the accumulation of body moisture in the insulation while at the same time maximizing the retention of body heat." This clothing looks bulky because it contains at least one inch of open-cell polyurethane foam, covered with a windproof fabric. The theory is that warm, moist air flows toward cooler, drier air. The greater the difference in temperature, the faster the air flows. Therefore, instead of your body's escaping heat having to cross a wicking layer, an insulating layer, and a shell layer to get out, it only has to pass through one layer of open-cell foam. Northern Outfitters maintains that because there is a greater temperature difference between your internal body heat and the outdoor air than there is between each successive piece of layered clothing, you will shed moisture faster with their system, thus staying drier and more comfortable. Other advantages are reputed to be its light weight and its ability to be worn for long periods of time without washing.

It is important to note, however, that this gear allows water to come in as easily as it is transferred out; hence, a rain poncho or other protective rain gear must be carried. Also, supplemental wind gear should be used when extreme cold is accompanied by high winds.

Hey, anyone know where a guy can get a cheeseburger around here?

Rick Swenson deadpanned when he arrived at Anvik in the lead during the 1989 race, thus winning the renowned seven-course "First to the Yukon" gourmet meal.

12

Food

Just a word of caution before getting into the details of what Iditarod canine and human athletes eat: all diets are different. The diets of Iditarod dogs and mushers are constantly changing and improving. There is a wide spectrum of personal preferences and scientific opinion on the subject of nutrition. Top drivers are sometimes reluctant to divulge the specifics of a highly successful feeding program. This chapter will cover a range of possibilities for satisfying the nutritional needs and palates of both the four-legged and two-legged competitors.

DOGS

Spectators who are new to sled-dog racing often comment on the slimness of the dogs ("They're so skinny! They look half-starved!"). Keep in mind that Iditarod dogs are world-class marathon runners. Have you ever seen an overweight distance runner? If the average household dog exercised as much as was good for him daily, the pet would probably lose 10 percent of his body weight. Carrying extra pounds strains the heart and joints. Sled dogs may look thin, but they are in fact well-fed, "lean mean racing machines."

Keeping Them Hydrated

The single greatest challenge in caring for sled dogs is undoubtedly keeping them sufficiently hydrated. Although it is the least expensive item on the menu, water is the most critical nutrient that a dog ingests.

When working, sled dogs are often unwilling to drink plain water, so mushers "bait" (flavor) the water with some type of enticing substance. Meat scraps, meat juice, chunks of beef by-products, canned dog food, fish meal, powdered whole eggs, corn oil, honey, and electrolyte powder are some of the bribes used to tempt the dogs to drink. In winter, baited water is usually served warm so that the dogs don't expend valuable calories rewarming themselves after having a cold drink.

In warm weather, some mushers provide water for their dogs on demand; in other words, water is always available to each dog. Libby Riddles, 1985 champion, suggests mounting water bowls in the roofs of the doghouses. Others supply their dogs with water at scheduled times. Generally, water is offered first thing in the morning, after every training run or race, and again in the evening. This does *not* include the water used to make their meals. Sled dogs drink from one to two quarts of water a day in cold weather or when they are inactive, and up to one gallon a day in hot weather or during heavy exertion.

An easy way to test for dehydration in a dog is to grasp a handful of fur and skin above the dog's shoulders, pull it up, and let go. The skin of a healthy dog will immediately snap back. If the dog's skin returns to its normal position slowly or stays up in a crease, the animal is dehydrated and requires immediate attention. Unfortunately, dehydrated dogs will often refuse to drink, thus compounding the problem. During the Iditarod, veterinarians are always available for consultation, and dogs that become too dehydrated to continue are dropped at checkpoints and then flown out to care facilities.

Along the trail, dogs often "dip" for snow (reach down and scoop up a mouthful), but this is not a significant source of water. Iditarod drivers heat water or melt snow at the checkpoints and out on the trail to ensure that each dog receives enough water to stay healthy and happy.

High-Octane Fuel

Just as race cars require specially formulated fuels, sled dogs need to be fed high-performance diets. Traditionally, arctic sled dogs were given what was available—walrus, seal, whale, bear, beaver, caribou, reindeer, and fish, for instance. When gold miners, trappers, mail carriers, and

Although it is the least expensive item on the menu, water is the most critical nutrient that a dog ingests. Mushers carefully monitor each dog to ensure that his fluid intake is sufficient.

dog punchers (those who transported supplies by dog team) began using sled dogs, they added cornmeal, oatmeal, or rice to the mix.

According to a recent study of sled-dogs' diets, an Iditarod dog consumes 11,200 calories per day while racing compared with 2,500 calories per day when at home in the kennel. To put this in perspective, that would equate to a 170-pound person eating 27,000 calories (or 50 Big Macs) per day.

Today a dry commercial dog food usually forms the foundation for sled-dogs' diets. The goal in formulating premium dry food is to produce a high-density diet, that is, one that contains a high nutritional content in a relatively small volume. In the past, mushers would feed their dogs as much as 85 percent fresh meat and supplements and only 15 percent commercial dry dog food. Now there are mushers and veterinarians who believe that a ratio of 80 percent dry food and supplements and only 20 percent fresh meat may be optimum. Of course, every competitor has his or her own preference, and depending upon the local weather, distance raced, and other variables, there is still a broad spectrum of dry food:fresh meat ratios.

There is also quite a bit of variation among types of commercial dry food. Mushers mention two percentages when discussing feed formulas—the first number is the percentage of protein in the food, and the second figure is the percentage of fat. Some high-performance dry feeds go up as high as 35/30 percent for use during the racing season, while others drop as low as 26/12 percent for off-season use. If you go to your local feed store and ask to see the label of a high-quality dry dog food, regular adult formula, the percentages will likely be in the 25/15 percent range. This is considered excellent for an adult household pet of average activity level. Puppies and expectant or lactating mothers require more protein and fat, while older or less active animals require less.

Mushers are careful to keep their dry food fresh, purchasing relatively small amounts frequently, rather than keeping tons on hand in a storage shed. Several bags are usually brought inside a heated building so that a ready-to-feed supply is always available.

The meat fed to sled dogs may consist of boned chicken, ground whole turkey, beef, lamb, game animals, salmon or other fish, and beef/chicken/turkey/pork liver. In the early years of the Iditarod, many mushers preferred to feed beaver because it is usually one of the last foods that a sled dog will refuse to eat. Because it is not widely available, however, beaver meat is not likely to appear on most sled-dogs' menus. The dogs' meat is often kept frozen in large blocks, making it difficult to keep on hand during the summer. Consequently, mushers may feed their dogs a higher percentage of commercial dry mix in the warmer months to alleviate the problem of storing fresh meat. A large variety of frozen meat is shipped ahead to the Iditarod checkpoints. Chicken tends to spoil if a warm spell occurs, while lamb (heavy with fat) is more likely to keep. Fish provides water for hot weather, and additional fat is required if the weather turns extremely cold.

Fat is also a significant addition to the dogs' daily meals. A good source of high energy in cold weather, fat must be soluble and can comprise as much as 40 to 50 percent of a dog's diet (including the fat content of the commercial dry food and fat supplements). Types of fat used include chicken, turkey, beef, or beaver fat; seal blubber; fish or seal oil; corn, vegetable, or safflower oil; and wheat-germ oil. In addition to being a good source of easily digestible fat, corn oil is rich in vitamin E, and wheat-germ oil contains vitamin B.

Some mushers add eggs to their dogs' meals because they are high in protein and contain a significant amount of fat as well. Other food supplements may include cottage cheese (which improves muscle tone), cream cheese, rice, honey, brewer's yeast, and bonemeal. Competitors who use bonemeal believe that it provides a valuable source of minerals (specifically, calcium), as well as other micronutrients and trace elements that the dogs may need. Unlike some minerals, however, excess calcium does not just pass through a dog's system; therefore, bonemeal must be given in carefully measured doses.

Nonfood supplements are discussed below. Needless to say, when deciding upon the elements of a dog's diet and the optimum proportions of each item, a musher should consult frequently with a veterinarian familiar with sled-dog racing. It is also important to remember that each dog must be fed in accordance with his individual needs. One dog may require more meat or fat or supplement than another.

How Iditarod Chefs Cook Canine Chow

Iditarod dogs generally eat most of the components of their complex diet in one delectably dripping concoction. Water is heated, fresh frozen meat is added, then additional fat and the dry food (as well as any supplements) are blended in. Once the whole mixture is served, the dogs lap it up greedily. Canine "dish-tippers" are discouraged during training because the liquid component of their meal is the most critical one for them to ingest.

When and how much the dogs eat changes on a seasonal basis. In the late spring and summer (the off-season), the dogs may get one meal a day. During serious training, this may increase to two meals per day and culminate in three meals daily throughout the racing season. This is in addition to baited water and snacks.

Out on the trail during the Iditarod, meal preparation becomes more challenging. Mushers usually have meal-size portions of commercial dry food shipped to the checkpoints, as well as frozen meat and any supplements that they choose to add. Preparation of these food drops prior to the race is a monumental task. It requires good arithmetic; hours of chopping, mixing, and packing; and a well-organized mastermind. In his third decade of racing the Iditarod, Rick Swenson still dreads this process and good-humoredly notes that his famous lead dog Andy, who died recently three days short of his twentieth birthday, was the only one who looked forward to food drops. Like most people's dogs, Andy must have been a real scrap hound!

Spectators who are new to sled-dog racing often comment on the slimness of the dogs. Iditarod dogs are world-class marathon runners: well-fed, fit, and healthier than most overweight family pets.

Using the contents of the drop bags, the musher prepares the meal by finding water and hauling it to the campsite (or melting snow if water is not accessible); heating the water over a portable stove; chopping up the frozen meat while the water comes to a boil (if the meat has not been shipped presliced); adding the meat; and when it has softened, mixing in the dry food, fat, and additives. Cold water may then be used to make the soup cool enough for the dogs to eat.

In his book *The Secrets of Long Distance Training and Racing*, Rick Swenson suggests that only water should be boiled in the cooking pot and that all of the other ingredients should be mixed together gradually in the cooler. Swenson chops up his frozen meat and places it in the cooler, then pours boiling water over it, puts the lid on the cooler, and allows the meat to thaw. He starts the next pot of water while he is waiting. He can then add the dry food and supplements, stir, and feed the dogs. The advantage of this system is that the cooking pot does not become contaminated with burnt dog food, which is difficult

Trisha, a handler for DeeDee Jonrowe, pours salmon oil into a concrete mixer along with commercial dry food, chicken fat, and powdered eggs. Although this meal is meant for her sled dogs, Jonrowe's Labrador Retrievers get fat from lying under the mixer waiting for scraps to appear.

to remove and makes subsequent batches of food taste bad. Swenson also stresses the importance of keeping the cooler clean so that it does not sour the dogs' meals.

While the team is enjoying the repast, the industrious musher prepares a second batch, which is stored in a three- to six-gallon insulated cooler for ready-to-eat use farther down the trail. Dogs are fed this type of meal at longer (four hours or so) rest stops to allow sufficient time for them to digest their food before returning to work.

Instant Energy

The primary difference between snacks and meals is that snacks don't require much time to digest and therefore can be given to the dogs at short rest stops. Throughout the history of the Iditarod, dogs have been offered a smorgasbord of snacks. One perennial favorite is the "water snack," which can consist simply of whitefish and water, but also may have gelatin and canned dog food added to the treat.

The high-fat, highly palatable "fish/fat snack" is another staple. This is a combination of salmon, whitefish, or herring with some type of vegetable fat (such as corn, flax, or coconut oil).

Some contemporary mushers prefer to make snacks by freezing chunks of the dogs' daily meal mix. As you may have noticed if you have a pet, once a dog realizes that tastier options are available, he may refuse to eat his customary rations. By feeding frozen portions of the usual food and avoiding the snack smorgasbord routine, mushers may keep their dogs eating well longer.

In desperation, however, most mushers will feed their dogs whatever is available (including their own food) to get them eating again. Sometimes giving a dog a special treat will reactivate his appetite, much like priming a pump. At home, dogs may get one snack a day during the training season, while out on the Iditarod Trail, they may eat a snack every hour or so between the checkpoints.

Supplements

As in any competitive endeavor, participants are constantly trying to gain an edge on the opposition. Some mushers believe that adding supplements to their dogs' diets enhances overall performance. A vitamin/iron supplement such as Vi-Sorbin® is a popular choice. B vitamins, or a blood-enrichment product like Red Cell®, are also used. Dogs are sometimes given vitamin C to maintain their health.

Another product favored by some dog drivers is a balanced dietary supplement (Pro Balance®, for example). Advocates claim that such products improve the dogs' haircoat, promote larger litters, reduce the incidence of stress diarrhea, and provide electrolyte-replacement properties. Critics contend that electrolyte-type supplements are not necessary.

A digestive-system enhancer such as ProBiotics®, which contains dried lactobacillus and acidophilus, may increase the efficiency of dogs' digestion and help reduce intestinal stress. Mushers using this product claim that they can feed 25 percent less commercial dry food because what the dogs are eating is being processed more efficiently.

There are mushers who do not believe in using any nonfood supplements. Competitors who do use them do so in close consultation with their veterinarians. The health of Iditarod dogs is too precious a commodity to be handled in a cavalier fashion. The diets of these animals are monitored constantly to keep the dogs happy and fit, as well as to maximize their potential as Iditarod athletes.

Upon arrival at a checkpoint, mushers fetch straw and their supply bags in order to make the dogs comfortable and prepare dinner for them. Volunteers at McGrath have stacked the food-drop bags alphabetically on the frozen Kuskokwim River.

HUMANS

According to a study performed by the Arctic Sports Medicine Institute at the University of Alaska, mushers should be chubby. An average person carries 10 to 15 percent body fat, but to run the Iditarod, about 19 percent would be optimum. Competitors have been known to lose twenty-five to thirty pounds during the race. They may consume as many as 8,000 to 10,000 calories per day in order to compensate for heat loss and heavy exertion.

With the exception of a few highly disciplined drivers, most Iditarod mushers neglect their own diet. This not only results in poor judgment and a lack of energy, but tends to make the person cold. Warm clothing cannot produce heat; the body requires fuel in the form of nutritious food in order to generate warmth.

Fueling the Fires Within

Iditarod food should supply high energy but be easy to prepare. This can translate into many interesting entrees. Favorite musher staples include steak, pizza, fried chicken, Mexican and Chinese food, pork chops, pasta, grilled sandwiches, soup, and dried meats.

In her book *Race Across Alaska*, Libby Riddles (with Tim Jones) details the culinary contents of her sled and supply bags during the 1985 Iditarod. To satisfy her protein needs, Riddles ate the following foods: steak, pizza, fried chicken, peanut-butter-and-jelly sandwiches, dried moose meat, bacon, cheese, commercial trail mix, kamamik (Eskimo ice cream), and seal oil.

Mushers are constantly discovering time-saving techniques for preparing their meals. When Iditarod drivers used to camp along the trail, they would wrap a steak in aluminum foil along with several large pats of butter and sliced-up potatoes and simply throw it over their fire. Fifteen minutes later, they enjoyed a juicy steak and fried potatoes. Because campfires are a thing of the past, boil-in-a-bag meals, which can be heated in the dogs' water, are now preferred.

Some competitors make grilled sandwiches ahead of time using a variety of meats and cheeses, and freeze them. Once thawed in a breast pocket along the trail, these precooked sandwiches taste better than the usual soggy-bread fare.

Survival Snacks

Riddles was criticized by the press for eating a lot of "junk food." Her snack options included french toast, corn muffins, ready-made popcorn, English muffins, carrot cake, pecan pies, pecan rolls, and a bar of Norwegian chocolate. In her defense, Riddles noted, "When I'm tired, I won't eat. I like to look forward to what's in the bag at the next checkpoint."

Other snack options include salami, beef jerky, and salmon strips. Dried and frozen fruits (such as grapes and peeled oranges), gorp (good old raisins and peanuts), nuts, and sticks of butter (yes, mushers crave fat so much that they will eat it straight!) are other favorites. One reporter who attended the prerace banquet was startled to note that a musher sitting at her table had eaten every scrap on his plate; her own was half-covered with large chunks of fat trimmed off of a generous serving of prime rib. Fruitcake, poppy-seed cake, sausage, Häagen-Dazs bars, chewing gum, and even lowly pilot bread (a dry cracker) round out the list.

One recent addition to the high-energy arsenal is a food supplement called Ultra Energy®. You can buy a four-ounce (500 cc) packet for about seven dollars; once it is mixed with water, the drink supplies 395 calories and 12.5 grams of protein. Besides providing high nutritional content quickly and easily, this product also reduces the amount of solid waste that a musher will produce (out on the trail, the fewer "restroom" stops, the better).

Fluid Replacement

Top-notch Iditarod competitors eat and drink on autopilot because they have trained themselves to do so. Most mushers, however, take care of their dogs at the expense of their own well-being. Dehydration is an especially difficult problem. Water loss results from sweating during hard exertion and also from merely breathing, because the lungs have to moisturize cold, dry air as it enters the body. The drivers' busy schedule and exhausted state compound this problem. Once a driver is dehydrated, he or she may simply feel tired and think that a little sleep will do the trick. The more tired the musher becomes, the more his or her judgment suffers. Iditarod competitors need to learn to take care of themselves *first* so that they can then care for their dogs properly. You have undoubtedly heard an airline flight attendant caution you to put on your own oxygen mask first if cabin depressurization occurs, so that you will then be able to place a mask on a young child traveling with you. It is the same principle: the caretaker has to be fit to care for the dependents.

Substances with high liquid content consumed by Riddles included fruit juices, frozen berries, frozen yogurt, powdered milk, and frozen melon balls. Of course, coffee is usually available, but serious competitors try to avoid caffeine because of its dehydrating effects. Caffeine or sugar also provides a short-term high, which can make mushers feel worse once it wears off than they would have felt without it. Similarly, drivers may bring brandy or other types of liquor with them, but front-runners stay away from alcohol because it is a depressant.

Generally, mushers carry boxed drinks or use a small thermos to keep fruit juice or decaffeinated tea readily available. They may pour boiling water into the thermos at a checkpoint, knowing that by the time they are ready for a drink farther down the trail, it will have cooled to a pleasant drinking temperature.

Seal Oil

Arctic peoples realized long ago that fat plays a crucial role in their diet, enabling them to endure the effects of extreme cold. In Eskimo communities such as Teller, Alaska, traditional feasts center around seal oil. Offerings at such an event might include dried fish and seal meat dipped in seal oil and then sprinkled with salt, greens in oil, carrots and turnips in oil, and berries with sugar or Eskimo ice cream (kamamik), which is made using seal oil.

Some mushers take seal oil, kamamik, or muktuk (dried chunks of whale fat and skin) with them to provide a long-lasting burst of energy out on the trail. During the blizzard near the end of the 1985 race, Libby Riddles washed down her Norwegian chocolate bar with seal oil while out on the ice of Norton Sound. Once Riddles reached land at Koyuk, she asked her hostess and personal friend Vera Napayonek for a refill of seal oil. Riddles relates Napayonek's reaction:

> She looked at me, surprised.
> "What you want seal oil for?"
> "For me, for the trail, so that I can keep warm."
> "Libby, you always have seal oil?"
> Then I gave her some moose jerky and a container of *akutug*, another word for *kamamik*, Eskimo ice cream, which I wanted her to have.
> "Libby, you always eat *akutug*? Who made this? You made this? Boy, dried moose meat, seal oil, *akutug* . . . I thought blondies never eat that. I know, I got daughter-in-law, she's blonde, and she won't eat seal oil. Next time you come around, I feed you Eskimo."

Sponsor Food

As a perk from sponsors, mushers will occasionally receive rather unusual additions to their trail menus. In 1990, one of Joe Redington, Sr.'s sponsors was Alaska Silk Pie. At every checkpoint, a silk pie awaited the Father of the Iditarod. Because he was also supplied with steaks from Mr. Prime Beef, and drinks from Maxwell House® and Tang™, he could make a meal out of his sponsors' largess.

That same year, rookie musher Larry Munoz, a sales/marketing representative for Kraft General Foods, received 250 frozen burritos from Mexico Restaurant. Whether he offered to trade a burrito for a steak after eating the first couple hundred is not reported.

At the Checkpoints

Villagers and checkpoint officials along the trail are famous for their hospitality. Mushers may be met with a lavish spread such as: moose stew, roast beef, ham, macaroni and cheese, rolls, salads, pies, cakes, cookies, and an assortment of beverages. In the larger villages, eating at a local bar, restaurant, or lodge is also an option, as long as the competitors pay for their own meals.

But the most memorable meals have been those served by individual hosts and hostesses in their own homes. Jim Wood, a professional property manager, felt that the people in the villages were the highlight of his 1990 rookie year. Arriving in Elim at 2 A.M., Wood was led by John and Darla Jimawok to their home, where Darla proceeded to feed him a meal of reindeer roast, potatoes, gravy, and biscuits. And as if that weren't enough, they then gave Wood their own bed so that he could take a quick hour-and-a-half nap!

Although mushers love to tell such "pre-corralling days" stories and eagerly anticipate the local offerings now made available to all, they are encouraged not to count on checkpoint food as they plan their trail supplies. Occasionally, however, bizarre things happen on the Iditarod Trail. Approaching the halfway point of Iditarod, a remote ghost town in the forbidding Alaskan Interior, 1993 race leader Jeff King must have thought that he was hallucinating when he saw a series of fast-food billboards! "After miles of mushing," the first one read, "Stop without rushing," advised the second. Sign #3 tempted, "Enjoy an Iditadog," and the final billboard proclaimed, "The best hot dog in Iditarod!" Naturally, once he had finished his checking-in and dog-care chores, King settled down to polish off two juicy hot dogs smothered with chili and onions. The entire population of the nearby town of Flat—eight resourceful individuals—set up this concession stand and operated it despite the ten-below cold. "The winter gets long in Flat," explained resident Tad Fullerton.

You begin to realize how alive you are when you're vulnerable. You begin to understand what survival is all about when you're close to the edge, pushing yourself harder than you've ever pushed before.

Bruce Hamler,
Anchorage Iditasport bike and ski racer

13

Mandatory and Optional Equipment

Iditarod rules list seven pieces of equipment under the heading of "mandatory items." According to the rules, mushers must have the following with them at all times: sleeping bag, ax, snowshoes, promotional material, dog booties, a cooker and pot, and a veterinary notebook. These pieces of gear are inspected by officials at every checkpoint with the exception of three of the early ones (Eagle River, Wasilla, and Knik) and the last checkpoint before the finish (Safety).

Many other pieces of equipment are required by Iditarod rules but are not referred to as "mandatory items" because they are not included in the checkpoint inspections. This chapter will examine mandatory items, other required gear, and optional equipment.

MANDATORY ITEMS

Sleeping Bag
Each musher must carry at all times a proper cold-weather sleeping bag weighing a minimum of five pounds.

Ax

An ax, with a head that weighs a minimum of one and three-fourths pounds and a handle that is at least twenty-two inches long, must also be in the sled bag throughout the race. Joe Runyan, 1989 Iditarod champion, has been seen putting his ax to a rather novel use: he stirs his pot of dog food with it!

Failure to produce any one of these seven mandatory items at a checkpoint inspection can result in disqualification. In 1990, two mushers had to backtrack to retrieve a misplaced ax. Linwood Fiedler, a supervisor at a day treatment center for emotionally disturbed children, forgot to include his ax when he changed sleds at McGrath. In spite of losing three or four hours going back for it, Fiedler placed eighth in his second running of the Iditarod. Bill Davidson discovered that he didn't have his ax when he was ten to twelve miles out of Unalakleet. Going back to retrieve it demoralized both musher and dog team. Leaving Unalakleet for Shaktoolik the second time, Davidson was depressed: "The dogs had zero attitude. It was a death march to Shaktoolik." Nevertheless, Davidson persevered and was able to finish his second race.

Joe Runyan puts his mandatory ax to a novel use —
stirring his potful of dog food!

In 1995, DeeDee Jonrowe carried this commemorative cachet out of Anchorage, across Rainy Pass, down Dalzell Gorge, along the Yukon River, through the severe weather of the Bering Sea coast, and finally across the finish line on Front Street in Nome.

Snowshoes

Many mushers fasten snowshoes to the outside of their sled bag. This frees up more room inside and leaves the snowshoes easily visible for inspection. Rules require that the snowshoes have "bindings, each shoe to be at least 252 square inches in size."

Promotional Material

Iditarod rules require each musher to carry "any promotional material provided by the ITC. All promotional material . . . must be returned to the ITC at the finish line, or in the case of mushers who scratch, to the checker accepting the musher's scratch form."

In her book *The Iditarod: Women on the Trail*, ITC archivist Nicki J. Nielsen explains the history and nature of this promotional material:

> In 1974, the second year of the race to Nome, the U.S. Post Office prepared cacheted envelopes for race entrants to carry

over the trail during the race. These cachets commemorated the historic role of the mail carrier who carried mail by dog team over the trail in the early years of this century. In an advertisement headlined "Mushers Reenact an Era" the post office stated: "This will be the first official dog team mail contract in twenty-five years. The mushers in the 1974 Iditarod Race will carry these specially printed envelopes all 1,049 miles from Anchorage to Nome. All cachets will be canceled in Anchorage prior to departing on the historic mail route and backstamped upon arrival in Nome."

The U.S. Post Office did not continue the practice for the 1975 race. In 1975 the Nome Kennel Club designed a special envelope for the race, and has continued having cacheted envelopes carried each year. These cachets are part of the official required gear that each musher carries and must show to official race checkers at each checkpoint along the trail.

If you would like to own one of these collectible cachet envelopes that has traveled out of Anchorage, over Rainy Pass, down Dalzell Gorge, along the Yukon River, through the severe weather of the Bering Sea coast, and finally across the finish line on Front Street in Nome, call the ITC at their 800 number (listed in the "Iditarod Trail Committee Hotlines and Catalog" chapter) and buy one that made the journey in the sled bag of your favorite musher. All proceeds benefit the not-for-profit Iditarod Trail Committee, Inc.

Dog Booties

The fifth mandatory item is "eight booties for each dog in the sled or in use." If a musher left Fourth Avenue (Anchorage) with the maximum of sixteen dogs, a total of 128 dog booties would have to be in the sled or on the dogs' feet. In practice, however, most competitors carry more than 1,000 dog booties to ensure that they will be able to protect each dog adequately throughout the entire race.

Cooker

A recent rule change has added a dog-food cooker to the list of mandatory equipment. According to race rules, each musher must have "one operational cooker and pot capable of boiling at least three (3) gallons of water."

In the early days of the Iditarod, drivers adapted the traditional two-burner Coleman stove. The fuel tank required frequent pumping,

Mushers' mandatory equipment includes items such as a sleeping bag,
snowshoes, and promotional material.

however, and the mechanical parts could be finicky in extremely cold conditions. Then the charcoal stove came into vogue. Used by Libby Riddles when she won in 1985, this simply consisted of a large pot into which she put charcoal briquettes, kindling, and Blazo® (a type of lighter fluid supplied by the ITC). A metal grating was placed over this lower pot, and a cooking pot set on top of the grate. The charcoal burned hotter and longer than the pressurized stove, but shipping charcoal or carrying it in the sled created unwanted extra poundage.

In *The Secrets of Long Distance Training and Racing*, Rick Swenson describes his prototype of the now-popular alcohol stove. Swenson used a 17" x 12" x 12" aluminum box as the base of his stove. He placed two one-quart cans filled with alcohol into this stove base; each can of alcohol had a piece of fiberglass insulation in it as a wick. A metal grate lay on top of this base box to provide a cooking surface. The dogs' water boiled in a second aluminum box resting atop the stove grate. Swenson also developed an aluminum tentlike lid that kept the heat rising from his alcohol "burners" against the sides of his cooking "pot." Swenson notes, "Starting with snow, I could have boiling

A handler may be required at the starting line. Keizo Funatsu drives his sled through the tunnel under Gambell & Inga streets in Anchorage, with his wife riding in the sled bag. Other mushers tow a second sled.

water for my 14-dog team in less than 30 minutes. It didn't matter what the outside temperature was."

The alcohol stove has no moving parts, weighs little, lights at any temperature, and burns hotter if it is windy. In concept, it is similar to the small Sterno® cans used by caterers to keep pans of food warm. The ITC now provides Heet®, a form of bottled alcohol, for mushers' use at the checkpoints.

Veterinary Notebook

The last item of mandatory equipment is a "veterinarian notebook, to be presented to the veterinarian at each checkpoint." Any dog needing special attention is written up, and if a dog requires follow-up care or close monitoring, this is also recorded in the notebook.

OTHER REQUIRED EQUIPMENT

Many other types of gear, some obvious and others less so, are required by Iditarod rules but are not inspected regularly.

Dogs

ITC rules specify, "The maximum number of dogs a musher may start the race with is sixteen (16) dogs. A musher must have at least twelve (12) dogs on the line [gangline] to start the race. At least five (5) dogs must be on the towline at the finish line. No dogs may be added to a team after the start of the race. All dogs must be either on the towline or hauled in the sled and cannot be led behind the sled or allowed to run loose."

To protect their well-being, dogs must wear "functional, non-chafing harnesses."

To identify loose or dropped dogs, "all dogs leaving the starting line will be electronically marked and tagged with electronic markers [microchips] and tags. Electronic markers will be installed by ITC personnel unless other arrangements are approved by ITC. Only current tags are permitted. Dogs must be listed by name and tag number/letter and electronic ID on the 'team list' provided by the ITC."

The amount of food required to be shipped for each dog is "a minimum of five (5) pounds of dog food per dog for each checkpoint designated Class A [14 checkpoints] and two (2) pounds to those checkpoints designated Class B [2 checkpoints and] must be shipped through the ITC. . . . Those checkpoints designated class C [1 checkpoint] may also receive food through the food shipment at the musher's option."

Upon arrival at the next checkpoint, if it is determined that a dog will be dropped from the race, "any dropped dog must be left with four (4) pounds of dog food and a reliable chain or [dog-drop] cable (16" to 18" in length) with swivel snap and collar."

Mushers

"Only one musher will be permitted per team and that musher must complete the entire race." However, in Anchorage the dogs are so crazed to go and so likely to get out of control that "a handler may be required at the start and/or restart at the discretion of the Race Marshal." This handler usually drives a second sled that is towed behind the musher's sled and acts as a restraint for the wildly careening, fresh team. The "Iditariders" (explained in the "How to Follow the Race" chapter) also provide additional ballast.

Another type of promotional material is a large bib with the logo of a major race sponsor and the competitor's starting-position number on it. Each musher is required to wear this bib at the start and restart and to wear it "in a visible fashion from the Safety checkpoint to Nome, and the winner shall continue to wear the bib through the lead dog ceremony."

Mushers are also expected to have at least one day's food for themselves in their sled at all times. Rules allow that each musher's food and other personal items may be shipped with the dog-food shipment as long as the competitor complies with the ITC's shipping directions.

Miscellaneous

Progress could not be made without a sled. Iditarod rules indicate that a musher has a choice of sled subject to the requirement that some type of sled or toboggan must be drawn. The sled or toboggan must be capable of hauling any injured or fatigued dogs under cover, plus equipment and food. Braking devices must be constructed to fit between the runners and not extend beyond the tails of the runners. As of 1992, mushers may change sleds no more than two times after leaving Knik.

The dog team is connected to this sled by means of a gangline (or towline). Mushers "must carry cable tie-out lines or have cable in the towline capable of securing the team." This rule ensures that dogs will not be able to chew themselves loose at prolonged rest stops.

On one occasion, all competitors were required to carry an item that is not listed in the Iditarod rules. Although the 1925 diphtheria epidemic in Alaska is the most famous one, it was *not* the only one. According to the July 1986 *Alaska* magazine, "In 1976 another diphtheria epidemic struck Alaska. Twelve people contracted the disease, resulting in one death. The state launched a massive inoculation program and immunized 180,000 Alaskans. That was 10 years ago. Booster inoculations for diphtheria need to be given every 10 years, so the state planned another immunization program, tying it to the Iditarod race. Each of the 55 finishers of the 1986 Iditarod Trail Sled Dog Race carried four vials of diphtheria serum across the finish line. . . . The first person in Nome to receive his serum was the mayor, inoculated with serum carried by winner Susan Butcher." Having your serum carried more than a thousand miles by dog team across the Alaskan wilderness might entice even the needle-shy to receive a dreaded shot!

OPTIONAL EQUIPMENT

From replacement krypton bulbs to photos of family and loved ones, nonmandatory gear is as diverse as the individuals who compete in the Iditarod. All of the items listed below are not necessarily transported in the sled. Many types of equipment are shipped in the food/supply drop bags to the checkpoints for use as needed. As the race continues to become more competitive, optional equipment becomes lighter in weight and more efficient. Drivers are constantly evaluating each piece of gear carried in the sled and shipped ahead, carefully balancing the desire to reduce weight against the need to travel safely and to function proficiently. Miki and Julie Collins, authors of *Dog Driver*, suggest that it is wise to remember the maxim: "Hope for the best, but plan for the worst!"

Traveling To and Fro

Competitors who cannot drive to Anchorage transport their dogs in airline crates, then rent or borrow a dog truck in the local area.

The most common means of transporting sled dogs is in a pickup truck with a dog box built into the bed. Susan Butcher's truck is parked at the Wasilla restart.

Conversely, once in Nome, noncoastal residents may arrange for the use of a truck after the finish, then fly their dogs home several days later when the banquet is over.

Team transportation ranges from fancy custom rigs and expensive specialized trailers to the back of an open pickup. The most common vehicle, however, is a pickup truck with a dog box built into the bed. A dog box has eight to ten individual compartments on each side of the truck in a two-layered arrangement. Each dog has his own cozy, straw-lined bed. Equipment is stored in a special chamber built into the side or back of the box, and sleds are tied on top of the whole affair. When asked what he considered the most important pieces of sled-dog racing equipment, one musher mentioned a good stereo in his truck because he used it so much traveling the race circuit.

One other item seen at the start and finish, but not during the race, is the stake-out chain or cable. Dogs are fastened to a long chain or aircraft cable with leads coming off of it so that they can be restrained in parking areas without chewing themselves loose. Because these chains or cables are heavy, mushers simply keep the dogs on the gangline during the race or use individual lightweight drop cables to secure them.

Camping Gear

In the past, mushers took tents and actually camped along the Iditarod Trail. The only tents that you see today are at the back of the pack (if there) or incorporated into high-tech sleeping bags.

Mushers generally carry a cooler to transport a second precooked meal for the dogs along the trail. Other cooking gear consists of the dogs' bowls, a ladle, and whatever cooking pots, dishes, cups, and utensils the driver uses to prepare his or her own food. Some competitors keep a thermos handy in the sled to combat dehydration.

Miscellaneous camping supplies might include matches in a waterproof container, and an old-fashioned waterproof poncho that can double as a ground cloth under the sleeping bag or be draped over a musher lying on top of the sled bag.

Spare Parts and Tools

Out on the trail, you'd better have what you need with you because the next checkpoint may be too late for an emergency repair. Mushers carry certain essential items in the sled with them, such as spare runner plastic, extra collars and harnesses, additional necklines

Bill Cotter, 1994 Humanitarian Award winner, dishes out a little mush to his dog team in the spacious interior of this dog box.

and tuglines, extra sections of gangline, hooks or snaps (a double snap can be used to replace a neckline snap that breaks), and any replacement parts that are difficult to obtain along the race route. Larger parts are shipped to the checkpoints, and the items listed above (which are often taken in the sled) may also be shipped in additional quantities with the food drops. Heavy wire, used to reinforce broken sled stanchions, is frequently included in the gear shipped ahead.

Mushers may keep a particularly useful tool or spare part on their person. Ubiquitous among Alaskan outdoorsmen and women is the Leatherman®, an all-purpose tool that slips into a leather case attached to one's belt. It is often worn next to a short knife in a second leather sheath around the belt. Also popular is a double-lead neckline (a short length of rope with a snap on each end). Joe Runyan, 1989 champion, uses one to clip a loose dog to his waist, enabling him to keep his hands free while switching the dogs' positions. A needle and dental floss for repairing the sled bag or other tears are often carried in the musher's clothing.

A tool kit is usually kept in a baggie in the sled as well. Essential elements include a screwdriver, open-end wrenches, bolts and nuts, a runner puller, a hacksaw blade, and some tie wire.

Safety Supplies

Many pieces of optional equipment are safety-related. To date, the ITC has not mandated that mushers carry an operational headlamp, but most do. Wearing a headlamp allows drivers to see the trail when they run at night. In the first few years of the Iditarod, mushers traveled during the day and camped at night. With experience, drivers realized that the cooler nighttime temperatures were easier on the dogs and consequently began resting more during the heat of the day and racing throughout the night.

A good headlamp should be lightweight, waterproof, shockproof, and bright. It should have a long dual beam, be reliable, and use lithium batteries and krypton bulbs. In *The Secrets of Long Distance Training and Racing*, five-time-champion Rick Swenson recommends buying only fresh batteries, shipping a set of them to checkpoints every fifty miles, and storing them in a pocket with a shake-and-warm packet to keep them viable. He also suggests keeping a small spare flashlight (or squeeze lights) handy to use when your headlamp goes out and you need to change batteries in the dark, and shipping extra bulbs to uninhabited checkpoints like Rohn, Ophir, Iditarod, or Cripple, where there are no stores to purchase replacements.

In addition to warming spare batteries, chemical handwarmers enable mushers to perform routine chores during extremely cold weather. Kotzebue resident Kate Persons, who received the Rookie of the Year Award in 1991 for her eleventh place finish, gave the following tip in *Mushing* magazine: "Chemical handwarmers used inside [a] lightweight glove liner inside a surgical glove allow for comfortable booting of [the] whole team and for applying ointment."

Having a knife easily accessible to cut through the necklines or tuglines in an emergency can save a dog's life if an animal is attacking the team. Mushers often pack a gun in order to scare off troublesome wild animals. Firecrackers or signal flares, fired by stranded competitors to reveal their location, are also occasionally used to frighten recalcitrant moose. Because the second half of the trail is not prime moose country, mushers will sometimes drop their gun as a weight-reduction measure.

The contents of a sealed emergency clothing bag (kept in the sled at all times) can save a driver's life if she or he takes an unexpected dip

Dogs are fastened to a stake-out chain so they can be safely restrained outside of the truck. Bill Cotter's dogs wait patiently for him while he transacts business at DeeDee Jonrowe's kennel.

in icy water. This bag contains dry underwear, a set of long underwear, socks, gloves, and a cap—that is, a complete change of clothing for the layer nearest to the skin. Even though it is so bitterly cold that the wet musher can't stand to think of stripping down to bare skin, doing so is not only worth the pain but can prevent hypothermia.

Keeping a ten-foot round nylon parachute with this emergency bag can make the change of clothes more bearable. The musher stands on the parachute with his or her back to the wind, pulls it up along the back, and throws it over the head as a makeshift shelter for the quick change. The parachute can also serve as a tent in a bad storm. One end is weighted down by the windward sled runner, and the rest of it is drawn over the sled, team, and driver, who huddle together in the lee of the sled.

Competitors may ship several pairs of dry socks, chore gloves, and surgical gloves to each checkpoint as an additional safeguard. Having dry clothes during the Iditarod is not merely a question of comfort!

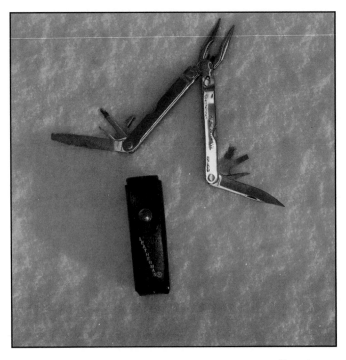

Ubiquitous among Alaskans, an all-purpose Leatherman® tool is usually worn on the belt. In the wilderness, it's important to have survival gear on your person!

The *ITC Musher's Handbook* strongly recommends carrying a basic survival kit on your person at all times, perhaps in a lightweight vest. Other survival items that can be kept in your clothing include a space blanket, a flashlight, matches and fire-starter material, a compass, heat packs, prescription drugs, eyeglasses, sunglasses, lip salve, energy food, minimal first-aid supplies, and a survival manual. As the handbook points out, "Lying on the side of the trail watching your dog team fade away in the snowstorm carrying all your equipment away from you can be fatal."

Although competitors usually concentrate on going as fast as possible, there are times when it is imperative to slow down the sled. In the past, drivers have used chains on their sled runners for steep downhill grades. Now snow-machine track drags, studded with carbide

tips, are favored. Dragging a studded section of track not only provides greater control on descents but also adds traction on glare ice.

During the 1985 race, Libby Riddles used another aid to traction—a
single ice creeper, a spiked device that straps onto the musher's boot.
This helps the driver negotiate icy uphills.

Joan Brockelsby, organizer of the North Pole Championship Sled
Dog Race and former co-owner of North Pole Optical, discussed
safety eyewear for mushers in an article in *Mushing* magazine. She
believes that:

> All mushers should use some type of eyewear to protect their
> eyes from trauma and the harmful rays. Those who do not need
> corrective lenses still need to protect their eyes, and those who
> wear corrective lenses should be sure they have the safest eye-
> glasses available.
>
> As far as impact resistance, polycarbonate is the safest mater-
> ial made. It is manufactured with a front scratch-resistant coat-
> ing and blocks 99.5% of the UV without being tinted.
>
> Many people are afraid of plastic and polycarbonate because
> they fear they will ruin them. Remember, you can always
> replace your lenses, but you can not replace your eyes. Whether
> you wear corrective lenses or not, sunglasses or goggles will
> protect your eyes from debris and branches along the trail.

First-Aid Kit

Another safety precaution is to carry a basic first-aid kit. For the
dogs, mushers take nail clippers, scissors, bandage material, a thermometer, various types of foot ointments, ophthalmic ointment, antiseptic ointment, and betadine solution. Other medications for the animals must be prescribed by race veterinarians. Competitors will
sometimes keep with them or ship ahead favorite varieties of canine
prescription drugs, such as antibiotics or antidiarrheals. This ensures
that their dogs receive what has previously proved effective, rather
than what a specific vet at a race checkpoint has on hand at any given
moment. Drivers occasionally use the dogs' ointments on themselves
to treat nicks, burns, or abrasions caused by various mishaps.

The musher's personal medical arsenal may include aspirin, an
upset-stomach remedy, some type of cold capsule, throat lozenges, eye
drops, a drug to relieve diarrhea, and any prescription medicines. Lip
salve, sunblock, and a moisturizing cream are sensible preventives.

A studded section of snow-machine track is often attached between the runners as a drag. When depressed by the musher, it serves as a secondary brake, providing greater control on descents and additional traction on glare ice.

Personal Paraphernalia

A cassette tape player helps mushers stay awake and fight trail boredom. Setting out for a night run during the 1985 Iditarod, Libby Riddles said, "I was wired for light and sound, stereo and headlamp, had sustenance easily available and two cassette tapes in my pocket." During the 1991 race, which he eventually won, Rick Swenson talked to KNOM (a Nome radio station) reporter Stacy Loucks at the Eagle Island checkpoint. Describing his run up the windblown Yukon River, Swenson said, "I've seen a lot worse. It was a nice time to listen to a tape and kind of nod in and out of reality."

Another comfort item used by mushers is called a "red sled." This is a four-foot-long child's plastic toboggan that makes it easier for competitors to haul the heavy food-drop bags and cooking pots full of water from their source to the team's campsite.

Some mushers keep a notebook with a pencil attached (the "musher's bible") to verify the contents of their supply drops or to follow a predetermined race strategy. Other personal items carried might include spare contacts or glasses, an alarm clock (especially the tiny kind that fits behind the ear and does not alert competitors to your timetable), a camera with film, premoistened wipes for freshening up, soap, toothbrush and toothpaste, comb and brush, razor and shaving supplies, vitamins, and a wallet with money (there are several stores, restaurants, lodges, and bars along the trail). Mushers often take postcards, musher cards (like baseball cards), and goodie bags with them to distribute to checkpoint residents and fans.

Special Events

Alaska magazine reported on an interesting piece of optional "equipment" transported from Anchorage to Nome during the 1987 race:

> Joe Garnie, who was the 11th musher to arrive in Nome, carried some special cargo this year: a copy of the U.S. Constitution to commemorate the 200th anniversary of the signing of the document. The four-page replica of the original Constitution, provided by the University of Alaska-Anchorage Chancellor's Constitutional Bicentennial Commission, stayed in Garnie's mail pouch until his arrival in Nome. Garnie, of Teller, [AK], presented the replica from the Philadelphia Free Library to Erin Hansen, student body president of Nome Beltz High School, and to two pupils in the kindergarten class, Jessica Brown and Brian Cannon. Cannon is Garnie's nephew.

During her fourth running of the Iditarod in 1990, Diana Dronenburg (now Diana Moroney) carried a different kind of special cargo: a quilt panel that became part of the National Names Project Quilt, a tribute to those who have died from AIDS. Dronenburg made this quilt panel specifically for her trip to Nome, and it was signed by many Alaskan friends. After finishing the race in twenty-eighth place, Dronenburg gave the quilt panel to her brother, who has AIDS. She also made a banner that read, "IDITAROD: A TRAIL OF HOPE. 1925 DIPHTHERIA 1990 AIDS."

Cheryl Holtzhouser of McGrath, Alaska, explains the "I Did It By Two! Race to Vaccinate" campaign sponsored by the Alaska Nurses' Association, University of Alaska Anchorage, and the American Nurses' Association:

> Our goal is to publicize the need for children from Alaska and all over the United States to be up-to-date on their immunizations to protect them from the nine deadly diseases that can be prevented by these usually free shots. Children under the age of two are under-immunized.

As part of this campaign, mushers carry immunization kits from Anchorage to Nome, a modern-day preventive version of the 1925 serum run. Dog drivers also appear in public-service announcements, and they autograph certificates that are awarded to children who have won "The Race to Vaccinate" and can say, "I Did It By Two!"

TRACKING
THE IDITAROD

It's a long way from Anchorage to Nome.
Now I know why they invented airplanes.

Bert Hanson
Iditarod Air Force pilot,
commenting on his 1990 rookie run,
mushing the Iditarod

14

How to Follow the Race

If you want to see a sporting event, you usually head for the local stadium, dome, or track. Admittedly, viewing the Iditarod is not as demanding as running it; nevertheless, even being an Iditarod fan is a challenge. The inaccessibility and grand scale of the race are part of its mystique, however. If 500,000 spectators could line the race course to watch the event, as they do at the Indianapolis 500 Motor Speedway, it just wouldn't be the Iditarod. For one thing, in order to have half a million spectators, every single resident of the state of Alaska would have to attend! Those noncompetitors upon whom the Iditarod has cast its spell can satisfy their need to know and participate in several ways.

READING, WATCHING, DIALING, AND SURFING

Many magazines cover the Iditarod in their February or March issues. Best bets include *Alaska* and *Sports Illustrated*, but ask a librarian to help you search the library's periodical information services if you want to read everything that's available. The number and variety of prestigious magazines that have carried articles on the Iditarod are impressive.

If you visit Alaska, be sure to stop by the Iditarod Trail Committee headquarters in Wasilla. You can look at a replica of a checkpoint cabin, many interesting displays, and a wide variety of race-related merchandise. In the summer, you can visit with sled dogs or go for a mushing ride.

Another possible source of information is your local newspaper. Unless you live in Alaska or in a snowbelt state, don't be too optimistic. Even in a large northern city like Minneapolis, the Iditarod usually only receives one small paragraph a day tucked away somewhere in the depths of the sports section. Die-hard fans can subscribe to Alaskan newspapers, but the delivery delay is aggravating.

A number of Iditarod mushers produce kennel newsletters. Write to the ITC, request the address of your race favorites, and send notes asking if they have a mailing list for fans. Then you can sit back and wait for fresh news from Alaska to arrive in your mailbox!

The cable TV sports channel ESPN often presents an Iditarod special after the race. Read the sports listings in your newspaper or *TV Guide* for program dates.

Local television stations will sometimes carry footage of the race and give updates. If you are interested in seeing more about the Iditarod, you will need to vocalize your wishes.

If you want detailed and up-to-date race information, the Iditarod hotlines are for you. The Iditarod Trail Committee's main hotline number is (907) 248-MUSH; there is also a toll-free number for ordering merchandise. Due to the remote location of the race, there is always some delay between when the racers arrive at a checkpoint and when the hotlines receive the standings. Please remember that most of the ITC's operators are volunteers, and be appreciative of their efforts.

In 1995, the Iditarod made the leap into cyberspace by collaborating with America Online's computer service. Subscribers could click onto such categories as "The Mushers," "Race Photos," "Diary from the Trail," "Race News & Results," "Alaska Weather Forecast," and "Iditarod Messages." The message board enabled fans to communicate with the Iditarod Trail Committee and with each other. Access to Iditarod information was also possible through World Wide Web, a part of the Internet. So, if you want to follow the Iditarod by surfing the net, check with the ITC for detailed instructions. See you in cyberspace!

BEING TAKEN FOR A RIDE

If you don't ever expect to own and drive a dog team, going for a sled-dog ride is the next best thing. In the snowbelt states, rides are often offered at local races. For a small donation, you may enjoy the sensation of following a six- or eight-dog team around a short, but beautiful, snow-covered loop. If you want to go on a several-hour, half-day, weekend, or extended mushing adventure, check sled-dog publications such as *Beargrease Hike!*, *Team and Trail*, or *Info* (the International Sled Dog Racing Association's newsletter) for advertisements.

Of course, in Alaska, there are plenty of opportunities to explore. In conjunction with the Iditarod, rides are often set up at Knik (accessible from Anchorage by car) and in Nome. Alaska tourism brochures generally list sled-dog tour operators. Businesses also advertise in magazines such as the *Iditarod Runner*, *Mushing*, and *Alaska*.

An *Anchorage Daily News* article by Susan Palmer, published March 5, 1993, entitled "Room to Mush," should be mandatory reading before you commit to a longer excursion. Palmer advises deciding in advance how much you want to spend (from $20 for a half-hour up to $15,000 for a month) and to what extent you wish to participate (from riding in the sled basket all the way up to mushing your own team). She also lists eleven Alaskan sled-dog outfits and gives guidelines for deciding which one is right for you.

Vern Halter, 1990 Yukon Quest champion, flashes a cheery smile at the Anchorage mushers' meeting. Fans are welcome to attend the first part of this gathering, which takes place at the Regal Alaskan Hotel.

Beginning in 1995, fans have been given a new opportunity to combine their love of the Iditarod and their desire to experience dog mushing firsthand. You can start the race either sitting in the sled bag of your favorite musher or riding on the runners of a second sled. By calling 1-800-IDITAROD, you can obtain an Iditarider bid packet. Bids are taken at a special prerace auction to match one Iditarider with each Iditarod driver. For $500 to $5,000, you can say that you ran the first seven miles of the Iditarod Trail. Most fans opt to ride in the sled bag, but those of you who have read too much Jack London can probably arrange (as Governor Tony Knowles did in the inaugural year of this program) to ride the second sled—upright, fearless, face to the wind, white knuckles on the handlebar.

Whether you go for a five-minute or two-week outing, ask questions and exercise caution, then have the time of your life. The beauty and exhilaration of dog sledding is something that can only be fully understood by experiencing it . . . so, go for it!

IN PERSON

Serious fans want to be in Alaska during the Last Great Race. Of course, this requires lots of money (depending upon where you are coming from), planning in advance (early reservations are a *must*), and warm clothing (the *average* temperature during March in Anchorage is 24° F and in Nome it is 8° F).

It also requires a special code of conduct among fans. The International Sled Dog Racing Association (ISDRA) gives the following tips for attending sled-dog racing events:

> *Never* bring your pets to the races or if you have to, leave them in your car. Drivers of teams cannot be responsible for the safety of your animals and races have been lost because of pets bolting onto the course. . . .
>
> All photographers should make sure that their activities will not startle the dogs or interfere with a team's progress. Sudden moves toward or away from the trail can cause a team to bolt, so pick your position and hold it until all teams in your area have passed your post.
>
> Never offer a dog treats and always ask before petting. . . .
>
> Keep toddlers in hand. Eager dogs, ready to run, may leap or rear up in anticipation of the race and it would be unfortunate to have an accident that was the fault of neither dog nor child.
>
> Please cooperate with race officials in staying clear of the trail. Stand well back as anyone too close may distract the dogs and cause them to bolt or balk.

A few additional notes about fans and mushers may be helpful. If you plan to attend the Iditarod specifically to meet in person a favorite musher, please do not change your opinion of your idol based upon one encounter. A gentleman from upstate New York traveled all the way to Anchorage to see a competitor about whom he had read extensively and, consequently, admired very much. At the prerace banquet, this fan waited at the side of the stage to get the musher's autograph. While most of the competitors patiently stopped and signed posters for the waiting throng, this particular driver evaded the crowd and declined to give autographs. The New York admirer was annoyed and deeply disappointed. Unknown to him, the Iditarod entrants had weathered a severely trying private meeting that morning, and many mushers felt angry and stressed. Throughout the rest of the year, this musher had gone above and beyond what is usual in dealing graciously with the public, and during the next week and a half of racing displayed considerable charm and openness to fans and the press. If you will only have *one* opportunity to visit with your favorite Iditarod driver, you may be setting yourself up for a disappointing experience.

Also remember that during the race these people are busy trying to finish well. It would be stunning if Mario Andretti chatted pleasantly with a devoted fan in the pits during the Indy 500. Can you imagine Michael Jordan signing autographs on court during the NBA finals? Mushers deal with a difficult paradox: most of them have chosen to drive dogs because they prefer to live in the wilderness and spend time alone with their animals; ironically, the reward for success at this endeavor is to be hounded by the press and mobbed by fans. If you do wish to talk to a competitor during the Iditarod, the ITC requests that you wait until she or he has spread straw for the team, removed their booties, and fed the dogs. After that, it's the musher's prerogative to grant an "interview" or not. There are many factors that can make even the friendliest driver speak to fans abruptly, including sick dogs, lack of sleep, a disappointing showing, and so on. Try to see the broader picture, and approach the musher again later if at first you do not succeed.

Finally, bear in mind that not everyone is an Iditarod fan. Some Alaskan residents used to be but have become disillusioned, and others simply can't get motivated about sled-dog racing. You may not care about the America's Cup or the U.S. Open or even the Super Bowl. One Nome taxi driver commented, "I'm always happy to see the race come every year, but I'm happy to see it leave." Life in the small-town checkpoints is turned upside-down during the Iditarod, and sometimes it just gets to be too much. On the bright side, though, there's probably no place on earth where you can go and strike up a conversation with a total stranger and be met with more warmth, openness, and hospitality than you will find in Alaska during the Iditarod. Just be receptive to all points of view and you may hear a different, but fascinating, perspective on the event.

If you do go, there are a number of ways to experience the race firsthand. Bring an appetite for adventure and your sense of humor, and you'll have a magnificent time!

An Anchorage fan goes all out in dressing for the race's starting festivities.

SEEING THEM OFF AND CHEERING THEM IN

The majority of race fans appear in Anchorage to experience the week of the start. There are many good reasons for this. Anchorage is easily accessible, food and lodging are reasonably priced, and a large selection of both is available. All of the mushers are in one place at one time, and you can figure out in advance when that will be. If you are going to watch the start on Saturday, plan to arrive earlier—at least by Wednesday.

On the Wednesday before the start, you can attend the mandatory vet check. It often takes place in Wasilla, so you may need to rent a car. While in Wasilla, you can also visit the Iditarod Trail Committee headquarters. There are a multitude of interesting displays, a full-scale replica of a typical checkpoint cabin, and the staff is as friendly as they come.

The first part of the mandatory mushers' meeting on Thursday morning is open to the public at the Regal Alaskan Hotel. Serious fans risk overheating when they see sixty-some Iditarod mushers in one room. Drivers tend to be relaxed and friendly because this is before the serious business of the race has begun.

That evening you can attend the prerace banquet at Sullivan Arena *if* you have purchased tickets well in advance (some may be available at the door due to cancellations; if you forgot or decide to go at the last minute, it's worth looking into). All of the competitors will be there to draw their starting positions, and if you are lucky, you may be able to speak with them (see "Prerace Details" for more about this banquet).

On Friday, you can sightsee in Anchorage and the vicinity. Although it is Alaska's largest city, Anchorage is strikingly beautiful with its ring of mountains and expansive shoreline. Tourism brochures can guide you to fabulous museums, shops, restaurants, and other attractions. Be sure to spend some time at the Iditarod Race headquarters at the Regal Alaskan Hotel. It's definitely *the* place to be during race week.

Get some sleep Friday night because Saturday is the big day. If you arrive downtown at about 7:00 or 7:30 A.M., you can walk along inside the starting chute and greet the mushers as they make their final preparations. By 9:30, you should have secured a spot so that you will be ready to watch the 10:00 A.M. start. Fourth Avenue and B Street is a good place to park downtown (a large garage is located there). After you've seen an hour or so at the start, you might want to drive to the bottom of Cordova Hill (at 16th Street) and to the tunnel under Gambell and Inga Streets at East 20th Avenue for other Anchorage viewpoints.

If you want to make a day of it, drive to Eagle River to see the mushers load their dogs into their trucks. With starting day's activities over, you may find that your favorite mushers are now relaxed and willing to chat. Stick around for lunch and use the afternoon to explore. Then, on Sunday, you can join the caravan from Anchorage to the 10:00 A.M. restart in Wasilla (expect to get stuck in a traffic jam).

Those who prefer to let someone else do the driving may wish to ride the Alaska Railroad Iditarod Restart Train to Wasilla on Sunday. This special excursion train leaves Anchorage at about 7:00 A.M. Sunday morning. It accommodates 600 fans in comfortable passenger coaches (complete with sandwiches and an espresso bar), connects with shuttles to the restart, and returns to Anchorage after the last musher has been cheered off. Tickets usually sell out in a matter of hours, so inquire early if you're interested.

Finally, those of you who drove up for the restart can now drive as far as Knik, where a huge tailgate party will be taking place as fans watch their favorite teams enter the wilderness at last. That's as far as you can go by car. Adventurous (and well-to-do) fans rent snow machines or charter a bush plane and go on to Skwentna and points beyond. It would be a shame to miss race week in Anchorage, but experiencing only the prerace activities and the start, and then going home, is not really seeing the Iditarod. To know what it's truly like, you need to be out on the trail yourself.

Attending the finish is a trickier proposition if you are coming from "Outside." The biggest problem is that no one knows when it will occur! You either have to guess and hope that you're lucky, or you need to have lots of vacation time and the flexibility to adapt your schedule to the mushers' progress. You could spend more than a week in Nome if you welcomed in every finisher. It's a good time to visit with mushers because the top finishers will be hanging around for several days after the race is over, waiting to celebrate at the mandatory postrace banquet. You can attend, but buy tickets early!

The best place to meet race competitors is at the Mini Convention Center, which serves as Nome's Iditarod Trail Committee headquarters. In addition to early finishers chatting at round tables, you will find a large Iditarod merchandise display, a wall-hung pocket filled with the latest race standings, a communications room, sponsor tables, an Alaska Air ticket counter, and a scrumptious spread of goodies on sale by the local PTA.

Keep in mind that Nome (population 3,430) has very limited accommodations and few restaurants. (Lodging in Nome is discussed further in the upcoming section entitled "Wing It.") It's not the big city, and it's probably not like other vacation spots where you have stayed. There are a number of Iditarod-month special activities that you might enjoy, including the world's largest amateur basketball tournament, the Bering Sea Ice Classic Golf Tournament, and exhibitions of traditional Native activities such as the blanket toss.

Be sure to check at the visitors center for a schedule of events; you may also watch wonderful Iditarod race videos here for free! While in town, don't miss the chance to see the Nome National Forest. Inhabitants include walrus, seal, penguin, polar bear, moose, pig, and a flamingo standing under a palm tree—all made from plywood cutouts and displayed among old Christmas trees that have been frozen into the ice out on the Bering Sea. As locals like to say, "There's no place like Nome."

DO IT

Volunteering to work with the ITC enables a fan to become a participant instead of just another spectator. You can get an insider's view of the Iditarod as a hotline operator, a checker, a dog handler, a cook, a crowd-control volunteer, or—if you have the special skills required—as a communications expert, a pilot, or a veterinarian (see the "Volunteers" chapter for more information). If you are interested, talk to the Iditarod Trail Committee to find out what you might be able to do. They'll find something for you. Volunteers are expected to arrange their own transportation to the race; the Iditarod Air Force then flies these volunteers to various checkpoints as needed. Short of mushing the trail yourself, there's no better way to see the Iditarod. Volunteers rank just under the competitors and the ITC staff in terms of access allowed and respect received. You will never meet a friendlier, more interesting group of people in your life.

HOOF IT

Another way to experience the Iditarod up close and personal is to walk the trail. In 1989, sixty-two-year-old John Kelly traversed the nearly 1,200-mile race route on foot. Patti Harper reported on Kelly's epic journey in the March 1990 issue of *Alaska*:

> "Being a basically lazy person," [Kelly] said, "I figured, I'm not going to fool around with dogs."
> Lazy? Kelly spent 84 days trekking through the wilderness.
> He wore out his only pair of boots and despite gobbling nearly 11,000 calories a day, dropped 30 pounds from his lean frame. He met the challenges of the wilderness and experienced its wonders alone. He tumbled down slippery bluffs in the Alaska Range. He walked behind wolves and met bison along the trail.

He had previous experience walking through snow and ice, once walking 60 miles to shower at an oil field camp in Prudhoe Bay.

SCHUSS IT

Those who find walking too slow can cross-country ski the trail, camping along the way. A ski-tour operator will charter a plane for you, drop you at a checkpoint along the trail, and pick you up a week later at another predetermined location. On one such trip, skiers began at Rainy Pass Lodge and traveled seventy-five miles against the flow of Iditarod mushers, completing their journey seven days later at Skwentna. *Alaska* magazine correspondent Don Cornelius, a participant in this outing, noted that "No longer were we just one of the crowd. Skiers out there in the middle of nowhere were as interesting to the musher[s] as they were to us. We heard of their difficulties, of broken sleds . . . of lost booties and encounters with cantankerous moose."

WING IT

Those of us lesser mortals who do not relish walking 1,200 miles or even skiing 75 are left with the option of flying. True to Iditarod tradition, even this is not easy. Oh, getting to Anchorage or Nome on a commercial flight is simple enough if you don't wait until the last minute to make your plane reservations (not to mention motel/hotel reservations). Making flight plans that follow the race and allow you to stop at villages along the route is another matter. Be sure to tell your pilot that you're an Iditarod fan on the smaller (eight to twenty-passenger) commercial flights. You might get a free flight-seeing tour of the Iditarod Trail if the weather permits and the pilot knows that you are interested.

If you want to fly on commercial flights to checkpoints along the trail, work closely with a good travel agent. Copy a map of the Iditarod Trail and mark the appropriate route (south for odd years, north for even). Explain to your agent where you would like to go and when, and see what your options are. Remember that most travel agents only deal with cruises and prearranged tours of Alaska. Don't be surprised if even an experienced agent asks you whether driving a car or taking a bus or train from point to point is a possibility. You'll have to explain that past Knik (checkpoint #3), there are no roads to Nome. With patience and shrewd planning, you can probably get to several of the interior and coastal villages without resorting to Plan B, which is chartering a private plane.

Your travel agent can also assist you in booking accommodations. Anchorage is easy, but after that you may have to do some of your own legwork. If you want to stay in a room with a bed, plan to have reservations by the Thanksgiving before the race. The villages and Nome fill quickly! Keep in mind that several of the checkpoints are nothing more than a tent for the checkers—you can't stay at every checkpoint along the way.

Many of the villages and towns on the race route will not be listed in sources accessible to travel agents. Call the ITC and ask a staff member for recommendations. Be sure to speak to someone who is objective about the various establishments, not just the proprietor, because there is a wide range of quality in what is available. If you do not make reservations early, the ITC staff or community leaders may be able to find you floor space.

Due to the limited facilities at the checkpoints, if you have booked rooms ahead, you may find yourself cheek by jowl with crews from cable TV network ESPN, KIMO 13 TV from Anchorage, the *Anchorage Daily News* reporters and photographers, and members of the press from across the nation and around the world. It can be a very heady experience.

If you do visit and stay in the villages, ask if a craft fair is being held while you are there. This gives you the opportunity to buy lovely Native and Alaskan handicrafts directly from the artisans for a very reasonable price.

If money is not a problem, and you are not afraid of small, single-engine planes, you may wish to hire a bush pilot to fly you check-point to checkpoint along the entire length of the trail. Three different air services advertise race tours in the *Iditarod Runner*. When you are selecting a pilot, look for someone who is humble and does not make unconditional promises. A good pilot will say, "I'll do the best I can, but I can't guarantee that I'll always be able to get you where you want to go." Remember the classic maxim, "There are old pilots and bold pilots, but no old bold pilots."

TAKING THE IDITAROD CHALLENGE

Since 1993, Joe Redington, Sr. has guided a group of tourists along the length of the Iditarod Trail each year behind the race competitors. Every participant in Redington's "Iditarod Challenge" drives his or her own team. Dog handlers and cooks accompany the intrepid novices so that at the end of a long day, the weary drivers can dine on steaks, stews, and cakes. In Nome, at the completion of his 1993 trip, Redington remarked, "No scratches, no dropped dogs. You can't beat that. And perfect weather all the way." The price per person for this remarkable outing is $15,000. If you'd like to go on one of Redington's tours, contact him through the ITC and express your interest. You may not receive an Official Iditarod Finisher's patch and belt buckle, but you don't have to own a 30- to 150-dog kennel and train for years either. Besides, it would definitely enable you to spin spellbinding tales for the folks back home!

SURVIVAL GEAR . . . ON YOUR PERSON!

You can't be cavalier about winter in Alaska; the arctic environment demands a healthy respect. If you plan to travel the trail on foot, skis, snow machine, or by small plane, you need to think of yourself as a musher—prepared to survive wilderness conditions. If your plane (God forbid) goes down, you'd better have what you need *on your person*. Minimal survival equipment includes a knife and/or Leatherman®, waterproof matches, energy food, warm clothing (wear your bibs, parka, and mukluks, and keep your hand and headgear in the pockets), and a survival manual. Additional suggestions appear in the "Mandatory and Optional Equipment" chapter under "Safety Supplies." As they say, prepare for the worst, then expect the best!

COLD-WEATHER PHOTOGRAPHY

A few technical suggestions will benefit those who wish to take along their trusty 35 mm. Buy the freshest batteries you can find and lots of them for your motor drive and/or flash. Store a backup set in a second battery holder (inexpensive to obtain at a camera store) in a

One clue that you are in Alaska is the cache, an elevated structure used to keep meat or other precious supplies out of the reach of wild predators.

pocket near your skin. If it's really cold, a chemical handwarmer can be used to keep the batteries viable. Serious shutterbugs may wish to buy NiCds—nickel cadmium cells—and lithium cells, or invest in a remote power pack for both body and flash.

The most critical point to remember is that the camera isn't bothered by going from your heated motel room to the bitter cold outside—it's bringing the camera back in from the cold to the warmth of a restaurant, motel, or cabin that will ruin it. Take one zippered plastic storage bag for each camera body and lens, and *be sure* to seal each one in a bag before taking cold equipment into a warm environment. This will prevent condensation from damaging your expensive gear.

If snow gets on a lens, use a small brush or lens tissue to remove it; blowing on a cold lens will ice it up. Remember that coming in contact with metal in extreme cold is dangerous. Consider wrapping tripod legs with foam, and camera surfaces that might touch your face with moleskin. Finally, don't neglect your wardrobe and diet! Two poly or silk glove liners and a pair of fingerless wool gloves will

Alaska is the only state in the United States where you will see a road sign that warns you to watch for caribou in the roadway.

allow you to operate even the smallest dials. Adequate footwear, headgear, and a neck gaiter are also indispensable, and waterproof pants permit dog's-eye-level shots kneeling in snow to be made in comfort. As you concentrate on composition and camera settings, don't forget that a high calorie intake and adequate hydration are necessary to keep *your* motor running. And if you're lucky enough to see the aurora borealis, set a wide-angle lens to wide open (f 2.8) and bracket exposures from eight seconds (for a very bright display) to sixty seconds (for low-light auroras). Good luck!

The Iditarod appeals to everything in me. There's some parts you'll never lose about waking up in your sled in the morning hundreds of miles out on the trail, with eight or ten of your favorite dogs staked out around you in the snow for company; rousing yourself up to start a fire, and passing your eyes over all the incredible country stretched out to the horizon in every direction . . . maybe you pick out a pale green mountain in the distance, and warm your insides with the assurance that before you camp again, you'll be on the other side of it looking back.

The late Bill Vaudrin
1975 Iditarod finisher
and author of
Racing Alaskan Sled Dogs

Previous Page: *Driftwood protrudes from the snow near Nome.* © *Charles Mason/Fairbanks AK.*

Above: *The Eskimos say, "One's heart beats differently when out on the ice." Here John Cooper crosses frozen Norton Bay.* © *Jeff Schultz/Alaska Stock Images.*

Below: *Fourth Avenue in Anchorage at dawn on the morning of the Iditarod start Mary Hood Photo.*

Above: *Tim Osmar's trip toward Unalakleet is burnished by a brilliant sunset.*
© Jeff Schultz/Alaska Stock Images.

Below: *A ghostly Rick Swenson and team are barely visible in this ground blizzard near*
Nome. © Jeff Schultz/Alaska Stock Images.

Above: *Two teams race along the Skwentna River.* © *Jeff Schultz/ Alaska Stock Images.*

Left: *Roger Legaard and his dogs on a rocky trail near Rohn.* © *Jeff Schultz/ Alaska Stock Images.*

Below: *Mushers combat the rugged Alaskan wilderness as well as each other.*
© *Jeff Schultz/Alaska Stock Images*

Above: *Tim Morlein and team sled into the setting sun near Unalakleet.*
© *Jeff Schultz/Alaska Stock Images.*

Below: *Bob Hickel steadies the sled as his dog team drops down onto Happy River.*
© *Jeff Schultz/Alaska Stock Images.*

Left: *These Unalakleet residents have large fur ruffs on their parkas to combat the arctic cold and coastal winds. Mary Hood Photo.*

Below: *Athabascan Indian Beverly Masek is one of the few Natives who has run the Iditarod in recent years. Mary Hood Photo.*

Right: *A young child enjoys the picnic atmosphere at Knik, in spite of the winter weather. Mary Hood Photo.*

Susan Butcher basks in the glow of her fourth victory with lead dog Elan. © Jeff Schultz/ Alaska Stock Images.

Libby Riddles, 1985 champion and the first woman to win the Iditarod, celebrates with her lead dogs Axle and Dugan. © Jeff Schultz/ Alaska Stock Images.

Above: *Two teams near Finger Lake.* © *Jeff Schultz/ Alaska Stock Images.*

Left: *Rugged Joe Redington, Sr. has defined the Iditarod for more than a quarter of a century.* © *Jeff Schultz/ Alaska Stock Images.*

Opposite Page: *Diana Dronenburg drives her team through Rainy Pass in the Alaska Range.* © *Jeff Schultz/ Alaska Stock Images.*

Left: *Glen Findlay's blue eyes pierce a heavy coating of frost from the -40° cold.* ©*Jeff Schultz/Alaska Stock Images.*

Below: *A dog rests comfortably in his compartment of a musher's truck. Mary Hood Photo*

Below: *The welfare of Iditarod dogs is the number-one priority. Vern Halter has placed jackets over his dogs as they rest at the McGrath checkpoint. Mary Hood Photo.*

Above: *Dogs resting under a starlit sky are enveloped by the warm glow of mushers' headlamps.* © *Jeff Schultz/Alaska Stock Images.*

Below: *Checkers record a musher's nighttime arrival at the remote Rohn checkpoint.* © *Jeff Schultz/Alaska Stock Images.*

Above: *Mushers' sponsors sometimes send large, brilliantly outfitted delegations of employees to assist as handlers at the early checkpoints (here at Eagle River). Mary Hood Photo.*

Below: *Mushers and their teams congregate at the icy blue ghost town of Iditarod.* © *Jeff Schultz/Alaska Stock Images.*

*Right:
The
northern lights
shimmer and pulse
over a dog team
resting at the village
of Kaltag.
© Jeff Schultz/
Alaska Stock
Images.*

Below: Paul Rupple rests under northern lights against the backdrop of the rugged Alaska Range. © Jeff Schultz/Alaska Stock Images.

Above:
Dewey Halverson muscles his sled through Dalzell Gorge.
© *Jeff Schultz/ Alaska Stock Images.*

Left:
John Patten pauses to give his team a little tender loving care.
Mary Hood Photo.

Right: *Lavon Barve's team leads him up "The Glacier" toward the towering Alaska Range.*
© *Jeff Schultz/Alaska Stock Images.*

Above: *A view from under the trail. Guy Blankenship near the Iditarod checkpoint.*
© *Jeff Schultz/Alaska Stock Images.*
Below: *Martin Buser winning his first Iditarod in 1992 in record time.*
© *Charles Mason/Fairbanks, AK.*

Right: *Tim Osmar nears trail's end: the burled arch on Front Street in Nome.* © *Jeff Schultz/Alaska Stock Images.*

Left: *Iditarod dogs' love of racing is hard to comprehend fully until you see their unbridled enthusiasm in person.* © *Jeff Schultz/ Alaska Stock Images.*

15

Trail Description

T he Iditarod Trail Sled Dog Race follows an historic Iditarod gold
miners' supply trail through the Alaska Range, over the Kuskokwim Mountains, and along the frozen Yukon River toward Norton
Sound on the forbidding Bering Sea. (Be sure to refer to the map
inside the front and back covers.)

According to volunteer ITC archivist Nicki J. Nielsen, historically:

> Roadhouses lined the trail . . . located at intervals of about
> twenty miles, approximately a one day journey. . . . All road-
> houses were required to keep lists of travelers in order to facili-
> tate finding the last known location of lost individuals. Territor-
> ial funds were set aside for staking trails and building shelter
> cabins to save the lives of travelers stranded by blizzards.

Some of these former roadhouses still stand today and are used by Iditarod competitors as shelter cabins during periods of severe weather.

The Iditarod Trail crosses many cultural and socioeconomic
boundaries. Along its route, mushers encounter four distinct cultures:
Anglo-Saxon, Athabascan Indian, Yup'ik (Eskimo), and Inupiat
(Eskimo). They also experience a wide range of population density at
the checkpoints. Some checkpoints are pristine wilderness with only a
tent erected by the ITC; others are ghost towns, relics of Alaska's former

The Iditarod Trail was designated a national historic trail in 1976. This sign describing it is near the Knik Museum and Dog Mushers Hall of Fame. Knik is the last checkpoint on the road system; from here on, drivers and dog teams will traverse more than a thousand miles of Alaskan wilderness.

gold-mining heyday. Many of the mushers' layovers occur at small towns and villages, but large metropolitan areas like Anchorage are part of the package, too.

The southern route, now run in odd years, traverses 1,161 miles. First used in 1978, the northern route brings the Iditarod to a second set of Interior villages and towns and covers 1,158 miles.

Spanning nearly the entire width of Alaska, the trail passes through numerous geographic regions as well. Often quoted from its press packet is this stirring summary written by the Iditarod Trail Committee:

> You can't compare it to any other competitive event in the world! A race over 1,049 miles of the roughest, most beautiful terrain Mother Nature has to offer. She throws jagged mountain ranges, frozen rivers, dense forests, desolate tundra and miles of windswept coast at the mushers and their dog teams. Add to

that temperatures far below zero, winds that can cause a complete loss of visibility, the hazards of overflow, long hours of darkness, and treacherous climbs and side hills, and you have the Iditarod. A race extraordinaire, a race only possible in Alaska.

Despite the hype, it's really true. The Iditarod is the world's most remote race. Rather than gathering at one huge oval in a convenient urban location to provide an afternoon's entertainment, Iditarod competitors spread out along a thousand-mile-plus race course over a period of weeks.

For winter-bound villagers along its route, the race relieves cabin fever. Checkpoint residents claim that the highlights of the year are Christmas, New Year's, and the Iditarod. In addition to much-needed entertainment, the Iditarod is an educational opportunity and provides a significant economic stimulus to these small Alaskan communities.

But ultimately, as Canadian musher Dave Olesen notes, "The Iditarod . . . is and always will be a solitary journey. Only some of it can be shared. The rest, the very essence of the race, can only be experienced."

1. ANCHORAGE to Eagle River 20 miles

Alaska's largest city, Anchorage (so named because originally it was no more than a place for ships to anchor) supports a population of approximately 250,000. The race begins downtown on Fourth Avenue at 10:00 A.M. If you gaze ahead down the avenue, it appears to be blocked by the impressive mass of the Chugach Mountain Range. In spite of the glorious mountains and encircling wilderness, however, Anchorage is a very American city—the race's starting banners hang almost directly in front of a McDonald's restaurant!

An average of sixty to seventy drivers line up on Fourth Avenue behind more than a thousand dogs for the start of the Iditarod. The eager huskies yelp, yammer, and jump "four off the floor," creating a deafening racket. Drivers carry an Iditarider in their sled basket and pull a second sled controlled by a handler in order to slow down these supercharged animals. Handlers are often the musher's spouse, and before the advent of Iditariders, sled-bag occupants have also included television cameramen, official Iditarod photographer Jeff Schultz, and ABC's commentator Donna DeVarona. Ten dog handlers usually restrain the canines as the countdown is announced, although rarely you will see a team standing quietly (with some dogs even lying down) and not a single dog handler in sight. Following a quick kiss for the wife/husband, children, girlfriend/boyfriend, mom, or grandma, each competitor sets off on the long journey to Nome.

The trail runs about a dozen blocks on Fourth Avenue before turning right and making a steep descent down infamous Cordova Hill. In places like the bottom of Cordova Hill, where the trail crosses a busy street, police officers stop traffic for the dog teams, and volunteers shovel snow back into the tire tracks after cars have driven across the trail. Having passed Mulcahy Park (a former Iditarod start location), following the bike trails of the Chester Creek greenbelt, and skirting Campbell Airstrip and Fort Richardson Military Reservation, the trail parallels the Glenn Highway on its way to Eagle River.

On a good surface, a sixteen-dog team can hit twenty miles per hour. This means that the mushers must be constantly vigilant or they may find themselves off of the trail helplessly tangled in the mother of all alder-tree snarls.

At about 12:00 to 12:30 P.M., the first team will crest a long hill and pull into the chute at checkpoint #2, Eagle River.

2. EAGLE RIVER to Wasilla 29 miles

With a population of 25,000, Eagle River has many amenities. So, if you grabbed your breakfast at the conveniently located McDonald's in Anchorage, you can continue your fast-food feast by driving to Eagle River and devouring another American favorite for lunch at the local Pizza Hut.

Due to the open water of the Knik and Matanuska Rivers and the traditional lack of snow on the Palmer Hay Flats, mushers meet their dog trucks and handlers at the Eagle River VFW Post and load up their teams and sleds. They will overnight somewhere in the vicinity and meet again Sunday morning twenty-nine miles farther north on the Glenn Highway at Wasilla for the restart.

3. WASILLA to Knik 14 miles

Home of the Iditarod Trail Committee's permanent headquarters, Wasilla is populated by 4,000 inhabitants. The restart of the Iditarod has been held "downtown" since 1989; prior to that, it was held farther down Knik Road at Settler's Bay, but traffic became unmanageable there.

At 10:00 A.M. on Sunday, the official race clock starts as the first team leaves the Wasilla restart through a narrow chute thronged by

10,000 to 15,000 avid Iditarod fans. As soon as they leave this chute, mushers must negotiate a busy highway and a railroad crossing. Snow is periodically redistributed on the Parks Highway to ease that crossing, and the railroad tracks are packed with snow and are closely monitored as well. Trains do have the right-of-way, but if a competitor has to wait for one, the time delay experienced is compensated for later in the race.

Once out of Wasilla, Iditarod dog drivers still have not left civilization behind them. The race trail from Wasilla all the way to Knik (and beyond) is lined by hardy spectators lounging in lawn chairs on the snow in front of campfires or grills, enjoying the day's festive atmosphere.

4. KNIK to Yentna Station 52 miles

Home to Joe Redington, Sr., the "Father of the Iditarod," Knik (pronounced "Kuh-NIK") is a town of 300 people. It's also famous for the Dog Mushers Hall of Fame, located in the Knik Museum and listed in the National Register of Historic Sites.

Commemorating Redington's accomplishments, a drawing for the Tesoro Alaska Joe Redington, Sr. Award is held in Knik. Each musher is invited to draw for the grand prize, a certificate for 2,500 gallons of Tesoro gasoline or a check for $2,500 (winner's choice).

On the day of the restart, this normally quiet town swells to a crowd of 2,000 to 3,000 tailgaters having one big party at the checkpoint near Knik Lake. Arriving competitors switch from a lightweight, empty sled to something more rugged packed with all of their mandatory and optional equipment. Second sleds and handlers are left behind here as the teams pull out of the last checkpoint accessible by road and head off into the wilderness.

The trail climbs through a forest before crossing an open area of frozen marshes and small ponds. Dropping onto the Susitna River and then winding back and forth from woods to swamp to river, the trail finally enters into Yentna Station.

5. YENTNA STATION to Skwentna 34 miles

A tent checkpoint set up by the ITC, Yentna Station is otherwise unpopulated. Mushers draw water for their teams through holes in the river ice. This is dangerous moose country. Running up and down the hills through spruce forest, or following the Yentna River (which can be a smooth, easy ride), the narrow trail leads into Skwentna.

6. SKWENTNA to Finger Lake 45 miles

Skwentna, population 120, is located at the convergence of the Skwentna and Yentna Rivers. It is the first major checkpoint. By now, the frantic dog teams are finally beginning to calm down and settle into their race routine. Mushers check in on the river below Joe Delia's cabin.

Leaving Skwentna can be confusing because of all of the local turnoffs and side trails. Once out of town, the route follows the Skwentna River for about forty miles before rising up into low hills covered by a spruce and alder forest. Trail elevation climbs from 100 feet above sea level at Skwentna to 800 feet at Finger Lake. One hint of things to come is the view of the Alaska Range, first visible from Skwentna.

All-around Iditarod volunteer Rich Owens has been a trailbreaker, food-supply planner, start/finish/banquet-logistics manager, ITC board member, and vice-president. Here, in 1993, he helps coordinate the race start.

Locally heavy snows of up to 200 inches (that's more than sixteen feet) can create what mushers call "bottomless trail." This loose, deep snow is extremely slow going for the dog teams, but eventually they cross the frozen lake and climb uphill into the Finger Lake checkpoint.

7. FINGER LAKE to Rainy Pass 30 miles
Through Happy River Valley

For many years, Finger Lake checkpoint was manned by the Leonards, who occupied its sole log cabin. Iditarod competitors park on the lake and sign in at a tent erected near the cabin.

The trail out of Finger Lake twists and winds for ten miles along the Skwentna River, rising from a 1,000-foot elevation at the confluence of the Skwentna and Happy Rivers to an elevation of 3,200 feet at Rainy Pass.

En route to Rainy Pass, the mushers cross a canyon created by the Happy River, first negotiating a steep descent and then scaling back up the other side. This crossing is one of the most infamous sections of the Iditarod Trail.

A narrow, treacherous trail lined with trees on both sides follows the edge of a cliff down the canyon, crisscrossing it three times during the course of the descent. Two major switchbacks add to the challenge.

If the driver doesn't crash, it's an extremely fast, wildly careening ride down. (If you've seen toboggans rolling over on television coverage of the Iditarod, it was probably here at Happy River.) Experienced mushers sometimes plan their schedule so that they reach this section during daylight; otherwise, they make certain to have a reliable headlamp with fresh batteries. Competitors also drag snow-machine tracks, and, of course, they furrow the trail standing on their brakes most of the way down.

Once down, the worst is not necessarily over. Some mushers claim that the steep, narrow ascent to Rainy Pass is as bad or worse than the descent. But at last, the weary teams reach frozen Puntilla Lake, where a gradual plain rises up to Rainy Pass Lodge. The entrance into this checkpoint can be rather exciting because of the dogs' reactions to a herd of horses kept here.

8. RAINY PASS to Rohn 48 miles
Through Dalzell Gorge

An unpopulated checkpoint in the winter, Rainy Pass Lodge hosts a guiding operation during warmer months. Most Iditarod participants

A race volunteer fills in mushers' times on a display board at Eagle River. Since the adoption of a two-day starting format, mushers' times from Anchorage to Eagle River have not been recorded. The race clock now officially starts at 10 A.M. on Sunday at the Wasilla restart.

agree that Rainy Pass ties with Rohn in having the most spectacular scenery on the trail. Mushers check in at one of the lodge's peripheral cabins.

The lodge is located at an elevation of 3,000 feet; from here, the teams climb a short distance to the top of Rainy Pass, which is 3,200-feet high. This pass divides South Central Alaska (the trail's first major geographic region) from the Interior (the second distinct section). Just to the north, Denali majestically rises to a height of 20,320 feet. In the pass, mushers may see caribou, moose, Dall Sheep, or ptarmigan, any of which can precipitate a wild chase by the dogs.

Over the next five and one-half miles, the trail drops 1,000 feet into the legendary Dalzell Gorge, then continues to drop another 300 feet in the subsequent six miles. This twisty downhill run rounds blind corners, hairpin turns, switchbacks, huge boulders, and passes through ravines enclosed by twenty-foot banks. As if that weren't enough, the teams also brave open water, ice bridges (which are prone to collapse), glare ice, and windblown snow. Surprisingly, the dogs actually seem to enjoy Dalzell Gorge, racing safely past all of these obstacles hell-bent for leather. It's the poor driver, desperately gripping the sled handlebar, who rides the end of "crack the whip."

The difference between Happy River Valley and Dalzell Gorge was put this way by one competitor: "The misery lasts longer on Dalzell." Rookie Jack Goode developed a novel approach to this descent during the 1993 race. He recounts, "What was really interesting was that we went down [Dalzell Gorge] in the dark at night. I thought that was a good idea because I couldn't be scared because I couldn't see all the scary spots." Goode did have his headlamp on, but said that even with it on, he couldn't see anything except his leaders.

Occasionally, if there's heavy snow, the trail is rerouted around Rainy Pass because of avalanche danger. Ptarmigan Pass, which has a gentler incline and decline, and thus less risk of avalanche, is used as an alternate route. Although a safer and lower pass, it does add thirty miles to the total race distance.

Having survived the descent, mushers drop onto the river, which is renowned for its open water and treacherous overflow. A number of sloughs veer off from the main course of the river, tempting the teams to take false trails.

Wolves are sometimes seen along this part of the race route, which is generally acknowledged to be one of the most beautiful sections. The northern lights often suffuse the night with their surreal glow, stars shine brilliantly, and as Iditarod writer Tim Jones observes, "the mountains go forever up into the clouds."

After one final stretch that winds through thick woods, the trail emerges into the picturesque Rohn checkpoint.

9. ROHN to Nikolai 93 miles
Through the Farewell Burn

Rohn (which rhymes with "bone") is an unpopulated checkpoint located in a canyon near the Tatina and Kuskokwim Rivers, surrounded by stately spruce and lofty mountain peaks. The ITC can't deliver the mushers' food-drop bags until the last possible moment or wolves will eat the food. A tent is set up for the checkers, and a 1930s cabin offers limited shelter. The landing strip here is dangerous even for experienced bush pilots.

Many drivers traditionally have taken their twenty-four-hour layover here, partly in order to recover from the twin horrors of Happy River Valley and Dalzell Gorge, but also in an attempt to prepare themselves for the dreaded Farewell Burn. To some race observers, Rohn is a litmus test. As *Detroit Free Press* columnist Mitch Albom remarked, "You reach Rohn anywhere in the top 10 and you're in the big leagues in Iditarod. As they might say in Georgia, your dogs can bark."

From Rohn to Nikolai, the longest journey between checkpoints (ninety-three miles), the trail passes through woods onto the frozen South Fork of the Kuskokwim River, back into the trees, across the Post River, up an overflow-covered hill affectionately referred to as "The Waterfall," and finally into the open, level Interior of the state.

In 1993, Bill Cotter, 1987 Yukon Quest champion, broke two ribs on the so-called "buffalo trail" or "buffalo tunnel" between Rohn and Nikolai. He told an *Anchorage Daily News* reporter that it was the worst section of trail he had ever seen: "No snow. Glare ice. Rock. Stumps. Narrow. Twisty. Scariest thing I've ever done."

If Happy River Valley and Dalzell Gorge are the Iditarod's Scylla and Charybdis, the Farewell Burn is its Hades. Formerly tundra and spruce forest bisected by streams, it was razed in 1977 by Alaska's largest wildfire, which charred an incredible 361,000 acres. Now its only features are blackened tree stumps and large tussocks that ruthlessly shatter mushers' sleds. In years of sparse snowfall, gravel and bare ground exacerbate the problem. The lack of anything to break the wind causes trail markers to be blown away, and to add insult to injury, the area is often frequented by buffalo. Iditarod racer Donna Gentry summed it up rather neatly when she said, "When I die, I'm going to heaven, because I've already been through the Farewell Burn."

Continuing toward Nikolai, drivers glimpse the tall towers of the FAA weather reporting and navigation system station at Farewell and cross the aptly named 28-Mile Creek when they are (you guessed it) twenty-eight miles away from Nikolai. Passing Salmon River and descending onto the Kuskokwim River, the mushers' first view of the village is its Russian Orthodox Church crowned by three crosses.

10. NIKOLAI to McGrath 48 miles

The trail's first Native village is a welcome sight after a series of wilderness checkpoints. Nikolai's 122 inhabitants are famous for their hospitality and for the excitement generated by the arrival of the race. The checkpoint is generally located at the community hall.

Most of the way from Nikolai to McGrath, the trail follows the Kuskokwim River. But the river bends too far to the south, and as a

The McGrath checkpoint consists of a canvas tent, wood stove, and a stack of firewood (you'll overheat inside the tent in your arctic clothes — it's like a sauna). Three feet of snow may cover six feet of river ice, and weather here is often "severe clear" — cloudless and bone-chilling cold.

result, the route frequently alternates between spruce-forest portages and river travel. Salmon-drying racks at summer fish camps perch above the banks as the teams wend their way to McGrath.

11. McGRATH to Takotna 23 miles

Located near the confluence of the Kuskokwim and Takotna Rivers, McGrath was founded in 1907 and named after the area's U.S. deputy marshal, Peter McGrath. The town used to be on the north side of the river but was relocated when the course of the river changed. On February 21, 1924, McGrath received the state's first air-mail delivery from Fairbanks. An airstrip built during World War II and an FAA weather station helped make the town a hub for the central Kuskokwim region. The current population is greater than 500.

Arriving mushers check in at a tent that sits smack in the middle of the Kuskokwim River. With six feet of ice below three feet of punchy (soft, deep, and uneven) snow, temperatures on the river tend to be

*Rick Swenson signs autographs for McGrath's young fans. Swenson arrived
in second place and only stopped here twenty minutes,
but he made time for these children.*

four to six degrees cooler than in town. Because McGrath is renowned
for its "severe clear" weather (as many as twenty-two consecutive
days below zero one year, reaching lows of -60° F), few competitors
stay here long. In the past, when the checkpoint was in town, this was
a popular twenty-four-hour layover choice. The excellent facilities
here (laundromat, hot showers, restaurants, stores, bars) still make the
town inviting to weary drivers, however.

Leaving McGrath, the trail runs along first the Kuskokwim and
then the Takotna River. Because of heavy snow-machine use locally,
the route may be marred by moguls (ruts as deep as six feet created
by the snow-machines' tracks). From a distance, mushers glimpse
Takotna's small air force installation; as they get closer, they will also
hear the village dogs barking and catch a whiff of that telltale hint of
nearby habitation—wood smoke.

12. TAKOTNA to Ophir 38 miles

Takotna was established on the banks of the Takotna River in 1914 as a mining and trapping center. Today it is home to about fifty people. Although it is small, the village boasts a school, a restaurant, a bar, and an air force installation. Mushers remember Takotna for its big welcome. For many years, villagers have sent each competitor back onto the trail with a lunch "to go."

As race strategy evolves and mushers let their teams run farther before taking their twenty-four-hour layover, the checkpoints of Takotna, Ophir, and Iditarod have become increasingly popular layover locales. All three checkpoints provide nearly undisturbed rest for musher and team because of their limited access and accommodations.

The trail out of Takotna climbs "twelve-mile hill" and then runs along a state highway built to allow access to the Distant Early Warning (DEW) Line. The trail then leads into the fabled gold country surrounding Ophir.

Leaving Ophir, mushers follow a southern trail in odd years and a northern route in even years. Textual description of the southern route is indicated by the letter "A" following the checkpoint numeral, while the description of the northern route is indicated by the letter "B".

13A. OPHIR to Iditarod 90 miles (southern route, used in odd years)

Now a ghost town, Ophir (pronounced "OH-fur") was previously the center of an important gold-mining district that was mined until the 1930s. It was named by prospectors after the lost biblical country of Ophir, reputedly the source of King Solomon's gold. A post office operated here until 1957; now there is only one year-round resident—Robbie Roberts, the "loafer from Ophir." The checkpoint is at Dick and Audra Forsgren's cabin.

The race route climbs gradually out of Ophir into the Beaver Mountains, a subsidiary range of the Kuskokwim Mountains. Mushers generally find it fairly easy going through this "big country" unless the wind is blowing, in which case the trail is quickly obliterated by drifting snow.

Partway through this long leg of the race, there used to be a roadhouse. It became badly dilapidated but was still used by Iditarod drivers as a shelter cabin. Having appreciated its protection, musher Don Montgomery donated the materials necessary to repair it, and in the off-season, Rick Swenson and Sonny Lindner built an essentially new cabin. Called "Don's Cabin," it was used as a checkpoint for several years.

After cresting seemingly endless, barren, rolling hills, the teams at length enter the broad floodplain of the Iditarod River. The two-and-one-half-story remains of the Northern Commercial Company store herald the mushers' arrival at the abandoned town for which the Last Great Race is named—Iditarod.

13B. OPHIR to Cripple 59 miles (northern route, used in even years)

For a description of Ophir, see #13A above.

Running through the foothills of the Kuskokwim Mountains, the mushers head north up the frozen Innoko River to the halfway point of Cripple.

14A. IDITAROD to Shageluk 65 miles (southern route)

Iditarod was named from the Ingalik Indian word "Haiditarod," which means "a far distant place." On Christmas Day 1908, gold was found here, beginning the last major stampede in Alaska. By October 1910, Iditarod consisted of eight saloons, six cafés, six general stores, six lawyers, five clothiers, three hotels, two doctors, two dentists, two banks, two tobacconists, a barber, a drugstore, a bathhouse, an undertaker, a sheet-music and musical-instrument store, a sweet shop, a post office, the usual number of freighters, suppliers, and warehouses, and a "restricted area" called the "cribs" inhabited by prostitutes.

To accommodate the traffic generated by the miners, the Alaska Road Commission cleared a trail north and south from Iditarod in 1910-1911. Originally called the Seward Trail after its southern terminus (Anchorage didn't exist then), it became known as the Iditarod Trail. By the time the gold petered out, $14 million of it had been mined in Iditarod, making this the state's third largest gold producer.

A U.S. Post Office operated in Iditarod from 1910 to 1929. At the height of its history, more than ten thousand people lived here. By 1940, only one remained. Today, Iditarod is a ghost town, a mute reminder of the fleeting glories of gold.

Traditionally, the checkpoint is located at Dick Wilmarth's cabin. Wilmarth became the race's first champion in the inaugural running of 1973. Water for the dogs must be drawn up through holes in the river ice. The ITC provides a heated weatherport or a shelter cabin for the mushers at each checkpoint, however, even at the unpopulated ones like Iditarod.

Iditarod is considered the halfway point of the race's southern route, and in recognition of this, the first musher to arrive here receives the Dorothy G. Page Halfway Award of $3,000 and a beautiful trophy. General Communications, Inc. (GCI) weighs out the three thousand dollars worth of gold nuggets, mined locally in the Iditarod area, in an antique scale. The recipient has also traditionally shouldered the halfway jinx, which so far has prevented all but three competitors who arrived first at the race's midpoint from going on to win in Nome. (Dean Osmar evaded the jinx in 1984, Jeff King overcame it in 1993, and Doug Swingley perhaps put it to rest in 1995.)

The trail out of Iditarod leads drivers down the Iditarod River toward a series of low mountains, where it heads west for the Yukon River. Having braved high winds in the hills, teams are grateful to drop into the shelter of a valley cut by the Innoko and Yukon Rivers. Eventually, the mushers descend to Shageluk Lake and pull into the race's second Native village.

14B. CRIPPLE to Sulatna Crossing 45 miles (northern route)

An unpopulated checkpoint, Cripple is really little more than a wide spot on the Innoko River. The ITC sets up a tent here, and General Communications, Inc. (GCI) presents the Dorothy G. Page Halfway Award described in #14A. The notorious jinx has plagued the northern route as well.

Although it is not one of the longest legs of the race, the forty-five miles between Cripple and Sulatna Crossing is so open and expansive that it seems endless to the mushers. Unfortunately, once there, Sulatna Crossing is not much to talk about.

15A. SHAGELUK to Anvik 25 miles (southern route)

The name of this small village (population 144) is an Ingalik Indian word that means (very appropriately) "the village of the dog people." The proper pronunciation is "SHAG-a-look." The checkpoint is located at the community hall, and mushers usually have access to the school gym (for sleeping), hot showers, and hot water for their dogs.

Drivers follow the Innoko River away from the village and then meander through deep woods on a narrow, winding trail. This area demands constant vigilance because of "sweepers"—low branches hanging over the trail that frequently smash mushers on the bridge of their noses. In this case, a little shuteye may result in a black eye!

Having crossed an area of marshy lowland, the trail arrives at the eastern banks of the mile-plus-wide, mighty Yukon River. Originating in Canada's Yukon Territory, it flows 2,300 miles before emptying into the frigid Bering Sea. Broadening to an almost unbelievable three miles in width, the river can be as shallow as one or two feet in depth. A highway for long-awaited barges bringing food, fuel, and supplies to the Interior in the summer, it is also an important source of salmon. In the winter, the Yukon becomes a thoroughfare for snow machines and dog sleds, as well as a landing strip for small aircraft. Because it lies lower than the adjoining land, the temperature on the river is often as much as ten degrees colder.

Iditarod drivers will race over the surface of this sleeping giant all the way from Anvik to Kaltag, almost 150 miles of river travel, all upwind! But for now, they only need to cross the Yukon to be welcomed by the friendly folks at Anvik.

15B. SULATNA CROSSING to Ruby 75 miles (northern route)

A tent checkpoint only, Sulatna Crossing is said to be the coldest spot of the entire Iditarod. Traveling up and down hills, mushers ride over a local road from Sulatna Crossing through Long to the village of Ruby. The Native village of Ruby is the first checkpoint on the northern route located on the Yukon River. For a description of the Yukon, see #15A.

16A. ANVIK to Grayling 18 miles (southern route)

The first checkpoint on the Yukon River along Iditarod's southern route is Anvik, population ninety-eight. Mushers check in at the city building. A formal seven-course gourmet meal is presented as the Regal Alaskan Hotel First Musher to the Yukon Award. Served on white linen by master chefs, this culinary delight is topped off by a $3,500 "after-dinner mint," plus a gold-pan trophy.

The trip up the Yukon River from Anvik to Kaltag is all upwind. With winds howling at fifty to sixty miles per hour and temperatures plummeting to -50° F to -60° F, this can be a truly nasty journey. Boredom is another downside to river travel. As musher Frank Teasley explains, "There's not much mental stimulation out there [on the river], and you fall asleep a lot. The dogs do, too. They get bored with it." Rough or punchy snow often covers the river, further complicating matters.

Drivers can't see the upcoming village of Grayling until they are almost on top of it because it is set back from the river bank.

16B. RUBY to Galena 52 miles (northern route)

Established in 1907 by the discovery of gold, Ruby served as a landing point for miners' supplies, which were then shipped overland. Now populated by 223 villagers, Ruby is the home of two renowned Native mushing families—the Honeas and the Peters. An interesting bit of trivia is that Ruby is the only settlement on the *left* (south) bank of the Yukon River along its last 800 miles in Alaska as it runs toward the Bering Sea.

The checkpoint is usually at the community hall. As in Anvik on the southern route, the Regal Alaskan Hotel First Musher to the Yukon Award of a gourmet seven-course meal is presented here (see #16A).

Out on the Yukon River, teams pass Cave-off Cliffs, travel west through the Koyukuk Flats, and finally approach the hidden town of Galena.

17A. GRAYLING to Eagle Island 60 miles (southern route)

Grayling has a population of 255 and is considered one of the trail's most picturesque villages, partly because of its many attractive log homes. The Iditarod checkpoint is generally at the community center.

The stretch of river between Grayling and Eagle Island is difficult to negotiate because of the many islands that must be circumvented. Mushers pass between the west bank of the Yukon and the first two of three Eagle Islands, then skirt Fox Point Island and Blackburn Island, where drivers sometimes stop at the Thurmonds' cabin. In addition to the islands, numerous sloughs and tributaries branching off from the Yukon make staying on the race trail a challenging proposition.

Nights on the Yukon River are usually cold and clear. A display of the northern lights often helps compensate for the discomforts, however. After hours of solitary travel, the Conasters' cabin at Eagle Island, with its annual feast prepared for the famished mushers, is a truly welcome sight.

17B. GALENA to Nulato 52 miles (northern route)

Galena (pronounced "gull-LEE-na") was founded in 1920 when local residents moved downriver from Louden in order to obtain better availability of firewood. Today, with 600 townspeople, it is one of the largest villages between Anchorage and Nome. Edgar Nollner, one of the original 1925 serum-run mushers, calls Galena home, as do the legendary Native dog drivers, the Huntingtons. Competitors check in at the community center.

Numerous snow-machine trails keep mushers and lead dogs on their toes as they leave Galena. The upcoming section of the Yukon River, from Galena through Koyukuk to Nulato and on to Kaltag, is the most heavily traveled stretch of the river.

Drivers pass Pilot Mountain, Bishop Rock, the fish camps at Yistletaw, and a small settlement at Koyukuk en route to the historic village of Nulato.

18A. EAGLE ISLAND to Kaltag 70 miles (southern route)

Ralph and Helmi Conaster opened their Eagle Island cabin to Iditarod mushers for many years. Since Helmi's death in October 1992, Ralph has continued the tradition on his own. The Conasters have created quite a reputation for their cheesecakes and other delectable edibles. The checkpoint is otherwise unpopulated.

On the way to Kaltag, teams endure the "twenty-two mile stretch" (twenty-two miles south of Kaltag), which is universally disliked on account of high winds, wide-open spaces, severe clear weather, glare ice, and occasionally, bare gravel.

Covering mile after mile of sameness, competitors are prone to hallucinate. A common mental delusion is seeing (and ducking) "sweepers," those face-mangling, low-hanging branches. Of course, on a mile-wide river, there aren't likely to be many trees growing!

The glow of Kaltag, situated high on a bluff overlooking the Yukon, brings tremendous relief after the tedium of long miles of upriver mushing.

18B. NULATO to Kaltag 42 miles (northern route)

The site of Russia's first occupation in the Interior, Nulato (pronounced "Nu-LAH-to") was established in 1838 as a Russian trading post at the confluence of the Nulato and Yukon Rivers. It was soon burned down by local Indians, but the Russian American Trading Company rebuilt it in 1841. Within ten years, it was burned again and the inhabitants were killed. Finally, in 1853, the Russians moved their trading post to the site of the current village, two miles upriver from the original location.

Iditarod mushers check in at the old village because the new one (population 450) is up on a hill.

After following the Yukon River southwest for forty-two miles, the northern route rejoins the southern route at the village of Kaltag.

19. KALTAG to Unalakleet 90 miles

Kaltag was founded in 1899 as a supply hub on the Yukon River for the Innoko gold fields. Today the village population is 278.

Arriving mushers are so pleased to be finished with their travel on the Yukon River that even the sixty-foot ascent of the river bank into the village doesn't faze them.

Astute observers will notice that the doorways to most homes along the Yukon River are several steps *down* from street level. This is because of the inexorable accumulation of snow throughout the long winter. Sometimes residents even use chain saws to cut the compacted snow into blocks so that it can be removed more easily.

All along the Iditarod's route, inhabitants of remote villages and towns are nearing the peak of cabin fever in early to mid March. This makes the arrival of the race a momentous occasion that is celebrated in style. Competitors sign in and enjoy the warm reception at a local

Unalakleet means "where the east wind always blows." The village also receives an abundance of snow. The combination of snow and wind creates dramatic scenes like this half-buried church. When the first musher arrives at Unalakleet, the church bells peal out a merry greeting.

checker's home. Most drivers try to take an extended rest here to fortify themselves and their dogs for the tiring ninety-mile journey to Unalakleet.

Rick Swenson claims that this is his favorite stretch of the trail because "it's off the river and before the coast." The trail out of Kaltag passes through a spruce forest and then along the Kaltag River until the mushers reach a low pass of about 1,000 feet.

This pass is called Old Woman Portage or the Kaltag Portage. Centuries before the influx of explorers and gold miners, this portage was used by Eskimos and Indians to cross from the Bering Sea coast to the Interior of Alaska. It later became a supply route and was chosen as the path of least resistance for stringing telegraph wires from Fairbanks to Nome. A telegraph station was built in the shelter of Old Woman Hill; this old cabin (and a new one nearby) is still used by Iditarod mushers today.

Descending from the pass, the trail runs over the Unalakleet River as it makes its way to the sea. The race now enters its third geographical and cultural region, the Bering Sea coast. This area is home to the Inupiat Eskimos. According to Sadie Neokok, an elder in Barrow, "Inupiat," which means "the only people," was so named because "we were so isolated that we always felt we were the only people."

Coming into the Inupiat village of Unalakleet, mushers rely on a superior lead dog to keep them on the Iditarod Trail despite the distraction of numerous intersecting snow-machine trails. After an interminable ninety miles, dogs and drivers alike are ready to receive some hearty village hospitality.

20. UNALAKLEET to Shaktoolik 40 miles

Pronounced "YOU-na-la-kleet," this town of 850 people huddles on the shore of Norton Sound, a large bay in the Bering Sea. The Inupiat word "Unalakleet" means "where the east wind always blows," which is a fairly accurate summary of winter weather here. The coastal section of the trail does not experience the extreme low temperatures of the Interior, but the wind combined with the cold produces blizzards, which are actually far more dangerous.

Remains of house pits dating back to 200 B.C. have been found here by archaeologists. Unalakleet is the first Eskimo community along the Iditarod Trail, and mushers receive a very warm welcome. The village siren sounds and church bells ring to announce the arrival of the race drivers. A large crowd assembles at the checkpoint in front of Leonard and Mary Brown's Unalakleet Lodge.

The Gold Coast Award, presented by the National Bank of Alaska, honors the first musher to reach the Bering Sea coast at Unalakleet. This trophy was founded by Jeff Hankerd, Burt Bomhoff, and Johnny Ellison and was first awarded in 1984. After a hiatus of several years, its sponsorship was assumed by the National Bank of Alaska in 1993. An impressive gold-bowl trophy is accompanied by $2,500 of real gold nuggets—barely enough mass to fill the palm of your hand, but so heavy that you feel truly rich.

Approaching Unalakleet from the air, you get the feeling that an outpost of civilization has somehow miraculously been dropped intact in the wilderness. A tight cluster of buildings faces miles of sea ice and open water to the west, and a series of low hills and a vast expanse of treeless, snow-covered openness in the other three directions. Its remote location makes the fact that Unalakleet ties with Galena as the largest community between Anchorage and Nome even more surprising.

Now that they have reached the coast, mushers start paring down their teams, operating on the principle that you are only as fast as your slowest dog. Many healthy, but slower, huskies will be dropped at Unalakleet.

Leaving Unalakleet can be challenging because of the presence of glare ice. Once out of town, the mushers ascend a series of low hills, part of a chain of mountain ridges called the "whalebacks," which separate the Bering Sea coast from the Interior to the east.

At last, the trail descends sharply onto frozen marshland. This open area is so cold, windy, and exposed that experienced competitors make a point of stopping in the lee of the hills to snack and rest their teams prior to setting out across the unprotected flats that characterize the remainder of the drive to Shaktoolik.

Having crossed a number of creeks, the teams arrive at Old Shaktoolik three to four miles south of (before) the current village. This can create chaos because many sled dogs will automatically stop, expecting a meal and a snooze, at anything that resembles a checkpoint. With luck, the mushers will guide their partners up onto a higher spit of land where modern-day Shaktoolik perches. When they see the snowdrifts towering above the houses and feel the wind funneling down the streets, drivers know that they have reached stormy Shaktoolik.

21. SHAKTOOLIK to Koyuk 58 miles
Across the sea ice of Norton Bay

Nicknamed "a resort for storms," Shaktoolik (pronounced "Shak-TOO-lick") is a village of 178 people. Racers check in at a trailer in front of the armory. The outcome of at least one race has been determined by a bold foray out of Shaktoolik into a wicked blizzard.

For the first ten to fifteen miles outside the village, mushers cross frozen marshland, where nothing is more than three feet high. Then they pass Lonely Hill, also called Lonely Rock or Little Mountain. If there is not enough solid sea ice, the trail will skirt the east end of Norton Bay, clinging to the shoreline and adding about fifteen miles to the route. Normally, however, the drivers will drop from the beach onto the ice pack of Norton Bay for the remaining thirty-mile run to Koyuk.

Sea ice is an interesting phenomenon. In places it is clear, in others drifted; it may be textured like washboard because of pressure ridges, or contain leads (gaps) of open water. The ITC sets laths with fluorescent flagging on them (not as visible as the pine saplings previously used) into the ice every 100 yards, but there is no guarantee that sections of the trail won't wash out to sea as the ice shifts and leads open. Pale green glare ice signifies that a section of ice has opened up and subsequently refrozen. To add to the mushers' apprehensions, the "permanent" shore ice groans and pops as the waves whipped up far out to sea roll in under its surface. Ice fishermen and women become accustomed and immune to these ominous noises, but for the uninitiated, it can be a hair-raising experience. This is the same stretch of sea ice that Leonhard Seppala crossed and recrossed during the 1925 serum run.

As they cautiously make this perilous crossing, Iditarod drivers see the lights of Koyuk as much as five to six hours before they reach the far shore. This is maddening and discouraging to the weary mushers, who are usually heartily sick of the sight of Koyuk by the time they arrive there. Nevertheless, after a particularly treacherous journey, competitors have been known to contemplate kissing the ground once they were again solidly planted on good old "terra firma."

22. KOYUK to Elim 48 miles

Mushers sign in at Koyuk's city hall. Although it has only 231 residents, the village has a new school and recreation center and a unit of the Alaska National Guard.

From Koyuk, the teams head west along the southern shore of the Seward Peninsula. After winding around steep, rocky bluffs, the trail traverses the Walla Walla Portage, where the rounded hilltops are covered by moss and tundra grass. Mushers pass Bald Head promontory, the Kwiniuk Inlet marsh, and an old FAA building at Moses Point before joining a spruce-lined road into Elim. Suddenly, having been hidden behind a rock bluff, Elim comes into view.

Scenes like this Native salmon-drying rack greet mushers as they pass through the beautiful Bering Sea coast region.

23. ELIM to Golovin 28 miles

Once the competitors reach Elim (pronounced "EE-lum"), population 264, they are beginning to think of the race as a sprint to the finish. As a result, having checked in at a villager's home, mushers generally do not remain in Elim longer than necessary.

After paralleling the shoreline for about eleven miles to the southwest, the race route runs inland across McKinley Portage. One of the hills in this area has become known as Little McKinley, partly due to the difficulty that mushers have climbing it and partly because of its proximity to McKinley Creek. Once they come down out of the hills, the teams are buffeted by vicious winds. Soon, however, they drop onto Golovin Bay and cross a short stretch of sea ice. Olson's large, white general store (owned by the descendants of serum-musher Charlie Olson) welcomes the Iditarod to Golovin.

24. GOLOVIN to White Mountain 18 miles

With a population of 131, the small village of Golovin (pronounced "GULL-uh-vin") offers arriving mushers a large helping of hospitality. Nevertheless, drivers hasten back on the trail, hoping to put distance between themselves and their pursuers.

The trail heads northwest across Golovin Bay, turns briefly onto the Nudyutok River, and soon rounds a bend that reveals the village of White Mountain nestled against the side of a hill.

25. WHITE MOUNTAIN to Safety 55 miles
Through the Topkok Hills

White Mountain was established in 1899 by C. D. Lane, who erected a large warehouse as a distribution center for area mining claims. The village takes its name from a nearby 500-foot-tall white "mountain." Many of the village's 180 inhabitants greet the incoming competitors down by the large oil tanks that power the local generator system. The checkpoint is at the community hall.

Only a checkpoint away from Nome, many mushers take time to lighten their sleds during their mandatory eight-hour layover here. Of course, the advantages of carrying less weight have to be balanced against the risks of facing potentially brutal weather in the Topkok Hills unprepared.

Drivers travel briefly on a river and then across a short stretch of tundra as they leave White Mountain. Passing an area called Big Timber, the teams reach the east side of the treacherous Topkok Hills. There's an A-frame cabin at the foot of these hills, but it's not suitable for shelter, other than from the wind.

Mushers sidehill through these barren, rounded hills and encounter strong blasts of wind as they crest the summits. One valley, called Topkok Funnel, channels the wind so strongly that dogs and drivers alike feel as though they are in a wind tunnel. Those who have fought their way through the "Topkok Blowhole" are quite emphatic in explaining that this phenomenon is not something that can be intellectually grasped; to really understand Topkok, you have to pay your dues there in the flesh. Each year Topkok exacts its vengeance . . . from the front-runners to the scores of middle- and back-of-the-pack mushers who get pinned down by a storm in this area nearly every year after the top twenty teams have finished. A shelter cabin constructed by the Nome Kennel Club stands on the Safety (west) side of these hills.

Following a long decline to sea level, the trail runs west along the shoreline toward Safety. Mushers realize that they are near Solomon when they see Tommy Johnson's cabin. Occasionally, drivers get off of the main trail and take an unintentional detour through Solomon, as both Libby Riddles and Rick Mackey did the years that they won the race.

Finally, having mushed by a protective sea wall and a collection of summer fish camps and cabins, the eager Iditaroders see Safety ahead.

26. SAFETY to Nome 22 miles

Serious competitors breeze through Safety, stopping only long enough to sign the checker's pad, eject all nonessential gear (which they can have shipped home to them), and pick up their mandatory finisher's bib (if they remember). They also may drop any dog that is not up to a hard sprint home.

Racing out of Safety, mushers round Cape Nome, often weaving around massive blocks of ice on the bay. The wind is generally fairly calm along this leg of the race, a real change of pace for coastal travel.

Miles from Nome, the front-runners begin to see spectators on snow machines lining the trail, as well as reporters and camera crews. A media helicopter is sure to make an appearance as well. Mushers know that they are only four miles from Nome when they pass Farley's camp. Leaving behind the Fort Davis Roadhouse, the trail drops once more onto the sea ice before finally running up a ramp that leads to long-awaited Front Street. Experienced drivers will tell you that the last few hundred yards are pure chaos. Libby Riddles said that she felt like she was driving through a hurricane. At long last, however, the triumphant team tows its grateful captain under the famed burled arch, where everyone who finishes wins a personal victory.

27. NOME

Mushers used to say, "All dog trails lead to Nome." Historically, four major routes converged here—from Seward, Dillingham, Nenana, and Cape South Wales (see the map). Gold was discovered on the beaches of Nome, of all places, creating an enormous rush that peaked in 1900. At the height of the stampede, 30,000 people lived in Nome; now the population is a more modest 3,430. In 1901, Wyatt Earp opened the Dexter Saloon in Nome, which is still considered a landmark today, now operating under the name of The Board of Trade.

Having your picture taken under the arch is mandatory for tourists in Nome.

The town's siren sounds to announce the arrival of each Iditarod finisher. After pulling under the "Red Fox" Olson burled arch, which reads "End of Iditarod Dog Race, 1,049 Miles, Anchorage [to] Nome," every musher is interviewed by KNOM radio.

For most mushers, to finish is to win. The task undertaken is so daunting that there is real honor merely in having completed it. Millionaire stockbroker Steve Fossett had an impressive résumé when he signed up to run the Iditarod. At age forty-six, he had already swum the English Channel, climbed the highest mountain on five continents, run the Boston Marathon, and completed cross-country ski marathons in ten countries. On his application form, Fossett indicated that he would consider it a superb accomplishment if he could finish the Iditarod. Fossett scratched during his first attempt in 1991 but went on to finish forty-seventh in 1992.

Many mushers experience post-Iditarod depression. Having finished the 1990 race in forty-eighth place, Bryan Moline commented, "It was the best sixteen days camping. It was kind of sad [when I got to Nome] because I thought, 'What am I going to do tomorrow?' " The "no-place-to-go" syndrome, coupled with readjusting to the "real world," gives some finishers the Idita-Blues.

Several days after the winner reaches Nome, the first of two awards banquets is held. Each first-time finisher receives the coveted Official Iditarod Finisher's belt buckle and a large Official Finisher's patch (obtainable only by completing an Iditarod), and is given the opportunity to speak to the assembled fans, sponsors, and co-competitors. The second banquet is celebrated after the last musher arrives (usually at least a week later than the champion). This hardy soul receives the Red Lantern Award, a humorous reference to the fact that this musher was so far behind that he or she needed a lantern to light the way home.

Once the last lamb has been welcomed into the fold, Iditarod officials extinguish the Widow's Lamp, which has burned brightly since 10:00 A.M. on the day of the start in its place of honor hanging from Nome's burled arch. Originally hung out at roadhouses along the trail to signify that a musher was expected, the Widow's Lamp has become a symbol of the Iditarod's philosophy that the Last Great Race is not really over until every single competitor is safely home, having successfully reached at last the end of the trail.

If you've stopped your car on a taxiway/road, someone's wingtips may pass over your roof momentarily if you dawdle.

IDITAROD CHECKPOINTS AND DISTANCES
(Southern Route - Odd Years)

		Total
Anchorage to Eagle River	20 miles	20 miles
Eagle River to Wasilla	29 miles	49 miles
Wasilla to Knik	14 miles	63 miles
Knik to Skwentna	86 miles	149 miles
Skwentna to Finger Lake	45 miles	194 miles
Finger Lake to Rainy Pass	30 miles	224 miles
Rainy Pass to Rohn	48 miles	272 miles
Rohn to Nikolai	93 miles	365 miles
Nikolai to McGrath	48 miles	413 miles
McGrath to Takotna	23 miles	436 miles
Takotna to Ophir	38 miles	474 miles
Ophir to Iditarod	90 miles	564 miles
Iditarod to Shageluk	65 miles	629 miles
Shageluk to Anvik	25 miles	654 miles
Anvik to Grayling	18 miles	672 miles
Grayling to Eagle Island	60 miles	732 miles
Eagle Island to Kaltag	70 miles	802 miles
Kaltag to Unalakleet	90 miles	892 miles
Unalakleet to Shaktoolik	40 miles	932 miles
Shaktoolik to Koyuk	58 miles	990 miles
Koyuk to Elim	48 miles	1,038 miles
Elim to Golovin	28 miles	1,066 miles
Golovin to White Mountain	18 miles	1,084 miles
White Mountain to Safety	55 miles	1,139 miles
Safety to Nome	22 miles	1,161 miles
Total		**1,161 miles**

NOTE: The ITC uses 1,049 miles as a symbolic figure. The distance traveled is always more than 1,000 miles, and 49 is added to signify Alaska, the 49th state.

IDITAROD CHECKPOINTS AND DISTANCES
(Northern Route - Even Years)

		Total
Anchorage to Eagle River	20 miles	20 miles
Eagle River to Wasilla	29 miles	49 miles
Wasilla to Knik	14 miles	63 miles
Knik to Skwentna	86 miles	149 miles
Skwentna to Finger Lake	45 miles	194 miles
Finger Lake to Rainy Pass	30 miles	224 miles
Rainy Pass to Rohn	48 miles	272 miles
Rohn to Nikolai	93 miles	365 miles
Nikolai to McGrath	48 miles	413 miles
McGrath to Takotna	23 miles	436 miles
Takotna to Ophir	38 miles	474 miles
Ophir to Cripple	59 miles	533 miles
Cripple to Sulatna Crossing	45 miles	578 miles
Sulatna Crossing to Ruby	75 miles	653 miles
Ruby to Galena	52 miles	705 miles
Galena to Nulato	52 miles	757 miles
Nulato to Kaltag	42 miles	799 miles
Kaltag to Unalakleet	90 miles	889 miles
Unalakleet to Shaktoolik	40 miles	929 miles
Shaktoolik to Koyuk	58 miles	987 miles
Koyuk to Elim	48 miles	1,035 miles
Elim to Golovin	28 miles	1,063 miles
Golovin to White Mountain	18 miles	1,081 miles
White Mountain to Safety	55 miles	1,136 miles
Safety to Nome	22 miles	1,158 miles
Total		**1,158 miles**

NOTE: The ITC uses 1,049 miles as a symbolic figure. The distance traveled is always more than 1,000 miles, and 49 is added to signify Alaska, the 49th state.

OUT ON
THE TRAIL

The unvarying routines, the hard work and the harsh cold, your dependence on the dogs and theirs on you, produce the framework for a world all its own, a world in which rest is rare and uncomfortable and sleep is shallow because you fear you might get left behind. It is a world in which life means motion and reality is the trail ahead and a half-formed idea of the finish line in a far-away place called Nome. It is a world of silence and ice — ice under your feet, ice stretching to the horizon, ice on your face as your exhaustion deepens with the cycle of the days and your world shrinks to a tight cocoon. Your time becomes detached from real time and finally even the haunting beauty of Alaska goes unseen. The repetitive, dreamlike quality of life on the trail can almost mask the fact that the race is even going on.

Sam Posey
ABC Wide World of Sports *commentator*

16

The Run/Rest Cycle

P erhaps the single most important decision that Iditarod mushers make is when to run and when to rest their teams. This chapter will examine exactly what happens during rest stops of various lengths and will discuss what it feels like to run the trail.

THE MENTAL-HEALTH MINUTE

Two-time champion Martin Buser has coined the phrase "the mental-health minute" to describe a very brief stop that he makes during the race right out on the trail. As part of his positive-reinforcement program, Buser explains: "I stop at a time when all the dogs are working at their peak, set the snowhook really secure, and pet and rub each dog from the wheelers to the leaders, telling them how proud I am of them and how good a job they are doing. By the time I am back in the sled, the dogs are barking, lunging, jumping and jerking in the harnesses to go on and get some more work done. The minute stopped translates into many minutes gained in overall traveling time."

Quick trailside pit stops are also made to inspect the dogs' feet, apply ointment and/or booties, and change the position of a dog, among other things.

THE SNACK STOP

Every hour or two, a longer break is taken to hydrate and recharge the dogs. Frozen fish is a snack favorite because it has a high water content and is usually snapped up greedily. Dogs are also given fish/fat snacks and premade patties for a quick pick-me-up.

If a snack stop occurs at a checkpoint, the driver is also required to sign in and show the checker all mandatory equipment. The musher will forgo straw and supply bags and will concentrate on feeding the team, praising and patting the animals, and gauging their general health. All of this can be accomplished in about twenty minutes; then, having remembered to sign out, it's time to hit the trail.

SUSTENANCE AND SOMNOLENCE

As they run, dogs (like other athletes) accumulate lactic acid in their muscles, which needs to be cleared out periodically during extended periods of rest. Generally, four hours is thought to be about the minimum amount of recovery time needed by a long-distance racing team. Competitors do pull off of the trail between checkpoints, in a sheltered spot if possible. Occasionally, large packs of mushers stop together.

This can have humorous results. For several years, Bill Cotter, 1987 Yukon Quest champion, had stopped at the same spot on the left side of the trail along a line of trees located just past a cabin near Ophir. His lead dog Zipper came to consider this her rightful parking place. One year, Zipper led the team in and discovered that Martin Buser had taken her space. Clearly astonished and annoyed, Zipper did not appreciate having to relocate. We humans are not the only creatures of habit!

For many reasons, however, the checkpoint is the preferred location for preparing and feeding a major meal. Upon arrival, the driver will check in, assist in inspecting the mandatory gear, select a parking place, secure the team, and immediately haul and spread straw to create a cozy nest for each tired canine. As soon as the sled stops moving, many huskies will rub their faces in the snow, shake, and have a glorious roll. Meanwhile, the weary driver may feel as though she or he has stepped off of a boat—the undulating motion of riding the runners makes the musher unused to the feel of solid ground.

*"Dog team!" a child shouted with excitement as Jeff King came into view —
the first musher to reach the McGrath checkpoint during the 1993 race.
King was also first into Nome that year.*

While resting, dogs are usually secured by their necklines only;
their tuglines are unhooked to make them more comfortable.
Obstreperous chewers and quarrelers may be secured separately. The
musher removes all booties and gently rubs down each dog. Once the
canines are happily napping, it's time for their human partner to get
busy cooking.

First, supply sacks and fuel are located (hopefully, the driver's bags
made it) and pulled on a small plastic sled from a central location to
the campsite. Next, the stove is set up and water is fetched. High on a
musher's wish list is hot water readily available at every checkpoint.
The other end of the spectrum is dipping a bucket through a hole in
the ice, then waiting while the water heats. As the water comes to a
boil, the chef chops up frozen blocks of meat (if the meat was not
shipped presliced). This is added to the water, or the boiling water
may be poured over the meat, which has been placed in a cooler.
While the meat cooks, supply bags may be sorted and the sled

repacked, or possibly runner plastic will be replaced. As soon as possible, commercial dry food, fat, and supplements are stirred into a rich soup. Cool water is mixed in until a pleasant warm temperature is achieved, and then "Voila! Dinner is served."

Some competitors believe that it is important to feed the leaders first, then work systematically back through the team. Others vary their chow-line protocol, but one nearly universal practice among Iditarod racers is to pat and sweet talk each dog while giving him his dinner. Even the most hardened trail veterans put home-loving pet owners to shame with an embarrassing outpouring of pure mush.

But there's no rest for the wicked. Though the hounds may be having haute cuisine, it's not dinnertime for their handlers yet. A second batch of food is prepared for the trail—so, more water hauling, cooking, and mixing must be done before the next meal can be stored in the thermal cooler. As this meal cooks and cools, dogs' feet are examined and ointment or booties are applied if necessary. Then the musher is required to dispose of all trash and return any unused fuel.

Finally, a few minutes remain to prepare some tasty, high-energy people food, have a brief chat with fellow competitors, consult with a vet about any concerns, and grab a quick catnap. Front-runners average about two hours of sleep per day, which works out to a forty-minute snooze during each four-hour rest stop.

Many checkpoints have heated buildings set aside for mushers to use. One possible side effect of coming in from arctic cold to the sudden warmth of such a shelter is a painful swelling of the sinuses. In *Race Across Alaska*, Libby Riddles complains that her head hurt so much from this condition that she often stayed outside rather than try to make the difficult adjustment. One time when she did sleep inside, however, Riddles set a tiny alarm clock that she had hidden in a special compartment of her fur hat so that when it rang, no one else would hear it and catch on to her game plan. Other racers ask a volunteer to awaken them, or have trained themselves mentally so that they can wake up at a predetermined time.

After a good, long rest, a dog team will be up barking and lunging to go by the time the driver steps on the runners and pulls the snowhook—or sometimes before then. Having already covered 600 miles of the Iditarod Trail, Doug Swingley stopped at the side of the trail between Ophir and Iditarod for an extended rest break. He planned to stay for a total of five hours. When Swingley had finished caring for the dogs, he fell asleep lying on his sled. Suddenly, a violent jolt awakened him, and he saw that his lead dog Bomber was

Often, as soon as they stop at a checkpoint, the dogs will have a glorious roll in the snow.

slamming into his harness, ready to go. Because only half of the allotted rest time was up, Swingley firmly told Bomber "No" and went back to sleep. But Bomber was bullheaded and pulled the team out onto the trail. He sat in the middle of it for two and one-half hours until the boss was ready. Not surprisingly, Swingley and Bomber went on to win the 1995 Iditarod.

Interestingly, as soon as a screaming, slamming team is underway, the dogs' racket ceases, and within a few moments all that can be heard is the tinkling of their lines and the voice commands of their coach.

ENJOYING THE RUN

Contrary to public perception, time spent traveling along the trail is not simply devoted to survival and strategy. Mushers actually do enjoy each other's company. Canadian competitor and author Dave Olesen explains in his book *Cold Nights, Fast Trails*: "We crave the opportunity to talk dogs, talk racing, talk strategy and contenders and breeding and sled designs. Like fanatics in every pursuit from stock cars to mountaineering, we are happiest when we are doing either one of two things—pursuing our passion, or talking about it with those who share it."

Racers joke around, have some fun, enjoy a campfire, and generally let their hair down once in a while, which is fine "as long as you don't get all romantic and dreamy and forget you're in a dog race," one particularly focused driver reckons.

In addition to appreciating direct contact with each other, mushers savor surprises tucked into their sleds and supply bags by loved ones at home. These may be notes, special snacks, a custom audio recording of favorite tunes, or other forms of support. Official Iditarod artist Jon Van Zyle faxes original cartoons to his long-time friend Martin Buser during the race.

Trail miles can also engender an appreciation of solitude and silence. Stan Smith, who finished forty-third during his rookie year in 1993 and moved up to twenty-seventh the following year, enjoyed his inaugural run and described it this way:

> We had left Puntilla Lake an hour or two after the team ahead. . . .
> As darkness descended, signs of all living things passed from
> view. The only sound was that of the sled runners and the gentle
> puffing from the dogs. What a place to be! . . . I felt the great
> inner peace and calm that only comes from being in the wild.

A STATE OF MIND

Over a thousand miles of trail . . . what's it like out there alone on the runners? Mark Chapoton, a rookie in 1993, wrote a detailed account of his experience, "No Home But The Sled," for the *Iditarod Runner* magazine. In it, he recounts going down the trail in a kind of trance: "Lots of people sometimes get in that trance when they drive a car at night, where they all of a sudden realize that they've come five miles from the last time they can remember driving. That sort of thing happened to me."

This sensation of floating in and out of reality is discussed in greater detail in a journal entry made by veteran musher Dave Olesen during his 1986 rookie run, reprinted in *Cold Nights, Fast Trails*:

An ITC sign directs mushers at a checkpoint to the location of food and water. Mushers will tend to their dogs' needs before seeing to their own.

On the Iditarod, time changes. The numbers on a clock or a watch become merely that—numbers, without the attached feeling of a day's start, middle and end. Is it 3 A.M. or 3 P.M.? Who knows? Who cares? Just run and rest, run and rest, feed them and water them and check their feet, change sled runners, tie down the load and take a nap and on and on as the miles fall away behind us. Evening comes and twilight brings the instinct to stop, make camp, build a fire, ward off the darkness and the cold. But this is the race, the Iditarod Trail. At dusk we check our headlamps, flick on the lights, follow the markers, keep moving.

It's a state of mind and after a while a state of being. Crazy? Certainly! But also somehow appealing and worthwhile in the lessons that come from it, in the state of mind I'm talking about.

Two-time champion Martin Buser looks forward to future Iditarods with faithful lead dog D-2.

Near the end of the 1994 race, between Golovin and White Mountain, Martin Buser became physically exhausted and decided to tie himself onto the sled for a quick nap. "I was mentally fine," Buser remembers. "I just needed to check out for a few minutes." Having told lead-dog D-2 that he was in charge until White Mountain, Buser entrusted the whole team to D-2 and co-leader Dave, totally relinquishing control for a period of twenty to thirty minutes. As he dozed, Buser felt "a big spirit ball" traveling with him, which he defines as "energy from all of my supporters, such as schoolkids, friends, family, and everyone else who is wishing me well." After a while, the sled stopped and Buser woke up at a checkpoint. "How long are you going to be here?" a member of the press inquired. Buser experienced a fleeting moment of doubt and panic. "Huh? How long am I going to be here? Isn't this where I have to take a mandatory eight [hour layover]?" Had infinitely reliable D-2 actually turned the team around and brought him back to Golovin? The ill-informed reporter then remembered that all mushers are required to stay eight hours in White Mountain and said, "Yeah." Flustered, but relieved, Buser said, "You guys are confusing the hell out of me."

The Iditarod state of mind is not always spooky and hypnotic. It can be a welcome relief from the relentless grind of daily life. Joe Runyan, 1989 champion, shares a lighter view. "For a lot of mushers," he relates, "the Iditarod is just a super long vacation. You're so *focused*. You've got 11 days and nothing to think about but getting down that trail. For 11 days, you don't think about taking out the garbage, or taking care of the kids." For many top competitors, mushing is a family business—all-consuming, requiring constant supervision, involving a steady influx of visitors, the phone incessantly ringing, and never a minute for yourself. The race is the reward for all of those months of training, an opportunity for the musher to do what he or she loves more than just about anything else in the world—travel in the wilderness by dog team. It's a reward for the dogs, too, because they get their master's undivided attention for a few weeks. Many people never have the chance to live out their dreams, but the individuals who run the Iditarod have made huge sacrifices of energy and resources to do so and have finally realized their goal. This sense of accomplishment sweetens the seemingly endless miles for the Iditarod adventurers out on the trail.

GRACIOUS HOSTS

The legendary hospitality extended to veterans and rookies alike as they pass through the trail's villages and towns has already been detailed. Coverage of life out on the trail would not be complete, however, without one more tale of a man who *literally* opened his home for the benefit of a needy musher.

Many Iditarod regulars competed in the 75th Anniversary All-Alaska Sweepstakes Race, held in 1983. At that time, the patented Quick Change Runner had not yet been invented, and a broken runner or damaged plastic could only be replaced by a laborious process that required the use of a drill. Arriving at the halfway point, entrant John Patten discovered that he was in this predicament. An area resident had opened his summer home for the race, and as soon as he found out about Patten's plight, he fired up his generator to provide power for a drill. When it became apparent that Patten did not have enough screws to complete the repair, this gracious soul backed the screws out of the windowsill of his cabin and donated them to the cause.

As the earth slowly tilts away from the sun, winter shadows begin to stretch out across the North Country. Each day less sunlight and less solar energy reach the land. Moisture falling through the cold air freezes into a crystalline comforter, covering the earth, tucking it in for a long winter's nap. Most forms of life respond to this roll of the planet by slowing down, conserving what little energy remains. Sap slips down into the roots of trees, beginning the long wait until spring's uprisings. Life seems to be silently settling into winter. But there is a creature whose season just begins with the first snowfall, whose life brightens into the low winter sun. This is the Alaskan sled dog, a husky who has anticipated the changing season since the first frosty nights of August.

Mary Shields
First woman to finish the Iditarod,
from her video
Season of the Sled Dog

17

Weather

In winter, when most of us draw inward, and even nature slows down, dog drivers and their frisky teams are gleefully embarking upon new adventures. The weather during the Iditarod does not always feel wintry, however. Within the two-week period of the race, temperatures can range from 45° F to -65° F. That's a variation of more than 100 degrees! Think like an onion and layer your wardrobe and you'll be ready to experience anything. Here we go.

TENNIS, ANYONE?

Warm weather on the Iditarod Trail usually comes as a surprise to mushers. Out on the sea ice near the end of the race, Diana Dronenburg (now Diana Moroney) enjoyed this phenomenon in 1990. In a postrace interview, she told Iditarod historian Nicki J. Nielsen, "The run from Shaktoolik across the ice to Koyuk was nice, not even a breeze. I only had to give the dogs breaks due to the sunshine beating down on them. What a welcome change." As Dronenburg points out, however, what is a pleasure for the musher is a hazard for the dogs. Commenting on the 40° F temperatures during the 1993 race, Bruce Lee explained to the *Anchorage Daily News* that "running dogs in this weather is like a person trying to play tennis in arctic gear." Competitors are careful to slow down their teams and give them extra rest in such unseasonably warm circumstances.

NO RAIN DELAY

In *Iditarod Classics* by Lew Freedman, Rick Swenson tells it the way he sees it:

> I think the key element in what makes the Iditarod special is that it's in Alaska, which means it may rain, it may snow. In some sporting events, if it gets cloudy, they stop. The caution flag comes out. There have been proposals that if the weather gets too bad, the race should be stopped. That's not the Iditarod. Weather is part of the deal. If you think it's too bad for your own safety, then don't go.

Occasionally, it does rain on the race. Many mushers dislike rain more than any other type of weather—including extreme cold, high winds, deep snow, heat, and even blizzards. Rain is dangerous because it saps both driver and dogs of heat and energy, yet to the inexperienced it may not seem as life-threatening as other conditions. Of course, it also soaks clothing and gear and generally demoralizes everyone. Rookies are advised to keep dry, rest the dogs, and double their own and their team's caloric intake. Fortunately, rain on the trail is rare and usually brief. Precipitation is more likely to fall in the form of snow.

QANIK, APUT, AND OTHER TYPES OF SNOW

If it's snow, the Eskimos have a word for it. "Qanik" is "snow in the air," while "aput" means "snow on the ground." Many other specialized types of snow have names, such as "aquillutaq" ("newly fallen soft snow"), "mauja" ("fluffy deep snow that fell without wind"), "qiasuqqaq" ("snow thawed and refrozen into an icy surface"), and "igluksaq" ("snow to build igloos with"). To Iditarod teams, however, snow means something that must be traveled through or over—one more offering from Mother Nature's bag of tricks.

Snow cover along the route may exceed 200 inches—a staggering sixteen feet of snow! While fresh, deep snow is difficult for the dogs to negotiate, once it's hard-packed, the number of inches under their feet is academic. Breaking trail through new snow, however, is no picnic and can cause tempers to flare.

McGrath had only received 121 inches of snow (light for them) when this picture was taken in early March 1993.

Without wind to whip it into a blizzard, running through a light snow can be enjoyable, rather like finding oneself *inside* a child's Christmas snow globe.

MERCURY, WHISKY, KEROSENE, AND DAVIS PAINKILLER

The ideal temperature for running sled dogs is generally agreed to be about minus 20° F. At some point during each year's race, however, the mercury is likely to dip much lower than that. Old-timers had an interesting method for gauging just how cold it was and what precautions should be taken as a result. In *Tracks Across Alaska*, Alastair Scott describes McQueston's thermometer:

It was common knowledge among bushmen of the time that mercury solidified at -40° (Fahrenheit *and* Centigrade, for at this

David Monson, 1988 Yukon Quest champion, once rolled in a snowbank to dry off after taking an unexpected dip in icy water.

point the two scales intersect) and that pure alcohol, such as Davis Painkiller, froze at -70° F. Certain other commodities had freezing points in between. McQueston's thermometer consisted of four small bottles and a note of recommendations placed on a shelf outside his trading post. The bottles contained mercury, whisky, kerosene and Davis Painkiller. Travellers shook the bottles in sequence. If the mercury was frozen, the note recommended not being caught out on the trail at night; if the whisky, it was unwise to leave camp; if the kerosene, a person should not leave his cabin; and if Davis Painkiller turned to ice, it was dangerous to step away from the fire.

The best antidote to cold is to dress properly and to keep well-fueled with high-energy food. David Monson utilized another technique to combat the cold when he took an unexpected dip during the 1987 Yukon Quest (the "other" 1,000-mile-plus race). On the last day of the race, Monson was running in third place when the leaders approached a frozen stream. As the first team crossed, the ice cracked. The second team passed safely but left the ice further weakened. Three's a charm: Monson and his team broke through and got soaked. Luckily, the weather had warmed up from -60° F to -40° F. In what must have looked like an act of pure lunacy, Monson threw himself into the snow and rolled around, then rose and calmly chipped the ice off of his clothing. In extremely cold temperatures, snow is very dry and will absorb moisture, so this is a good trick to know. After heating a meal for the team (which can also be dried the same way) and having a hot drink, Monson went on to finish eight minutes behind the winner.

Racers are not the only ones affected by cold weather. The January 1994 *Iditarod Runner* contains a humorous "Help Wanted" notice that offers to provide volunteers with "transportation, food, and a place to stay. The food may be cold, as is also the case with the transportation and lodging." For the most part, however, Iditarod fans and participants actively enjoy chilly Alaska and share author Gary Paulsen's delight in "the raw-cold joy of going again and again inside the diamond that is northern winter."

THE AURORA BOREALIS

March is a good time to see the aurora borealis, or northern lights, in Alaska. Thought to be produced by particles from the sun colliding with earth's atmosphere, their mysterious display is a privilege to see. Huge bands of emerald green, lemon yellow, and cherry red swirl and pulse in the night sky. They are said to make a noise like silk rustling and are considered to be a harbinger of good luck. Even no-nonsense Rick Swenson has confessed to lingering on the trail to appreciate their luminous beauty.

AN ILL WIND . . .

The strength of a gale-force wind is a power to be reckoned with. In a March 1983 *National Geographic* article, Susan Butcher spun the story of her 1982 race, including an encounter with a wicked coastal storm:

Groping from tripod to tripod, I finally reach Shaktoolik alone and with a frostbitten face.

Lucy Sukpelik welcomes us to her home. Even the dogs. It is too cold outside for them to rest easy. And I can't feed them outdoors because their pans blow away.

By morning, winds are gusting up to 80 miles an hour, piling up 30-foot drifts. Splitting wood for Lucy's stove becomes a challenge: Someone must stand downwind to catch the chunks as they fly by.

Firewood is not the only thing tossed about by tempestuous winds. Struggling through the Topkok Blowhole (a sort of Devil's Triangle of the Iditarod Trail) in 1987, Dave Olesen bucked winds up to 100 miles per hour. He remembers that "the dogs were being tossed *sideways* through the air, picked up in pairs and set down again four feet to the south." It didn't take Olesen long to decide that making camp and riding out the blast was the better part of valor.

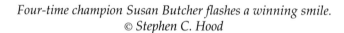

Four-time champion Susan Butcher flashes a winning smile.
© *Stephen C. Hood*

THE WINDCHILL FACTOR

When the air is still, an aura of warmth (one's own escaping radiant heat) surrounds an individual and acts as a buffer against the cold. When the wind kicks up, this protective cocoon is stripped away, leaving the unfortunate victim exposed to the arctic environment.

The windchill factor is an index of the combined effects of wind and low temperature on a person. So, for instance, on a pleasant, sunny day when the mercury reads 20° F, if you factor in a thirty-five-mile-per-hour wind, you suddenly feel as miserable as if the actual temperature were -20° F. Or if you start at most mushers' favorite temperature to run dogs, -20° F, and whip up a forty-mile-per-hour breeze, you will now experience the bone-chilling sensation of -87° F.

Early white observers of the Eskimos reported that Native peoples had many successful ways of dealing with such severe conditions. One was to sit down, back to the wind, doubled forward, and fall asleep. Only a small surface of the body was presented to the wind, and entering a state similar to hibernation, precious energy was conserved.

Faced with windchills as low as -130° F, modern Iditarod mushers adapt the best they can. Like Dave Olesen, many other competitors have made the decision to hole up for the duration. A complete cataloging is not available, but numerous human lives have undoubtedly been saved by crawling in a sled bag or into a hastily dug snow cave, which can actually get quite toasty and warm. Sled-dogs' double coat, constitution, and metabolism enable them to curl up under a blanket of snow and emerge nonchalantly stretching and yawning once the worst is over.

One dog driver claims to actually benefit from the ravages of windchill. Hearty Martin Buser boasts, "Every year I get what I call my Norton Sound Facelift. I get a new layer of skin. Instead of getting older, I get younger every time I race. Two weeks after the race, I got a layer of baby skin on my face, courtesy of the Iditarod Trail Committee with no extra charge."

BLIZZARD!

On several occasions, the Iditarod has been won by an intrepid individual who set out into the teeth of a blizzard. In 1985, Libby Riddles captured the attention of the world, changing the Iditarod from a little-known Alaskan event to an international media fest.

Libby Riddles won the 1985 Iditarod and received the coveted Leonhard Seppala Humanitarian Award for outstanding care of her winning team. © Jeff Schultz/ Alaska Stock Images

As Riddles pulled into the coastal village of Shaktoolik with a lead of several hours, the chase pack was hot on her heels. A temperature near zero and winds gusting to seventy miles per hour created a windchill of -56° F. Darkness was approaching as Riddles deliberated what to do. Wavering, she telephoned mushing partner Joe Garnie for advice. "Get going," he said. "Get your butt out of town."

In her book *Race Across Alaska*, Riddles reveals the turning point:

I made myself get ready to leave, not believing I would. I packed the new sled and got all my dried clothes from the Takaks' and booted the dogs, all fifty-six paws. When everything was done, there was nothing left to do but leave. Still I hesitated. Then [Lavon] Barve rolled into the checkpoint. The wind whipped snow around him and his boots crunched on the cold snow as he walked up. His face was raw from the wind.

"What are you doing?" he asked. "If it's anything like what I just came through, it's impossible."

That set me. "Impossible?" This was the whole point of all the work and energy I'd put into the past five years. Everything aimed toward one thing: Iditarod. I lifted the snow hook.

"Okay, gang. Let's go."

I allowed only one thought: to keep my lead at all costs, taking it inch by inch if necessary. Winning the Iditarod was the dream that had driven me since I first raced. It was the dream that had rousted me out of a warm bed on many a dark, cold winter morning and dragged me over the tedious miles of training. My goal was attainable now, and so long as I was capable of putting one foot in front of the other, no storm was going to prevent me from achieving it.

Having formed this resolve, Riddles clawed her way along the trail from one marker to the next. Visibility, she remarked, "was something like you'd find in a blender full of powdered milk, only this powdered milk was frozen and sharp and cut your face." She would keep the marker behind her in sight until she located the next one. If she couldn't see it, she'd hook the team within view of the previous stake and walk ahead of them until she was sure which direction to go. Then she'd retrace her steps to the sled, pull the hook, and guide the leaders forward, repeating the process stake to stake until it became too dark to see. "Nothing else existed in the world, just the team and me in this sea of a storm," Riddles remembers.

When darkness fell, Riddles made camp next to a trail stake. After feeding each dog a frozen whitefish, she removed everything from the sled except her heavy parka and sleeping bag. Laying the sled crosswise to the wind, she stacked her gear on its leeward side and climbed into the sled bag. Stopping often to warm her fingers against her skin, she removed her damp jacket and bibs, wriggled into her warm parka, and finally burrowed down into the sleeping bag. All of this took place inside a 5' x 2' x 2' sled bag!

Twelve hours later, Riddles emerged ready to go. After layering on every piece of dry clothing that she had, she turned to the dogs. Riddles explains:

When I looked in the direction where the dogs should have been, I saw only a blank white expanse of drifts. The dogs were nowhere to be seen. I leaned into the wind and plowed over to where I had left them the night before.

"Brownie? Where are you, old boy? Come on, Sister. Dugan? Up you go, Duke." As I called their names, they began standing up through the snow, ghostly creatures rising out of the ground. They shook and smiled and stretched happily despite the weather.

Another whitefish snack and the outfit was in motion. Later in the day, Riddles realized that she needed to force herself to eat. Choosing the most high-energy snacks available, she washed a Norwegian chocolate bar down with a bottle of seal oil, followed by a frozen fruit-juice chaser. This time the team ate fat-rich slabs of lamb.

Throughout its history, the Iditarod has only been "frozen" (temporarily stopped) three times. There were two race freezes in 1985, the year that Libby Riddles won. And just after Vern Halter finished eleventh (shown here), the 1993 race was suspended due to severe weather.

Continuing on, all went well for a while until suddenly there were no more trail markers. This section of sea ice was pale green glare ice and looked newly formed. Riddles' leader Sister refused to head right as instructed. "Gee, Sister," Riddles yelled. "Aw, come on, Sister, give me a break. Gee! You stubborn old rattlesnake!" At Sister's mercy due to the slick ice, Riddles kept veering left. Even swearing didn't help matters. In a few moments, she glimpsed something dark in the distance. Her stubborn lead dog had delivered her directly to an Iditarod Trail stake. An apology was quickly made as Riddles realized that an open lead of water must have carried a section of the trail away, leaving the new glare ice frozen in its place.

The rest of the trail to Koyuk was uneventful. Leaving there, the lead that Riddles had fought so hard to retain enabled her to become the first woman musher to win the Iditarod. As she passed under the arch, a reporter reached a microphone to her and asked, "How does it feel, Libby?" Her famous reply, "What I feel is, if I died right now, it'd be okay" seems to sum it all up. Riddles was awarded the Leonhard Seppala Humanitarian Award for giving her dogs outstanding care throughout the entire 1985 race.

I'll say one thing: you finish this race and you feel like you could spit in a tiger's eye.

Terry Adkins,
who retired from Iditarod competition in 1994
after running the race twenty times

18

Dangers of the Trail

The variety of obstacles and challenges that racers encounter along the Iditarod Trail is almost beyond belief. Anchorage resident Joseph W. Albrecht eloquently expresses fans' awed admiration when he notes that, "For many of us onlookers, the annual classic is the benchmark for endurance, skill, and courage by which all other contests are judged."

WHAT'S THAT MASSIVE BULK ON THE TRAIL?

A number of enormous wild animals live in Alaska, and many of them can be seen right here, standing in the middle of the trail in front of you!

Moose
Certainly the most dreaded sight is that of an unyielding moose. Unfortunately, deep snow makes browsing an ordeal for moose, and they seek the path of least resistance: the hard-packed surface of roads, railroad tracks, snow-machine thoroughfares, and often, the Iditarod Trail.

The most serious moose incident involved Susan Butcher near the beginning of the 1985 race. Butcher was running what she considered to be the best dog team that she had ever entered. As a result of a moose attack, however, Butcher was forced to scratch. Libby Riddles claimed the victory in 1985, taking her place in Iditarod history by becoming the first woman to win. Race watchers wonder whether the outcome might have been different if Susan Butcher's team hadn't met a moose on the trail that fateful night.

Buffalo

During his rookie run in 1990, Larry Munoz saw about fifteen buffalo just before the Farewell Burn. His team gave chase, and because he was on glare ice, he couldn't stop them. Instinctively, he reached for his gun but thought better of it because there were so many of the glowering giants. "I felt like a cowboy on a dogsled," Munoz laughed. His team came within ten yards of the behemoths before they turned off of the trail. "It was a little spooky," he confessed.

Caribou

Governor Hickel's son Bob also ran his rookie race in 1990. He had a close encounter with caribou. Two of them were standing in the trail and Hickel's wheel dogs either couldn't or wouldn't stop until the team was only about seven feet away. Remembering his stare-down with the ungainly ungulates, Hickel vows, "I'll never forget looking at their wild eyes."

Canine Cousins

Imagine riding the runners, passing through a heavily wooded section of the trail. Almost imperceptibly, you become aware that you are not alone. Muffled footfalls, the snapping of a twig in the undergrowth, an increased alertness among the dogs, and finally a glimpse of gleaming eyes: a pack of wolves is pacing your team.

Wolves have been known to do this but seem to be merely curious. Perhaps they are just trying to figure out what their canine cousins are up to.

MOTHER NATURE'S ARSENAL

Television commentator Sam Posey, who covered the race for ABC's *Wide World of Sports* for many years, tersely expressed the paradox of battling nature when he observed that "the wilderness threatens, yet beckons" as it "casts a spell" upon the mushers.

Lovey Dovey

Not all problems with animals on the trail are caused by wildlife. Many a musher has looked on in dismay as a besotted male dog finally manages to mate with an irresistible bitch. This brings everything to a screeching halt for about twenty minutes until the lovebirds are through. Drivers try to separate females in heat from their lascivious teammates, but it's hard to stop a determined dog. This wouldn't be a problem if the females were spayed, but professional racers are reluctant to give up the option of breeding a successful animal. So it makes life just a bit more exciting.

A Wake-Up Call

Mushers hate sweepers, i.e., tree branches that hang over the trail. Volunteers and locals at the checkpoints are often aghast to see the bloody noses and bruised visages of drivers who have lost a battle with a solid branch "sweeping" down low over the trail. All it takes is one moment of inattention. Near McGrath in the 1990 race, Mike Owens recollects, "A sweeper hit me right in the headlight. Nearly cleaned my clock out. A wake-up call. It nearly knocked me out."

Usually the musher is the one who has problems with trees. Not so for Richard Burmeister back in 1979. Having been raised and trained in Nome, Burmeister's team was accustomed to treeless tundra. On the first day of the race, his poor lead dog nearly lost control because she had never run through a forest before. Canine claustrophobia, perhaps. She had to be dropped, but the rest of Burmeister's dogs adapted and went on to finish forty-first.

Dangling over the Canyon

Lavon Barve, 1994 Yukon Quest champion, was leading the race in 1985 near the infamous Happy River Canyon when his leaders missed a hard left turn in the trail. Almost immediately, Barve noticed that there was no sign of a trail in front of him. He turned his team around and continued on the correct route. The next musher to approach the tricky turn, Burt Bomhoff, was not so lucky. His dogs followed the scent of the previous team but continued beyond the point where they had turned around, until suddenly Bomhoff's dogs began disappearing from view over the cliff. Fortunately, Bomhoff was able to pull his dogs back up. Bomhoff took a few minutes to chop the branches off of a spruce tree and build a fence to block the false trail. "I thought somebody would get killed," he said.

On Thin Ice

Into a tree, over a cliff, or through the ice, perhaps? Pick your poison. Susan Butcher's legendary lead dog Granite justified his reputation during the 1984 Iditarod as her team crossed Shaktoolik Lagoon near Unalakleet. Abruptly finding themselves on a section of unstable ice, the dogs became spooked when the ice began billowing beneath them. Realizing that it was merely a matter of minutes before they fell through, Butcher forced herself to remain calm and quietly gave Granite the command "Haw" ("Go left"), because that looked like the most direct route to shore. Granite responded instantly, veering the team left with him. With waves of ice rolling behind them, Granite reached land and quickly clawed his way up. Just as he gained a good footing, the sled, Butcher, and the rearmost dogs fell into the frigid water. Granite's tenacity and momentum enabled the rest of the team to emerge from the sea, soaking wet but safe and grateful for his decisive leadership.

My Boots Overfloweth

When lakes and streams freeze, the shallow sections become solid; however, underground springs continue to flow. Eventually, they well up through the ice barrier and spread across the surface above. "Overflow" is the term used to describe the water, saturated snow, or slush that floods an otherwise frozen body of water. Overflow can result in dropped dogs and frozen feet, not to mention iced-up sled runners. Consequently, competitors are constantly on the lookout. When they do take a dip, drivers are careful to dry dogs and themselves thoroughly. The danger of overflow is not taken lightly.

It Rained Ash

On Sunday, March 4, 1990, Mount Redoubt, an active volcano located nearly 100 miles south of Anchorage, erupted. Ash rained down on the mushers and their teams, who were now halfway through the second day of the race. Drifting from six to eighteen inches, the coarse, glassy ash wreaked havoc in many ways. Dogs dipping for snow ingested ash instead, paws required extra protection from the abrasive grit, drivers who wore contacts risked ruining them, while goggles worn to keep off the blowing particles became indelibly scratched when wiped clear. Even snow machines stopped

In addition to thin ice, open water is a danger of river travel. A good lead dog can take a team and musher around such obstacles.

running when the fine dust plugged their engines. Hopefully, it will be many years before this volatile mountain spews forth during the Iditarod again.

Whiteout

Mother Nature threatens Iditarod volunteers and race supporters, not just the competitors. Trail vets, ITC personnel, checkers, cooks, dropped-dog caretakers, news reporters and cameramen, and professional photographers all "fly over some very big country in some very small airplanes," as a recent *Iditarod Runner* magazine observed.

On the ninth day of the 1992 race, volunteer pilot Chris McDonnell flew Iditarod photographer Jeff Schultz from Koyuk toward White Mountain so that Schultz could shoot race leader Martin Buser's arrival at the checkpoint. As Schultz says, "It was the 20th annual running of the Iditarod Trail Sled Dog Race, my 12th year in a row to cover the action of this magnificent, mystifying race between men and dog[s] struggling through God's most beautiful, treacherous and unforgiving wilderness called Alaska."

Just past Golovin, the flight ceiling became so low that the pilot began using small shrubs on the ground for reference. Suddenly, there was a total whiteout. The next thing they knew, McDonnell and Schultz were standing on bloody ground outside the aircraft. Somehow, in spite of serious injuries, both men had managed to crawl out of the tiny plane. Operating on autopilot, they set up an overnight camp complete with sleeping bags, pads, and ground cloth. McDonnell thought that he had broken both of his ankles, and he had a gash on his scalp that nearly encircled his head. Schultz's face had smashed into the back of the pilot's seat even though he was wearing a seat belt.

Having confirmed that the emergency locator transmitter (ELT) was activated, Schultz began to radio for help. He called all channels that he thought might be monitored, including the Iditarod Air Force channel, the emergency channel used by commercial aircraft, and local village channels. In his story, "On Friends, Human Kindness, God and Survival," published in the June 1992 *Iditarod Runner*, Schultz writes:

> I tried "mayday" on all of them. I kept repeating over and over, "This is Piper Super Cub 7685 Delta. We have crash-landed on Golovin Bay five miles beyond Golovin towards White Mountain. Pilot Chris McDonnell and passenger Jeff Schultz. We have injuries; we need snow machines to come from Golovin to rescue us. Please help."

The plane had gone down between 4 and 5 P.M.; at about 7 to 7:30 P.M., a Bering Air commercial pilot named Will answered Schultz's distress calls. He informed Schultz that he would make repeated passes over the area, and when the aircraft's strobe lights became visible or the sound of its engine was audible, Schultz should radio back immediately. Then Will could fix the crash position on his long-range navigation (LORAN) device and send snow machines from Golovin directly to the scene. Using this technique, Will circled overhead until the Golovin villagers arrived, pried the radio out of Schultz's reluctant grasp, and assured the pilot that they now had things under control.

A dedicated photographer to the last, Schultz tossed two cameras into the backpack that contained his gold mine of exposed film and asked the snow machiners to grab his main equipment bag. He lay down on a nine-foot-long utility sled, which villagers use to haul various supplies

Despite a dreadful plane crash and serious injuries in 1992, official Iditarod photographer Jeff Schultz was back in the finish chute on Front Street in 1993. Schultz's irrepressible cheerfulness, humility, and willingness to help others in need make him an inspiration to those who know him.

behind snow machines, and endured the bumpy ride to Golovin. McDonnell and Schultz were then airlifted to Anchorage's Providence Hospital.

McDonnell had surgery the morning after the crash; his injuries included a fractured ankle, a sprained ankle, a broken wrist, and a laceration on almost the entire circumference of his scalp. He says that he has now recovered fully, and that his plane has been salvaged and will fly again.

Five days later, Schultz had two surgeries. Six permanent titanium plates, held by twenty-four titanium screws and a wire, were implanted in his face. In spite of all this, Schultz flew the trail again in 1993 and continues to do so. His irrepressible cheerfulness, humility, and willingness to help others in need make Jeff Schultz an inspiration to those who know him.

MECHANICAL MALADIES

According to Tim Jones' account of the 1979 Iditarod, *The Last Great Race*, sixteen mushers broke the brush bow of their sleds on the same tree, which was protruding from the snow on a tight bend in the trail near Gene and June Leonard's cabin at Finger Lake. Equipment failure during the race is a given. Competitors carry tools and spare parts so that they can improvise a repair on the trail, then try to fix the problem at the next checkpoint. Sometimes a new sled has to be shipped in, delaying the driver. Major wrecks may result in a scratch.

Errant equipment can cause serious injury. During a wild descent of Happy River Canyon, Libby Riddles' sled somersaulted. While the sled was upside down, the snowhook flew loose, slashed Riddles' jacket, and slammed into her hand. One knuckle did not return to normal size until a year later.

A manmade maelstrom engulfed Lavon Barve in 1990. A network news crew hovering in a helicopter was photographing Jerry Austin just ahead of Barve, and the downdraft from the rotor simulated blizzard conditions. The Iditarod press really do make an impact on the race!

OPERATOR ERROR

In *Cold Nights, Fast Trails*, Dave Olesen quotes an old maxim that the FAA uses to admonish new pilots to stay alert: "Good judgment comes from experience. Experience comes from poor judgment." Iditarod racers are certainly not immune to this problem.

You Snooze, You Lose

Rookies Jim Wood and Bob Hickel were traveling together during the 1990 race. At 2:00 A.M., Hickel abruptly stopped on the trail in front of Wood. When Wood asked why, Hickel said sheepishly, "I'm falling asleep." After the race, Wood reminisced about how "they stopped and talked a while under the full moon at minus 40 degrees, wondering what their friends were doing while they were spending $40,000 sitting out in the cold falling asleep in midsentence."

Patty Friend didn't stop soon enough in 1979. She nodded off while riding the sled, then *fell* off. Her errant dog team ran for two hours before they became tired and lay down for a nap. Eventually, driver and dogs were reunited.

Falling asleep can have dire consequences even if you do manage to stay on the sled. Many parts of the Iditarod Trail are used heavily by other types of traffic, and hard-packed local offshoots may confuse a team's leaders. Without direction from the driver, the dogs may stray from the proper path. Sometime later, the musher wakes up and discovers that the team is lost. Being lost in the wilderness is a spooky experience. Competitors and their canines feel frustrated, disgusted, and demoralized. It's a big price to pay for a little shuteye.

Escapees

Bill Peele, a fifty-five-year-old pharmaceuticals businessman from North Carolina, was changing the position of one of his dogs near the Farewell Burn in 1991, when the opportunistic pooch slipped away. Having accumulated three years' worth of vacation and borrowed $30,000 from his retirement fund in order to run the Iditarod, Peele was not about to give up easily. He spent hours calling Charlie, coaxing and tempting him with treats, to no avail. Finally, Peele drove the remainder of his team to Nikolai (the next checkpoint), arranged for their care, and hired villagers to drive him back to the spot where he had last seen Charlie. Against all odds, he found the recalcitrant animal and was allowed to continue racing. His team now intact, Peele forged ahead to Grayling, seven checkpoints farther on, where he ended up scratching from the race.

The situation was more serious when Joe Garnie lost his entire team near the end of that same race. Garnie tells what happened in Lew Freedman's *Iditarod Classics*:

> It was getting dark and starting to snow, but it wasn't storming. I got to a fork in the trail and it was obvious that they went back together, but I was feeling good because I was in striking distance of fifth place or fourth. I wanted to be on the hard, main trail, the one with markers, and I ran down there to take a look and I kept going a little farther and a little farther. And I hadn't put my snow hook in. When I came back, my team was barreling down the other trail.
>
> Losing my team was a screwup. I had about fifteen different lies dreamed up by the time I got to Elim, but I had to tell the truth. I just didn't put my snow hook in. . . .

Eighteen hours later, after walking in search of his dogs and sleeping overnight under drifted snow, Garnie was able to wave down a snow machiner and find his team. He finished twenty-third. That one little omission—planting the snowhook—cost him nearly twenty places and could have cost him his life.

On a lighter note, Libby Riddles enacted a Monty Python-esque scene when her dogs departed McGrath in 1985. She had changed sleds, transferred her gear into the new sled bag, put booties on the dogs, filled her pockets with snacks, installed a new headlamp battery, and even selected a cassette tape for her Walkman™. Ready for action, she stood on the runners and the crazed team charged forward—without Riddles or the sled! In the process of switching sleds, she had neglected to fasten the gangline carabiner to the sled bridle. Luckily, a fellow musher apprehended the runaways and assisted Riddles in hooking them up.

The Code of the Trail

Race fans are surprised to learn how often dog drivers lose their teams. In the first half of the 1992 race alone, Joe Garnie, Loren Weaver, Joe Redington, Sr., Beverly Masek, Susan Butcher, and Claire Philip (now Claire Alezra) all lost their teams. There have been a number of instances in which teams were lost and mushers helped other competitors in need. This is the unwritten "code of the trail." "Life and death take precedence over sport," Lew Freedman notes. "You can't dial 911 most places along the Iditarod Trail. In many cases, mushers only have each other to rely on." Freedman summarizes this philosophy by quoting long-time Iditarod driver Jerry Austin, who claims, "There's not much choice in the matter. Anybody alone in Alaska has got a problem. You're not supposed to be alone out there. I would always stop. Even five miles out of Nome."

TOUGH LUCK

Even if you stay alert and exercise good judgment, danger still lurks along the trail. Often, Lady Luck is conspicuously absent.

Trail Travail

In his 1914 book *Ten Thousand Miles with a Dogsled*, Archdeacon Hudson Stuck frequently discusses the importance of a good trail to the mushers who lived in the early years of this century. An unbroken trail required snowshoeing, whereas the passage of even two or three teams gave a "bottom" to a trail. Parties traveling in opposite directions

gave each other the "gift of a trail" when they met. Sometimes, however, drivers would delay their departure until another team set out—
perhaps the monthly mail run or a missionary—in order to avoid the
arduous task of trailbreaking.

The Iditarod Trail Committee creates and marks a trail for the racers,
but bad luck can intervene. Occasionally, competitors get so far ahead
of the rest of the pack that they outrun the ITC trailbreakers, or a snowstorm may drift over a recently packed trail. You may also remember
that Libby Riddles found that a whole section of trail had been carried
out to sea on an ice floe! A pair of snowshoes is mandatory equipment
for modern mushers so that they can assume the role of lead dog when
necessary, as Archdeacon Stuck did all those years ago.

Stray Supplies

The trail may be in, but your supplies may not be. Given the volume of food-drop bags shipped by the Iditarod Air Force, it really is
miraculous that most mushers find their sacks waiting for them at
each checkpoint. Unfortunately, however, the law of averages dictates
that it will one day be your turn. Which bag is missing? The one with
your dogs' food? You may have to borrow some. The one with your
headlamp batteries? Maybe you can follow another driver whose
light is on. Your spare socks and boot liners? Welcome to the cold foot
club. Usually such losses are merely aggravating, but they do disrupt
race routines, may cause serious delays, and may leave competitors
ill-prepared for the trail. Hopefully, whatever you need will be safely
ensconced in your next food drop.

Canine Contagion

Another checkpoint complication is canine virus. Like children
bringing home sickness from school, dogs from one part of the state
(or from other states) may become ill when exposed to new viruses as
they congregate. There isn't much that can be done to prevent this
except to vaccinate the dogs religiously and travel to other areas during the training season. Dog caretakers and Iditarod veterinarians are
on hand at every checkpoint to lavish love on any sick pups.

Inexplicable Collapse

Sudden illness can strike the mushers, too. In 1989, Jamie Nelson
was following fellow rookie Mike Madden when he abruptly fell off
of his sled. As she examined him, she was joined by three other rookies (Mitch Brazin, Linwood Fiedler, Kathy Halverson) and veteran

racer Jerry Austin, all of whom pulled off the trail to help. Unable to determine the nature of his illness, they built a fire, wrapped Madden in a number of sleeping bags, administered fluids, and sent two of the drivers ahead with Madden's team to the checkpoint of Iditarod to get medical assistance.

Twenty-five miles from Iditarod, with a temperature of -25° F, the dedicated group fretted over Madden. Slipping in and out of delirium, he would say, "Put me in the building," or "I'll have the coffee now," when, of course, there was neither building nor coffee. Toward morning, a fifth rookie, Bernie Willis, joined the rescue crew, relieving the now-exhausted three on duty.

Finally, a helicopter brought Austin and Fiedler back with a doctor. Kathy Halverson expressed her relief in a chapter of Lew Freedman's *Iditarod Classics*:

> The doctor who touched down with the helicopter said, "Well, Mike, thank goodness for friends like this because another two hours and you wouldn't have been here." Another two hours and he would have been . . . gone.
>
> By Unalakleet, we heard Mike was OK. [He was successfully treated in Anchorage for salmonella poisoning.] He was at the finish line with tears in his eyes to thank each of the people who helped him. He knew exactly who we were, and he and his father were there to greet us.
>
> They had a beautiful Iditarod Good Samaritan Award made for us. And the other mushers voted to give us the Good Sportsmanship Award. I think what we did and the feeling we have means more to us than some rookie-of-the-year award.

Each one of the so-called "Selfless Six" finished the 1989 race in positions ranging from twenty-second to thirty-second. Mike Madden has since returned and garnered two top-twenty finishes.

A "Ruff" Experience

Before the start of the 1995 Iditarod, Doug Swingley put in his extended-wear contacts, assuming that he would be able to wear them comfortably until after the finish of the race. On his way to Safety, Swingley's right eye started bothering him. After checking his eye, he decided that he must have lost a contact. This is a major problem, because, as Swingley notes, without corrective eyewear he's "as blind as a bat." Swingley had a spare pair of contacts easily accessible—

Doug Swingley, 1995 champion, is a fifth-generation Montanan. He started mushing as a result of helping his younger brother Greg prepare a dog team to compete in the John Beargrease Sled Dog Marathon. "Dog mushing is a giant vortex and I stood too close to the edge and got sucked in," Doug remarks.

but they were frozen solid. Was it worth it to stop at Safety long enough to warm them up and put them in? Because he was on the verge of winning his first Iditarod (in record time), Swingley decided to make do with his emergency glasses. As you can imagine, wearing glasses in arctic weather poses a problem. With his warm fur ruff up, Swingley's glasses fogged, which was a distraction. When he dropped his hood, however, he became cold. Alternately frosting his glasses and freezing himself, Swingley made it from Safety to Nome, becoming the first Iditarod champion from the Lower 48. Shortly after he finished, Swingley's wife Nelda examined his eye (which was still bothering him) to see if the contact had slid up under his eyelid. She successfully removed the cause of Swingley's discomfort—a long piece of wolverine hair that had worked loose from the ruff of the parka and encircled his right eye.

Crash and Burn

Another dramatic moment occurred when 1991 rookie Chris Converse rolled his sled down a switchback in Happy River Canyon. He didn't realize until he was a little farther down the trail that his sled was on fire. Flambé, anyone? Apparently, the impact of the crash had been forceful enough to ignite Converse's box of wooden matches. Luckily, the fire was contained by the plastic bag in which the matches were stored.

Boozehounds

Suspension of disbelief is also required for the next anecdote. In 1991, Nome's own Matt Desalernos came charging into the finish chute in seventh place, just ahead of DeeDee Jonrowe. At the last second, his team swerved off the trail and headed straight for the door of the historic Board of Trade Saloon. Although the maneuver cost him $2,000 (the difference in pay between eighth and seventh place), Desalernos took it in stride, quipping, "Nome dogs."

Pesky Pups

Other people's dogs can wreak havoc, too. Six beautiful black puppies chased Lavon Barve out of Unalakleet during the 1991 race. They stayed with his team, nipping at his lead dogs' heels for nearly an hour. Near Shaktoolik, reindeer herder Paul Sagoonick chased them off and excused their behavior with the observation that, "They're pups, just like kids. They see something exciting, they try to get in on it."

A Buffalo Buss and a Confusing Kiss

According to the June 1994 *Iditarod Runner*:

> In 1965, eighteen bison (buffalo) were relocated to . . . the Farewell Burn . . . . The herd has been maintained at between two and three hundred since 1972. Mushers have been astonished when taking a nap in this area to wake up to a buffalo kissing their cheek. The animals seem to be curious about the mushers and their teams, but to date have never caused a musher any problems.

A kiss nearly caused Mary Shields a very big problem as she prepared to take a twelve-dog team out for a run. Husband John gave

Mary a goodbye kiss, which her eager dogs misinterpreted as the smacking noise that she often uses to start the team instead of a verbal command. A desperate leap saved Shields a long walk.

IF I DIED TOMORROW

Wild animals, the caprices of nature, equipment woes, misjudgment, and bad luck—the Iditarod is fraught with peril. One sponsor claims in an advertisement that the Iditarod "is perhaps the only sporting event where the desire to win is eclipsed only by the will to survive."

Iditarod mushers are a hardy breed, though, and Terry Adkins speaks for most of them when he says, "You forget the frostbite and you forget the heartaches and you just remember the good parts. If I died tomorrow, I'd have had a full life just running the Iditarod."

A note to rookies: Enter a long race with three goals. Winning is not one of them. Try to finish the race. Learn as much as you can. And enjoy yourself, your dogs, and the magnificent country through which you travel.

Miki and Julie Collins
Dog mushers and authors of
Dog Driver

19

Strategies and Ploys

From serious attention to training and technical details to devious psychological ploys, competitors pull out all the stops during the Iditarod. Brace yourself for anything—you're in the big leagues now.

EQUIPMENT

Design and Quality

The Iditarod has its share of technophiles. These drivers are almost obsessive about having the latest innovations in equipment design and materials. If the budget allows, purchasing the highest-quality gear and experimenting with new products can give a musher an edge in the race. When your arch-rival is breathing down your neck as you sprint along the coast, every little advantage counts.

Sailing and Rolling along the Iditarod Trail

Between Kaltag and Unalakleet, an area famous for its wind, imaginative Martin Buser raised a makeshift sail during the 1992 Iditarod by inverting a wind parka over a set of ski poles. The result of this experiment pleased him so much that he had a sail with a window custom-made for the 1993 race. By 1994, Rick Swenson had added a sail to his list of optional equipment. Although not yet forbidden by the rules, Buser's sail was banned by the race marshal during the 1995 Iditarod. A rule revision addressing this issue is likely to be made.

In 1994, Iditarod champion Jeff King created a stir when he announced to the press that he had a secret weapon that would be revealed at the Farewell Burn. As it turned out, the Burn had good snow cover for a change and King didn't need the controversial invention until he hit the barren trail along the coast. There he attached wheels to his sled, just in front of and behind where he stands on the runners. The race marshal consulted the rules, which specify that drivers must use "some type of sled or toboggan." This still did not resolve the question until *Webster's Dictionary* was invoked and clarified that a "sled" is "a vehicle on runners for moving over snow, ice, etc." No mention of wheels. Oh well—back to the drawing board.

There seems to be a consensus among competitors that innovation is necessary and desirable, but boundaries are needed. After all, this is the Iditarod Trail Sled *Dog* Race and should be won on the basis of mushing dogs. Raising your jacket on ski poles may be resourceful and clever, but hoisting a forty-foot parasail and loading the entire team into the sled for a ride up the coast would not be sled-dog racing. A consistent standard for evaluating such contrivances should be devised, which would respect the urge to improvise while preserving the quintessential nature of dog mushing.

Night Vision

Most Iditarod competitors utilize the brightness and efficiency of a headlamp when running in the dark. Others, however, have excellent night vision and prefer not to compromise their peripheral view. Switching off your light also increases the stealth factor, which may enable you to slip past the competition undetected. Near the end of the 1983 Iditarod, Rick Mackey turned off his headlamp and passed arch-rival Eep Anderson in the night. Mackey won the 1983 race, joining his father Dick as the first (and only) parent/child champions in Iditarod history.

TRAINING

Dog Barns

Champion Jeff King swears by the benefits of dog barns. He expounded on the virtues of a barn in the January/February 1994 issue of *Mushing* magazine:

*Jeff King's dog barn has pens built into it that are used for confining bitches
in heat and mothers with young pups.*

I do think that having a dog barn has really helped my training. The dogs are fully capable of maintaining body heat outside
at 30 below, but if you let those dogs sleep indoors at 50 degrees
after a training run, more bodybuilding is going to occur, and
they are more ready to go the next morning. The barn enabled
me to build better mentally and physically prepared dogs.

In addition to bringing dogs in after training runs, the barn is used to
house huskies that may need a little extra care or attention. It is also a
convenient place to conduct veterinary examinations and administer
any necessary treatment.

Stake Training
Progress along the trail in blizzard conditions slows to a stake-to-
stake search. To prepare for this contingency, mushers may want to
replicate this process in training. Stakes are set up at similar intervals
to the Iditarod, and leaders are taught to take "Gee" and "Haw" commands to find them. A little experience at home can provide invaluable confidence on the trail.

System, Order, Organization

In *Racing Alaskan Sled Dogs,* Bill Vaudrin quotes 1967 Iditarod Centennial participant Bill Sturdevant, who maintains that "If you intend to be a winner, self-discipline must permeate your lifestyle. This takes dedication. You're going to have to have rules to live by. System. Order. Organization. You can't be slipshod in anything that has to do with dogs, in your choice of handlers or collars, what time you feed, in your shots, watering, worming or feeding, or any other aspect of care or preparation."

Computerizing mushing records, lists, and files has been an enormous aid in this regard. Strategy is not something that you save for the race; it pervades every aspect of a musher's life.

A Robot at the Checkpoints

Astute prerace planning can result in time savings during the Iditarod. The racer establishes a rest stop agenda and practices it. Year-to-year experience also helps. Eventually, some mushers become so efficient that it psyches out the competition. Rick Mackey, 1983 champion, describes his colleague, four-time victor Susan Butcher, in action: "Bang, bang, bang, she wastes no time. Susan is like a robot at the checkpoints. There's no goofing around, I'll tell you."

Drop Details

Five-time champion Rick Swenson also excels at organization. In his book *The Secrets of Long Distance Training and Racing,* Swenson makes several suggestions about preparing food drops. Send four lighter bags instead of two heavy ones. Then, if one gets lost, you will still be able to function. Use clear liners so that you can find what you need easily. Keep a notebook and pencil with you listing the contents of each bag, and drop a label inside each one. Such forethought can eliminate many trail headaches.

NBA Finals

Once a musher has made a commitment to a major race strategy, such as feeding a different dog food, taking new equipment, or seeing the results of a season's worth of alternate training techniques, the die is cast. Joe Runyan, 1989 champion, admits, "That's frustrating. In many sports, you get another weekend to try it again. I love watching the NBA finals. They lose one game, they get time to make an adjustment for the next game. In the Iditarod, you have to wait a year to make an adjustment."

Jeff King brings dogs into the barn after training runs.

The Minor Leagues

Occasionally, drivers will run young dogs with them or have a handler enter a second team consisting of yearlings in order to build an experienced Iditarod team. One proponent of this plan is two-time champion Martin Buser, who has utilized both methods. In an interview with *Mushing* magazine, he explains: "I had yearling teams finish the Iditarod to give these young dogs experience without pushing them too hard. . . . I think they need to be in the minor leagues before they go into the major leagues." This strategy seems to be spreading: in 1995, competitors and their assistants running a second team included Swenson/Milne, Buser/Pattaroni, King/Lyrek, Osmar/Adkins, Halter/Whiton, Austin/Westman, and Butcher(not racing)/Church.

How Good Can I Feel?

Ultimately, the goal of training is to enable the musher to face any challenge offered by the trail. Though you expect to enjoy it, adventure is something that you prepare for totally. If your equipment, training, and organization are all up to snuff, you may actually enjoy taking it as it comes during the race. The long-range objective is to see "How good can the dogs and I feel when we get to Nome?"

TRAIL DETAILS

Trail Scents

Burt Bomhoff's dogs got off the trail and ended up in a precarious situation as a result of following another team's tracks (see "Dangers of the Trail"). Usually, though, drivers consider it helpful for their huskies to have the scent of a previous team by which to navigate. In fact, competitors will choose to run in second or third place for this reason, deferring the lead to others.

Midnight to 6 A.M.

As discussed in "The Run/Rest Cycle," various stratagems are employed to ensure that dogs are well-rested and enthusiastic about racing. Reflecting on his 1993 victory, Jeff King noted, "I was getting into the checkpoints at noon, and consistently the teams trying to catch me were having to run one or two hours in the hotter part of the day. If I can, I don't want to travel between midnight and 6 A.M. I know people and dogs shut down metabolically at that time of day. Ideally, I want to run between 6 A.M. and noon, and from 6 P.M. to midnight." Other run/rest tactics are covered in the "Major Strategies" section below.

A Photographic Memory?

Running the 1985 race, Libby Riddles noticed that Rick Swenson always seemed to find the best place to rest between checkpoints—a nice sheltered spot out of the wind, with water available nearby. Is he gifted with a photographic memory? Perhaps, but it's more probable that his decades of trail experience and good notes enable him to remember the location of that perfect campsite.

As Fast as the Slowest Dog

If you count the number of dogs on each team at the start of the Iditarod, you will find that most drivers leave Anchorage with a sixteen-dog string. The advantages of a big team are greater power, more dogs from which to choose later when reducing the dog count (sometimes called "taking the bench along with you"), and, as the race reaches the halfway point and beyond, the intimidation factor ("How come they're still running sixteen dogs and I only have . . . ?"). The down side is that sixteen dogs have sixty-four paws to inspect, salve, and boot. Each dog also requires a time investment for strawing, massaging, feeding, and cleanup. As the competitors reach the coast, an old mushing maxim comes to mind: "You're only as fast as your slowest dog." Taking that into account, dogs are often dropped near the end of the race simply because they can't maintain the pace of the rest of the team. Mushers have finished the race with as many dogs as they started with; but if you count the number of dogs on each team at the finish of the Iditarod, you will find that most drivers enter Nome with a significantly smaller string of dogs.

One Last Fling

In addition to reducing the number of dogs that they are running, toward the end of the race, drivers also divest of all unnecessary gear. The trick is to know what you will need and what you can do without. Because the weather is so variable along the coast, this can be a dangerous strategic call. By the last checkpoint—Safety—nearly everyone elects to eject.

MAJOR STRATEGIES

36 Minutes

Joe Runyan had run the Iditarod four times when he sat down to formulate a scientific approach to the 1989 race. Having carefully studied data from previous years, he filled a notebook with a schedule of where he wanted to be and when. Taking longer rest stops than most of the other mushers, Runyan stayed on schedule even when it meant watching his competition leave from a checkpoint ahead of him. This approach carried Runyan to victory under the burled arch in Nome within thirty-six minutes of his projected arrival time. Not a bad estimate, considering that he had just traversed 1,200 miles over an eleven-day period. Runyan is the only dog driver to date who has won distance racing's so-called "Triple Crown": the Iditarod, the Yukon Quest, and the Alpirod.

Rabbits

Others have decided to get out front, set a blistering pace, and see what happens. Maybe a storm will intervene between them and the rest of the pack. In 1987, Dewey Halverson and Jerry Austin were the "rabbits" from Rohn all the way to Unalakleet, the first village on the coast. There they were caught by Susan Butcher (who went on to win), Rick Swenson, and Tim Osmar, whose teams were better rested. Halverson finished third and Austin came in fifth.

*Martin Buser avows, "I named my kennel Happy Trails Kennel because it
fits my philosophy. I want racing to be fun.
When it stops being fun, I'll quit."*

Joe Runyan tried a variation of this plan when he and co-conspirator
Doug Swingley delayed taking their twenty-four-hour layover until
Ruby during the 1992 contest. The two enjoyed sharing a seven-
course meal, but their satisfaction soon soured as the competition
arrived only hours later. Runyan and Swingley had to wait twenty-
four hours before they could leave, while the other teams who had
taken their layovers at a more traditional location (Rohn, Nikolai, or
McGrath) could depart when they wished. Rookie Doug Swingley
finished a respectable ninth; Runyan scratched three checkpoints later
at Kaltag.

This technique has succeeded, however. In 1980, Joe May and Herbie Nayokpuk traded the lead and put a bout of bad weather behind
them. May went on to win, setting a new speed record. For his speedy
second-place finish, Nayokpuk earned the nickname "The Shishmaref
Cannonball." (Shishmaref is Nayokpuk's home village.)

In 1995, Doug Swingley vindicated his and Joe Runyan's 1992 strategy by waiting until Iditarod to take his twenty-four-hour layover (long after everyone else had taken theirs) and then going on to win the race in record time with a comfortable margin. Swingley believes that being a rabbit is a sound strategy—you just need to have trained the dogs properly to be able to implement it.

The Master Plan

Rick Swenson, often called "the master" of the Iditarod, has been the bane of "rabbits": always running near the front but hanging back just enough to conserve his dogs' strength. By giving his team the best possible care, racing conservatively until he reaches the coast, and allowing others to make mistakes, Swenson lies in wait . . . watching the competition dissolve away. "You don't have to have the fastest team," he observes, "but you have to be consistent, steady, and careful, and if you make a mistake, you can't let it get you down. You have to wait for the right opportunity. You kind of have to be like a vulture." Iditarod reporter Lew Freedman summarized the Swenson style when he said, "Contenders must always race with the fear he is lurking. Bluff? Or full house? Every new face will learn you don't play poker with the man whose brand is on the deck." Because Swenson announced at the end of the 1995 race that he won't be running the Iditarod again until 2000, the competition can breathe a little easier for a few years.

Racing Relaxed

You can run by a set schedule, sprint ahead, or lie in wait near the front—or perhaps you would prefer to race relaxed. Martin Buser advises, "Tune in to your dogs. Disregard the competition and do what's best for your team. Establish a rest-run pattern that is geared to your dogs and not to whomever you're racing against." Amplifying his run/rest strategy, Buser explains:

> I often marvel at the fact that we can be sitting in the middle of nowhere taking a break, sipping a fruit juice, the dogs are all sleeping, yet we are in a race where every minute counts. I call it "racing relaxed." One has to learn that the rest stops are every bit as important as the travel phases. The team will let you know when they need a break. One must tune in to their subtle signals and stop before they really need the rest.

These various strategies are not mutually exclusive, and as long as the welfare of the dogs is put first, methods can be mixed and matched.

Your Personal Best

A final major strategy reminds competitors to keep things in perspective. Veteran musher DeeDee Jonrowe maintains that the goal of running the Iditarod is "to showcase your dogs at their very top performance and achieve your personal best." Any dog driver who can accomplish both of those goals is a real winner and deserves as much respect as the first musher to cross the finish line.

ATTITUDE

Visualization

Although it's an intensely physical event, race insiders claim that 90 percent of the Iditarod is a mental proposition. Attitude can separate the champion from the contenders.

One confidence-building technique favored by athletes is visualization. This involves imagining in minute detail exactly what you are going to do in order to successfully accomplish your goal. If you can imagine it, you can do it.

When It Stops Being Fun

It is important for competitors to keep things in perspective. If you have a pet, you may have noticed that he quickly senses and reflects your feelings. Iditarod dogs will not perform well for a driver who is morose, resigned, or frustrated. Upbeat Martin Buser avows, "I named my kennel Happy Trails Kennel because it fits my philosophy. I want racing to be fun. When it stops being fun, I'll quit."

The Zone

The Holy Grail of the sports world, being "in the zone" is every athlete's dream. Operating at this level, baseball great Ted Williams claimed that he could see the seams on the baseball as the pitch approached him. When Iditarod champions are asked the reason for their success, the same response is often given: "Everything just clicked."

SCRATCHING

One Contraction at a Time

One moment everything is going fine, then suddenly you are wet or lost, or you are traveling in the wrong direction to retrieve a piece of mandatory equipment from the last checkpoint. Whatever the problem, you are profoundly depressed and want to quit. You're ready to throw in the towel, cry "uncle," get the hell out of Dodge, wave the white flag—in Iditarod lingo, to scratch.

What you need is a scratch strategy. Probably the best thing for you to do is to lie down and take a good long nap (after caring for your dogs, of course). Then, eat a truly righteous meal. Nine times out of ten, eating well and sleeping soundly will give you a new lease on life. If you're still in doubt, talk to other mushers at the checkpoint and to race officials, and call your friends and family for advice. If the dogs are healthy but reluctant, try switching their positions, using a different leader, and giving them lots of extra rest. Above all, remember the natural-childbirth coach's mantra: "You can do it! Just take it one contraction at a time." On the trail, all you have to do is make it to the next checkpoint, just taking it one checkpoint at a time.

We'll Be Back Another Day

While determination and perseverance are admirable, there are times when you just shouldn't go on. Because scratching is such an anathema, it's difficult for competitors to make an objective decision. Dog driver/veterinarian Dr. Terry Quesnel observed that "There is a tendency in every musher's mind to think you are the most important animal in the team. You need to be able to look at your dogs, judge how they are feeling and then say, for their benefit, 'We'll be back another day.' " Trail vets and other experienced personnel are present at each checkpoint to assist in this process.

PLOYS

Mind Games

If 90 percent of the race is mental outlook, then 90 percent of your competitors' ploys are probably psychological posturing. In *The Speed Mushing Manual*, Jim Welch lists ten common psych-outs [paraphrased here] that may be used against you:

1. The Superiority Complex—"If I am better than you in one thing, I must be better in just about everything else. If you can't be better than me in something trivial, how do you think you can beat me in a race?"
2. The Confidence Strut—"He seems really sure of himself. He must have a really good team to be that confident. Maybe it will be hard to beat him. I don't know if I can beat him. I would probably have to push my dogs really hard to beat him. He probably pushes his dogs really hard. I don't want to be that kind of a driver."
3. Distraction—Your opponent tries to make you mad, worried, or focused on anything other than winning the race.
4. Ignoring You—Some people stew so much about being snubbed that they can't see straight.
5. Ready-Made Excuses—"Oh, that's really too bad about . . . " Nice-guy sympathies become self-fulfilling prophecies.
6. Create Overconfidence—All that prerace praise swells your head and affects your judgment.
7. Helpful Advice—May not be so helpful.
8. Magnanimous Congratulations—"You're doing really well. It's great to see you advance almost to my level. You needn't win the race."
9. Publicly Proclaimed Race Plans—You adopt a questionable strategy that the proponent never uses.
10. The Turn-Around—You beat a former buddy who now becomes a jerk.

Iditarod racers specialize in subterfuge. They distribute disinformation. They declare that they'll be taking their twenty-four-hour layover, then pull out of the checkpoint twenty minutes later. They sneak back onto the trail after a long rest when the competition is snoozing (maybe literally). They run with their headlamps off. They hope that it's getting to you.

A Rush Job
In 1987, Susan Butcher pulled into Elim, a checkpoint less than 100 miles from the finish, leading the race. Before she had finished feeding her dogs, Rick Swenson appeared. To her surprise, thirty minutes later he was back on the trail. Butcher cut short her stop to pursue Swenson, fearful of letting him establish a lead this late in the race. Guess what she found just outside of Elim—Rick Swenson encamped beside the trail. In this case, the ruse ultimately failed to work, as

Butcher went on to claim her second victory. This is a dangerous ploy, though, because it tempts even experienced drivers to cut short their team's rest. Once a musher's run/rest cycle is disturbed, it may be difficult to get back on track.

Sandbagging

Dick Mackey and Rick Swenson traveled within about 100 yards of each other for the last 800 miles of the 1978 Iditarod. In *Iditarod Classics*, Mackey explains:

> I let Rick lead. The only time that I was in the lead was where it was easy to be in the lead. When it was difficult to be in the lead I let him lead. Difficult in terms of trailbreaking. He was perfectly content to do that.
>
> Now don't get me wrong. Rick and I are good friends, but at that time in his life he was pretty sure of himself—"I'm the defending champion and you're number two." I was willing to play that game until we got to Nome.

By hanging back in second place and giving the impression that his team was exhausted, Mackey lulled Swenson to sleep. Instead of making an early attempt to outrace Mackey, Swenson waited until the two teams were on Front Street to turn on the heat. By then it was too late. In a photo finish, Mackey edged out Swenson, snatching his victory by a *one-second margin*.

45 Dogs, One Irate Woman, and a Musher
Who Didn't Know Beans from Catsup

David Monson was just getting to know Susan Butcher when they both ran the 1981 Iditarod. During the race, he ended up off the trail in the brush. Butcher had become tangled in the same brush before Monson and his team got ensnared, and Emmitt Peters joined the snarl shortly thereafter. Monson recalls, "We had 45 dogs in there, one irate woman, and a musher who didn't know beans from catsup. That was me. When we finally got out, she told me, 'You've got to rest your dogs.' I said, 'Gee, sure. OK,' and that was the last time I saw her in the race." Butcher finished fifth, and Monson—having taken her advice—finished twenty-first, a respectable showing for a rookie. Apparently, Monson wasn't bothered by Butcher's less-than-objective advice because he married her four years later.

*Sometimes [the dogs'] breath inverts and hides them —
you'll be crossing a lake on a moonlit 30-below night and
it's like you're being pulled along by a steaming roast.*

*Gary Paulsen
Iditarod finisher and novelist*

20

Hallucinations

You haven't slept well for days. You've been stoking your system with snacks and strong coffee. You haven't figured out yet that you are dehydrated. You are starting to suffer from the stress of competition and the loneliness of the trail. You begin hallucinating. In his book *Woodsong*, Iditarod finisher Gary Paulsen warns, "Nothing can prepare you for your first hallucinations in the race because they are not dreams, not something from sleep or delirium; the intensity of the race . . . makes for a kind of exhaustion in the musher not found in training. The hallucinations seem to roar at you. They come while you are awake, come with your eyes open, and are completely real."

Dehydration and lack of sleep seem to be the most critical factors. As he relaxed in the finish chute after completing the 1993 race, Rick Swenson was asked by the press, "Any interesting hallucinations this year?" "No," Swenson replied, "I got too much sleep. We had all those [additional mandatory] rest stops."

AN ASSORTMENT OF APPARITIONS

From the man who saw late-model automobiles to the woman whose dogs turned into lobsters and swam away ahead of her—what triggers hallucinations? One driver came upon a large, beautifully lit church when he was crossing the sea ice, and another desperately dragged his team to the side of the trail to avoid being flattened by an oncoming train. Who knows what they were thinking about?

Other illusions are more strongly grounded in Iditarod experience. Because they are a very real danger, sweepers often figure prominently in mushers' fantasies. Drivers have ducked insubstantial sweepers so violently that they smashed their noses on the sled's handlebar. Or having stared at it too long, racers watch the horizon transform itself into a stick that is about to knock them out. Weary of such specters, a competitor may stop at a cabin that appears to be a checkpoint, only to discover that there is neither cabin nor checkpoint. Welcome to the Iditarod, where phantasms thrive.

A SWENSON CHIMERA

Paranoia can activate a musher's mirage. Throughout the last few hundred miles of the 1994 race, nervous leader Martin Buser reported, "I saw Rick Swenson passing me. It was impossible. I was going 14 mph and his team was doing 25 mph. It was clearly not reality. I knew it was a hallucination." Perhaps the specter of Swenson overtaking him helped push Buser on to his second victory. When you enter other drivers' subconscious thoughts and figure in the figments of their imagination, you know that you have established a daunting reputation.

CAN'T SEE THE FOREST FOR THE TREES

At a speaking engagement shortly after the 1986 race, Susan Butcher charmed her audience with this narrative:

> We had no time to sleep or think of anything this year. The sleep I had at Kaltag was the longest sleep I had in the whole race. Usually, I was getting two hours of sleep a day, so I did a lot of hallucinating this year. We were out on the coast where there are no trees—you're above the arctic tree line—and I was standing on the back of the runners and the trail's not marked very well at all, and we were in a blizzard and I couldn't see very well in front of me and my dogs got off the trail. Joe Garnie was right behind me and he followed me off the trail. I put in

the snowhook, which stops the sled, and I walked back to Joe and I said, "Joe, this is going to be so hard . . . the trail's over there and we've got to go through this forest over there." And he goes, "What forest?" And I go, "We've got to line the dogs through all these trees." And he goes, "Susan, there aren't any trees here."

Despite the phantasmagorical forest, Butcher wended her way to her first Iditarod victory.

WHITE LIGHT

Alaskan artist Jon Van Zyle has used his two Iditarod experiences as the inspiration for his art work. In Lew Freedman's *Iditarod Classics*, Van Zyle recounted a mystical occurrence during his second race:

Another neat thing happened in 1979 going down the Post River. I left Rohn in late afternoon, stopped and fed my dogs. I had not slept in approximately two days. But this "thing" has nothing to do with a hallucination. I don't practice an organized religion. I don't practice any religion but I consider myself religious and quite spiritual.

I fed my dogs and went on. The Post River had open water with thin, dark glare ice and no moon. My headlamp battery was dead. There were lots of holes, and because it was so dark, I couldn't see far enough ahead to call my leaders around them. We nearly slid into a couple of openings in the ice. That's when I decided to walk up front with my leaders. I turned my sled on its side to slow the team. A spiritual person had told me if I ever felt as if I was in dire straits, I should ask for protection from the White Light. I did. We made it around this mile or two of dangerous trail. It was scary—not a comfortable situation.

A little farther down the trail I stopped and was feeding the dogs when this musher caught me. He said something about being able to see me on the river. And I said, "How did you do that? I didn't have a headlamp." He said, "I was behind you quite a ways and all of a sudden, it was like somebody had turned a light on you."

It was the White Light.

"WHERE ARE YOU?"

Unlike many other mushers, two-time champion Jeff King says that his hallucinations are primarily auditory. "I hear my children talking to me," King explains. During the 1995 Iditarod, King clearly heard the voice of his eight-year-old daughter Tessa saying, "I love you, Daddy." Startled, he jumped, and turned around to look for her, calling, "Where are you?"

When King does have visual hallucinations, they are grounded in his love of wildlife and in his experiences with animals near his Denali Park home. For instance, he once saw a large brown wolf charging up to his Iditarod team. When the wolf stopped in the trail and King could focus on it, he realized that it was only a stump. Another time, bands of caribou were flowing across the trail. They turned out to be willow bushes.

"I HEARD SOMEBODY CRYING"

In the hours just before dawn, suspended in that mysterious limbo between the blackness of the previous night and the brightening of the new day, 1988 Iditarod rookie John Patten glimpsed a familiar form trudging toward him. It was a Finnish exchange student who had married a close friend of Patten's. Patten was deeply moved that this young woman had walked so far to wish him well. As the figure approached, Patten could see that the woman's husband and three children had come on foot all the way from Finland to join her in cheering Patten on. Describing this emotional reunion, Patten recalled: "I was so happy to see them! And then I heard somebody crying and I didn't know who it was." Patten didn't realize that he was hallucinating until he felt hot tears streaming down his own face and found that he was sobbing with joy.

INSIDE
INFORMATION

I've been mushing since before I was born.

Ramey Smyth
Iditarod finisher, whose mother Lolly Medley
was one of the first two women to complete the race

21

Iditarod
Traditions

Over the years, many customs associated with the Iditarod have become time-honored traditions. Mushers reach deep into an enormous boot or hat to draw their starting-position numbers at the prerace banquet. Mention of Fourth Avenue conjures up images of pandemonium in Anchorage, while Front Street suggests the thrill of victory or the immense satisfaction of achieving a personal goal. The burled arch welcomes the weary to journey's end, while faithful friends such as the Skwentna Sweeties, the Delias, and the Forsgrens ease the passage along the way. Whether upbeat, superstitious, humorous, creepy, or comforting, long-standing Iditarod practices are part of the race's lore and mystique.

IT'S ALL IN THE FAMILY

Iditarod fever seems to be hereditary. Fathers have passed it to sons: Joe Redington, Sr. to Raymie and Joee; Dick Mackey to Rick and Bill; George Attla to Gary; Dan Seavey to Mitch; Richard Burmeister to Aaron and Noah; John Barron to Laird, Jason, and Will; and Dean Osmar to Tim. Mothers have also inspired their sons to conquer the race course. Roxy Wright-Champaine (formerly Roxy Woods) and her son Ramy Brooks have both finished the Iditarod. Ramey Smyth comes by his love of mushing from both parents—father Bud Smyth is a five-time finisher, and mother Lolly Medley was the second woman to complete the Iditarod. Ramey's younger brother Cim won the 1994 Junior Iditarod and in 1996 became the fourth family member to earn the finisher's belt buckle. One mother/daughter pair has also finished the race: Barbara and Lisa Moore.

Brothers have waged war against each other, including early participants Rod and Alan Perry, and Babe and Eep Anderson. As mentioned, Redington, Mackey, and Barron siblings have also vied for victory. Rose Albert and her brother Howard (Athabascan Indians from Ruby) each finished the Iditarod.

A number of married couples are well-known Iditarod drivers. Norman Vaughan and his wife Carolyn Muegge-Vaughan, Dewey and Kathy Halverson, Jim and Susan Cantor, Bill Hall and Pat Danly, and, of course, David Monson and Susan Butcher come to mind. Many other couples and former couples have made this race a joint adventure. Some have even popped the question or tied the knot right on the trail.

KINDERGARTNERS AND CARDBOARD AXES

Various villages and towns along the trail have created ongoing Iditarod activities. One of the more novel village ventures is McGrath's Mini-Iditarod. First-grade drivers hitch up one husky and settle a kindergarten handler in the sled. Having stowed their commemorative cachets and a cardboard ax, they leave "Anchorage," pass the checkpoints of "Rohn," "McGrath," and "Unalakleet" (where checkers examine their mandatory gear), and arrive at last in "Nome." Moose lollipops are awarded to all participants, for as in the real race, all who finish are winners.

SIGNING CEILINGS

For years, mushers signed their names on the ceiling of a cabin at Cripple. Although it is no longer part of the checkpoint, the cabin and its graffiti remain intact. At a small shelter cabin in the Topkok Hills, Rick Swenson left his mark during the decisive 1991 blizzard. Confident that he was about to make history by grasping his fifth victory, Swenson etched on the wall: "3-14 91 R. A. Swenson stops here to dry out on my way to Idit. V!" The next day, his self-assurance was vindicated.

John Barron has run the Iditarod seventeen times. Barron's sons Laird and Jason have also completed the Iditarod, and his youngest son Will may bring the family-finisher count to four.

THE HALFWAY JINX

A substantial award is given to the first musher who reaches the race's halfway point: Cripple in even years and Iditarod in odd years. Superstitious drivers avoid winning this award because it comes with a jinx—if you're first at the half, you'll not be first into Nome. In the twenty-plus years of the Iditarod's history, this jinx has only been overcome three times: in 1984 by Dean Osmar, in 1993 by Jeff King, and in 1995 by Doug Swingley. As Rick Swenson has remarked, "The odds are against you greatly, let's put it that way."

A HAUNTED HOUSE?

About forty miles past Kaltag, Old Woman Cabin offers shelter to those bold enough to accept it. Legend has it that years ago an old woman was buried by an avalanche near here; some are convinced that she still haunts the area. Mushers report that they have seen a competitor's headlamp following or preceding them to the cabin and later discovered that no one was anywhere in the vicinity. A hallucination, perhaps? Others have said that they were unable to rest well inside the structure, and one driver actually claimed that he became so sick that he could hardly function until he came outside again, whereupon he recovered immediately. In an attempt to soothe the spirit of the old woman, mushers leave offerings of candy bars or other snacks. You never know.

I DO . . . YOU BET!

Athabascan Indian Beverly Jerue met Czechoslovakian musher Jan Masek when he came to her home village of Anvik in 1979 to buy fish. Love blossomed. On March 5, 1984, Jerue waited at the Finger Lake checkpoint for her fiancé to appear. She recalls:

> He arrived in the late afternoon. He fed the dogs, made sure they were OK. And then we got married. We had one of the older racers [Norman Vaughan] do the ceremony, and several of the other mushers came and watched. It was beautiful, out in all that scenery. I had a bouquet made out of branches and flowers I collected in the woods. We said "I do." And then, a few minutes later, he was back in the race.

During his rookie run ten years later, Iditarod Air Force pilot Bruce Moroney planned to pop the question to his girlfriend Diana Dronenburg, a race veteran. Unfortunately, he became ill early in the competition and was unable to catch up to her. Undeterred, Moroney allowed a television crew to videotape his proposal, which he made while kneeling on his sled runners. As soon as Dronenburg pulled under Nome's arch, the conspiring cameramen replayed the request for her. Laughing with delight, Dronenburg replied heartily, "The answer is yes, a definite yes. You bet!"

IDITACHICKS

Mushers finishing the race in recent years may think that they've finally lost it after all those days on the trail: a vision of poultry in motion welcomes them to rowdy Nome. Not to worry—it's just the Iditachickens. Yes, five otherwise responsible adult women hidden by their chicken costumes act eggstremely silly and receive startled looks from the unsuspecting. Padded by pillows and accessorized with huge orange feet and red crests, the chicks waddle and strut, enlivening the carnival atmosphere of the race's culmination.

A LITTLE BUBBLY

At some point in their career, most mushers do business with Rae's Harness Shop in Anchorage. As a thank-you from owners George and Patricia Rae, George has flown to Nome almost every year since 1978 to present each finisher with a bottle of champagne. The champion and the Red Lantern winner receive a more expensive bottle, and nonalcoholic champagne is given to those who prefer it.

THE WIDOW'S LAMP

Years ago, when trappers, miners, missionaries, and mail carriers relied on dog teams for transportation, mushers stopped at a series of roadhouses along their route. As a safeguard, they would send word ahead to their destination. The roadhouse or village would then light a kerosene lamp and hang it outside, signifying that a team was expected.

Each year, the Iditarod Trail Committee lights such a lantern at 10:00 A.M. on the Saturday of the race's start and hangs it on the burled arch in Nome. This "widow's lamp" will continue to burn until the last musher finishes. So if you're still out on the trail, we'll leave a light on for you.

I'm from Texas and a cowboy at heart. Dorothy Page said mushers are toughest of the tough. I set out to prove her wrong. I found out she was right.

John Barron
Iditarod musher since 1979

22

Trail Trivia

Originally, what was the name of the Iditarod Trail Sled Dog Race?

When a fifty-mile version of the Iditarod was first run in 1967, it was called the Seppala Memorial Iditarod Trail Race, in honor of serum musher Leonhard Seppala. This first race is also sometimes referred to as the Centennial Race because it celebrated the one-hundredth anniversary of the United States' purchase of Alaska from Russia.

Who is the first dog driver in seventy-five years to begin mushing the Iditarod Trail at Historic Mile 0?

Mitch Seavey grew up listening to his father Dan Seavey tell tales of his top-five Iditarod finishes in 1973 and 1974. So, in 1982, Mitch ran the race, placing twenty-second. Thirteen years later, Mitch decided to travel the trail again, but this time he would start from Historic Mile 0 in Seward. In the early 1900s, the trail originated at the seaport of Seward and was called the Seward Trail. In order to reach the gold strike at Iditarod, the trail was extended up from Seward and down from Nome. It eventually connected the state from south to north and changed its name to the Iditarod Trail. Mitch left Seward one week before the start of the 1995 race, mushed to Anchorage following the historic trail, and went on to finish his second Iditarod "in the money" in twentieth place.

What's the most exotic location in which an Iditarod team has been trained?

Eagle Point, Oregon, resident Terry Hinesley traverses the Pacific coast sand dunes on his training runs. "It's a great place to train dogs," Hinesley maintains. "The sand massages their feet and the salt water toughens their paws. And with all the sand dunes to weave around, it's a great place to train gee-haw leaders."

What's an even more imaginative way to train a leader to go "Gee" or "Haw"?

One musher noticed that when he brought his leader into the house, the dog followed him from room to room. The opportunistic driver taught gee/haw commands as the animal accompanied him. You can't help but wonder how long it took before the trainer was comfortably ensconced on the couch, sending the husky to the kitchen for a cold one. Another musher could take his team into an open, snow-covered field and, by giving the canines voice commands, write his name in the snow.

What does "Outhouse Bombing" have to do with the Iditarod?

The Copper Valley Lions Club sponsors the annual Gulkana Air Show, which includes competitive events such as short field takeoffs, short field landings, and the ever-popular outhouse bombing, in which an assistant tries to drop a bag of flour on an outhouse while the pilot flies over it. Pilots and outhouse bombardiers are often members of the Iditarod Air Force and usually place high in each of these events.

How is running the Iditarod like neurosurgery?

Three-time Iditarod finisher Cliff Roberson, a neurosurgeon from Seattle, notes that several aspects of his medical background transfer well to the trail. "Being somewhat used to sleep deprivation helps," he says, "and keeping your cool when things aren't going well." And you thought mushing a team of dogs wasn't brain surgery.

When did Denali move to West Palm Beach?

In January 1994, the theme of the South Florida Fair was "North to Alaska." Organizers built an 80' x 22' replica of Denali, a Southwestern Native lodge, a mining tunnel, an ice cave, and simulated the aurora with a laser light show. Iditarod finishers Dewey and Kathy Halverson attended with their canine ambassador "Lumpy."

Norman Vaughan, who accompanied Admiral Byrd to the South Pole in 1928, finished the 1990 Iditarod at age eighty-four.

How did the Make-a-Wish Foundation of Richmond and Western Virginia make an Iditarod dream come true?

This group enabled fifteen-year-old Becky Venning, a leukemia patient (along with her father, mother, and brother), to attend the 1995 Iditarod. Venning's itinerary included the prerace mushers' banquet, a visit to ITC headquarters, seeing the start of the race, going for a sled-dog ride, flight-seeing over the trail near Skwentna, and visiting early race checkpoints. Being true fans, Venning's family took twenty-two rolls of pictures! Because of a bone-marrow transplant received from her brother, the outlook for Iditarod fan Becky Venning is promising.

Who else competes on the Iditarod Trail besides sled-dog drivers?

Each year in mid-February, a group of self-proclaimed "ididiots" use the Iditarod Trail to compete in the 210-mile Iditaski (for cross-country skiers), the 210-mile Iditabike (for mountain bikers), the 105-mile Iditashoe (for snowshoers), the 80-mile Iditafoot (for runners), or a triathlon for the truly rugged. One writer noted that the sled-dog race could be renamed the Iditadog.

Also in February, the Gold Rush Classic Iron Dog Snowmobile Race allows mechanized speed demons to motor 2,098 miles from Anchorage to Nome and then back to Big Lake, located just outside of Anchorage. Five-time dog-driving champion Rick Swenson traded his canines for an Arctic Cat Cougar and ran the 1993 Iron Dog. By the time he arrived in Nome under dog power, he had traveled the Iditarod Trail three times that year!

How do you say good-bye to a musher during the Iditarod?

"See you in Nome!" conveys your confidence that the competitor will finish the race. A nonrace farewell is "Happy Trails!"

Unlike other professional sports, is it true that older mushers excel in the Iditarod?

Judge for yourself: in 1994, nine of the top ten finishers were over thirty-five years of age, as were seventeen of the top twenty! Why? Older drivers may have more money at their disposal, may have developed more stamina, and definitely have more experience than their younger cohorts.

Who has proven that even old age is not a barrier to finishing the race?

At age seventy-one, Joe Redington, Sr. led the 1988 race for almost 500 miles from Rohn to Kaltag and achieved a fifth place finish—his highest ever.

In 1990, eighty-four-year-old Norman Vaughan completed the Iditarod for the fourth time, much to the delight of his many fans along the route.

Isn't Norman Vaughan the one who went to Antarctica?

Yes. In 1928, Vaughan was a member of Richard Byrd's Antarctic Expedition, acting as chief dog handler. In his book *My Life of Adventure*, Vaughan describes how he returned to Antarctica in 1994 to climb 10,302-foot Mount Vaughan, which Byrd had named after him. Three days before his eighty-ninth birthday, Vaughan reached the summit.

Have any other Iditarod mushers participated in arctic expeditions?

Japanese musher Keizo Funatsu traveled 3,741 miles by dog team in the 1989-1990 Trans-Antarctica Expedition. He completed his first Iditarod in 1993.

Having been the first woman to solo by dog team from Resolute Bay to the magnetic North Pole, Iditarod finisher Pam Flowers completed her "In the Tracks of Anarulunguaq" journey in 1994. Following the route of Anarulunguaq, a Native woman from Greenland who had accompanied Northwest Passage explorer Knud Rasmusson seventy years ago, Flowers mushed more than 2,500 miles alone with her dogs from Barrow, Alaska, to Gjoa Haven in the Canadian Arctic.

Did I hear something about sled dogs climbing Mount McKinley?

The first climbing expedition to reach the top of Denali with sled dogs included Joe Redington, Sr., Susan Butcher, climbing guides Ray Genet and Brian Okonek, and photographer Rob Stapleton. Describing his experience that morning in May 1979, Redington said, "It was a perfect day on the summit. . . . It was 8 below zero, and we spent four hours on the summit, just laying there in the sun. [The dogs] were still barking when we got to the top. When we first reached it, the lead dog looked over the other side, but there were no more hills to climb."

Don't they keep sled dogs at Denali National Park?

Yes. As a matter of fact, the sled dogs are Denali Park's most popular attraction, aside from the mountain, of course. In 1921, soon after the park had opened, dog teams provided the first superintendent with a means of winter travel. Denali's dogs now perform winter patrols to deter poachers and to maintain contact with recreationalists. In the summer, they also entertain thousands of visitors during sled-dog demonstrations (using wheeled carts). If you visit Denali, be sure to see these dependable, dedicated dogs.

Which mushers have appeared in presidential inaugural parades?

In 1981, Herbie Nayokpuk, Joe Redington, Sr., and Norman Vaughan drove dog teams in President Ronald Reagan's inaugural parade. That same year, Vaughan also gave a mushing lesson to Pope John Paul II during a papal visit to Anchorage.

Emmitt Peters, Norman Vaughan, and Jan Masek, along with Gene Leonard, brought dog teams to Washington, D.C., for President Reagan's 1985 inauguration.

Is it true that an Iditarod champion is an honorary crew member of an Indy 500 team?

That's right. Martin Buser has assisted with Gordon Johncock's pit stops as part of the Hemelgarn/Runyon race team. He observes, "There are many similarities between the sports. If you ask anyone what the ultimate in auto racing is, they would say winning the Indianapolis 500, and if you asked anyone involved in sled-dog racing what the ultimate is, they would say winning the Iditarod."

Why did the Oscar Meyer Wienermobile attend the Iditarod?

In the early 1990s, Kraft General Foods salesman Larry Munoz ran the race twice, and his company wanted to show support in a dramatic and unforgettable manner. The giant wiener gave new meaning to the phrase "Iditarod dog."

When was 13 a lucky number during the Iditarod?

Emmitt Peters wore bib #13 when he drove to victory in 1975, as did both father Dick and son Rick Mackey in 1978 and 1983, respectively.

How did the most unusual wedding announcement related to the Iditarod read?

"The Bride Wore Mukluks and the Groom Wore Bunny Boots" is the title of an article that appeared in the March 1988 issue of *Alaska* magazine. It describes the New Year's Eve wedding of Norman Vaughan and Carolyn Muegge. Guests arrived by dog team, snow machine, bush plane, and helicopter. Vows were spoken outside amidst falling snow. At the end of the reception, Vaughan climbed in the sled bag, Muegge-Vaughan stepped on the runners, and they mushed into the twilight to honeymoon in their nearby cabin.

What did Susan Butcher get when she won a bet with her husband David Monson that she'd finish first in the 1986 Iditarod?

Monson had to shave off his beard.

Of all the scenes that could have been chosen by a major rental company to portray Alaska on its trucks, the one selected was an Iditarod musher driving a team of huskies. Mush on!

Who has named their children after race checkpoints?

Martin Buser and wife Kathy Chapoton have named their two sons Nikolai and Rohn.

Who named a child after their favorite lead dog?

Rick and Kathy Swenson's son Andy is named for the legendary lead dog that guided Rick to four of his five Iditarod victories. Susan Butcher and David Monson named their first child Margarethe Tekla in honor of Butcher's first famous leader, Tekla.

Who is the youngest Iditarod finisher?

Technically, you have to be eighteen to enter the Iditarod. A number of eighteen-year-olds have finished, including Karl Clauson,

Rome Gilman, Ramey Smyth, Simon Kinneen, and Aaron Burmeister. Burmeister can claim to be the youngest to have crossed the finish line, however, since his father Richard scooped up four-year-old Aaron at the end of the 1979 race and put him in the sled bag just before passing under the burled arch.

What's the most unusual piece of optional equipment that a musher has carried?

At the beginning of the 1994 Iditarod, the *Anchorage Daily News* ran the following story:

> Matt Desalernos showed up for the restart of the Iditarod Trail Sled Dog Race on Sunday in a refriga-wear suit, a headlamp strapped around his Day-Glo orange cap, and a briefcase in his hand. Yes, a briefcase. Perhaps he planned to attend a few formal business functions on his way to Nome? You know, lose the dogs for a couple hours and close a few deals, schmooze the big-wigs in Nikolai and Ophir or the other cosmopolitan spots along the trail.
>
> Was there a necktie stashed away in that sled somewhere?
>
> Desalernos scoffed. "Presidential stuff," he said, explaining the briefcase.

In addition to mushing, Desalernos has recently been serving as president of the Iditarod Trail Committee.

Out on the trail, what kind of music do mushers play on their Walkmans™?

DeeDee Jonrowe enjoys contemporary Christian rock 'n' roll, Rick Mackey turns up Credence Clearwater Revival, Tim Osmar gets into Led Zeppelin, and Rick Swenson takes twenty tapes that range from country-western to the Stones. Susan Butcher generally sings to her dogs but does enjoy Broadway tunes, especially *Les Miserables*.

Jeff King uses his radio to get the latest race information but otherwise feels that it's too much trouble. He usually finds himself singing Disney classics such as "Davy Crockett," "Zorro," "Andy's on the Road," or "Mike Fink, King of the River." A visit to King's home makes this all come clear—if you stay long enough, you'll hear "Disney Children's Favorites" played at his girls' request. You may find yourself performing a rousing rendition of these catchy tunes on your way home.

What is a musher's least favorite job?

No, not shoveling you-know-what. Soliciting sponsors. Nobody likes calling and writing people they don't know asking for money. The amount of image-building and hype necessary to do it right is analogous to going through the process of a job search. You can end up feeling like you're selling your soul for money.

Aren't there any little-known facts about dogs?

Sure. Did you know that the name of the rock group Three Dog Night comes from the Australian Aborigines and refers to how cold the weather is? At that temperature, it takes three dogs huddled close around you to keep warm. By extrapolating, you could assume that out on the Iditarod Trail, when the windchill plunges to something like -100° F, it would be a Fourteen Dog Night.

If you're ever standing near the trail in the dark (perhaps at a checkpoint waiting for a musher to come in), look at the dogs' eyes as a team approaches. Light striking the huskies from a checker's head-lamp or a news crew's flood will make a blue-eyed dog appear to have red eyes, while a brown-eyed dog's eyes will seem green. It's a rather unsettling sight to see a string of red- and green-eyed canids charging toward you through the blackness.

Is it true that dogs trash talk out on the trail?

Yes, at least Martin Buser says that his dogs trash talk. In the 1995 *Iditarod Race Program*, Buser explained:

> One of the funny things they do now, my guys, they kind of pull up behind a team and then right on the heels of the musher. Three or four dogs that do that—Dave, Tyrone, IBM and D-2— they will, as if on command, bark loudly at the driver and the team. Then they put it in overdrive and excitedly keep on going past the team—barking, tails wagging high up in the air, hackles up, barking as they're passing the team. And as soon as they get back on the trail after they pass, they kind of bounce into each other, rubbing shoulders and, every now and then, you can see them steal a glance back. You just know that they just love that moment. And, of course, I feed on that too, you know. I chuckle and praise them for doing that.
>
> [Interviewer Bill Sherwonit] Kind of like, "In your face on the Iditarod Trail."
>
> (Laughing) [Buser continues] I know, the dogs do some trash talking of their own.

If there are 30,000 bears in Alaska, how come no one has ever seen one during the race?

There may be flowering trees and spring bulbs blooming in your yard in March, but in Alaska, it's still winter. The bears are blissfully snoozing.

Could you cite some of the staggering numbers involved in putting on the Iditarod?

According to *Alaska* magazine's March 1994 issue, the numbers (approximate) are:

> Pounds straw for doggie beds = 65,897
> Small airplanes patrolling trail = 25
> Foreign reporters = 20
> Pounds prime rib served at mushers' start banquet = 813
> Wooden trail stakes = 9,000
> Fresh strawberries served at end-of-trail banquet = 9,030
> Spectators = 26,102
> Yards Day-Glo trail marking tape = 5,000
> Dog booties = 70,344
> Pounds dog food = 120,000
> Gallons aviation fuel = 20,000
> Entry fee in dollars = 1,249 [1,750 as of 1995]

And that's only a sampling!

What happens to extra food-drop bags left behind by mushers at the checkpoints?

Upon mushers' request, personal gear is shipped home to them at their expense. Otherwise, leftovers become the property of the Iditarod Trail Committee and are made available to succeeding competitors and, once they have all passed through, to local residents. Volunteers occasionally hit the jackpot and find a stash of particularly tantalizing trail treats.

How do the mushers relieve themselves out in the middle of nowhere in that cold?

Several strategies are used. Obviously, mushers try to time pit stops to coincide with the checkpoints, most of which have facilities. Also, drivers may design their diets with the goal of minimizing the amount of solid waste produced (high-energy drinks like Ultra Energy® are useful in this regard). Otherwise, it's just like primitive camping in the wilderness. You're not in Kansas anymore.

Who's the guy who greets the finishers as they stand under the arch?

He's the mayor of Nome. From 1973 to 1991 that was Leo Rasmussen, and starting in 1992, Rasmussen's nephew John Handeland took over the job of mayor and welcome committee.

Where do they get yellow roses for the champion's lead dogs when it's beaucoup degrees below freezing?

Sorry to disillusion you, but unlike the sunny south, when you run for the roses up here, you're vying for some plastic posies.

Is there any tougher race than the Iditarod?

Recently, *Outside* magazine ran an article about the toughest sporting event in the world, based on how far the racers have to go, how tough the course is, and how hard the competitors have to work. Their first panel ranked the Iditarod number one. A second panel, however, decided that too high a percentage of Iditarod entrants finish the race and dropped its ranking to number three. In the published article, number one was the 3,000-mile Race Across America bicycle race, and number two was the Vendee Globe 24,000-mile solo sailing race. In an *Anchorage Daily News* piece about this article, disgruntled mushers noted that the bicyclists are only sleep deprived for a few days and get total support (from vehicles with food and drink, for instance). They also pointed out that the race is not run in the winter and the cyclists need only tend to themselves, while mushers care for sixteen other athletes in an arctic environment. As for the percentage of finishers, Iditarod entrants set their own level of challenge, and not all of them are really racing. So . . . you make the call.

Who was the first musher to finish the three longest races in Alaska all in one season?

Bob Holder, from Fairbanks, placed eighth in the 1995 Yukon Quest, thirty-first in the 1995 Iditarod, and seventh in the 1995 Hope Friendship Run. The three races, run from mid-February to early May, total nearly 3,000 miles.

Wasn't traveling the Iditarod Trail on the agenda of some adventurous Brits?

A unit of the British Army in charge of security for the royal family undertook the Roof of Americas Expedition 1994, in which they planned to travel 2,500 miles. By dog team and snow machine, they set out from Nenana, following part of the Iditarod Trail on the Yukon River and along the coast to Nome; then they continued on to Barrow. The expedition's 20 members were selected from 300 applicants. This is only the first of six expeditions; the others are to scale Mount McKinley, kayak in the Grand Canyon, raft through the Amazon Basin, climb Mount Aconcagua, and cross the Southern Patagonia ice cap to Cape Horn. These folks take their training seriously.

Didn't an Englishman who was one of Joe Redington's tourists run the Iditarod?

Max Hall of Manchester, England, joined Redington on his first Iditarod Challenge in 1993. All five of Hall's 1993 trailmates flew to Anchorage to give him a grand send-off as he began the 1995 Iditarod. Along the coast, Hall got pounded by winds up to fifty miles per hour and numbed by a windchill of -70° F. Commenting on the weather between Safety and Nome, Hall admitted, "This is bad, but you should have seen Topkok." Three other mushers who had been running with Hall were holed up in a cabin just past Topkok. As Nan Elliot relates in an *Anchorage Daily News* article on Hall's ordeal, the three heard a knock on the cabin door:

> "A polite little knock," said [Kjell] Risung, a transplanted Norwegian.
> The mushers opened the door and there was Hall looking like the ice man cometh. When Risung later told this story to fellow Scandinavian Lena Hall, who happens to be Max's wife, she burst out laughing.
> "I can't believe he knocked—that's so British," she said. "Anyone else would have flung the door open and fallen in."

Although the storm followed him all the way to Nome, Hall gave it the stiff upper lip and finished his rookie run in forty-sixth place.

Isn't there a golf tournament in Nome in mid-March?

You could call it that. As Iditarod finishers are still trickling in, the Bering Sea Ice Golf Classic gets underway. The six-hole course is

Many mushers earn additional income by offering rides to tourists. Joe Redington, Sr. made his roadside advertisement memorable.

located just offshore on the frozen Bering Sea. According to Lew Freedman, "The greens are swatches of carpet. They are circular, several feet in radius and, truth be told, resemble amoebas under a microscope the way they lie on the ice and contrast with the whiteness around them. Each hole is drilled into the ice, and the cup the ball rolls into whenever a golfer can negotiate the obstacle bumps under the rug are made of tin cans. Hey, if you're going to play arctic golf, you've got to be adaptable."

Is President Clinton really going to run the Iditarod?

Chitchatting with seven other world leaders at a summit meeting in Naples, Italy, during July 1994, President Clinton suggested that he and Boris Yeltsin could raise money for Russia by running the Iditarod. "Someday what we should do is go up there and raise money by participating in the Iditarod race; you know, the dog race," Clinton told Yeltsin. "It goes on for days and days and days, all across Alaska." Gesturing to the press, Clinton added, "See, Boris and I, we have enough body fat, we can survive." On a more serious note, the

In 1995, the Iditarod made the leap into cyberspace by collaborating with America Online's computer service. Subscribers could click onto categories such as "The Mushers," "Race Photos," "Diary from the Trail," "Race News & Results," "Alaska Weather Forecast," and "Iditarod Messages."

President confessed that he has dreamed of entering the Iditarod. As soon as this news broke, the Iditarod Trail Committee sent President Clinton a formal invitation. Keep your eye on the trail and one day you may detect a presidential presence!

Are there very many rabid Iditarod fans, or is this a pretty select group?

You wouldn't suspect that Detroit, Michigan, was a hotbed of Iditarod fans, but it proved to be during the 1991 race. *Detroit Free Press* columnist Mitch Albom had flown to Alaska to cover the action and had gotten as far as Rohn when he was told to come home so that he could fly to Florida for baseball's spring training. More than 300 incensed readers phoned Albom's boss, protesting this decision. Three days later, Albom landed at Kaltag and went on to write six more fabulous installments of his race diary.

Has the Iditarod really entered into America's mainstream?

Several sources supply a resounding "Yes!" to this question. What comic is more mainstream than the long-running "The Family Circus"? During the 1994 race, the famous circle portrayed mom overseeing her children as they hitch two family mutts to a traditional wood sled. The child driver, standing on the sled, informs mom, "We're gonna have an Iditarod in our yard!"

Next time you rent a truck, if you get the orange brand with pictures painted on the sides representing a particular state, see if one of the vehicles on the lot shows Alaska (or keep your eyes out for one on the highway). Of all the scenes which could have been chosen to portray Alaska, the one selected was an Iditarod musher (complete with identifying bib) driving a team of huskies. Mush on!

Have very many magazines done articles about the Iditarod?

An amazing cross-section of periodicals have written up the race. They include *Reader's Digest, Sports Illustrated, National Geographic, People, Time, U.S. News & World Report,* and *Newsweek.* Coverage has also appeared in *Boys' Life, Smithsonian, Dog World, Vogue, Hotel & Motel Management, Road & Track, Women's Sports & Fitness,* and *Weekly Reader. Editor & Publisher, Footwear News, Flying,* and *Air Conditioning, Heating & Refrigeration News* have featured pieces on the Iditarod, too.

Controversy is the cauldron in which truth is distilled.

Alan D. Hyde
Attorney-at-law

23

Controversy

BATTLE OF THE SEXES

The most high-profile aspect of the Iditarod historically has been the phenomenal success women have had, and the rivalries (both real and imagined) that this has engendered. As many sports writers have observed, the Iditarod is one of the few events in which men and women compete together on equal terms.

There has been much speculation about why females do so well. Some have suggested that the innate nurturing ability of women gives them an edge when working with dogs. Others contend that a lighter-weight driver gives the team a strategic advantage. Women respond that weight is not a critical advantage but that judgment, strategy, and the ability to work with dogs are true equalizers.

Of course, most of the blame (or credit) for the fray has to be assigned to the media, who are always ready to satisfy the public's insatiable appetite for controversy. For a recap, read on.

1973 - 1984: Women Make Inroads

All twenty-two mushers who finished the first Iditarod were men. In 1974, Mary Shields and Lolly Medley entered the Iditarod and received a somewhat less than warm welcome. Shields laughs with satisfaction when she recounts that male fans were betting on how

Mary Shields, the first woman to finish the Iditarod, holds her half-Labrador lead dog Cabbage. © Evelyn Trabant, Fairbanks, AK

soon the women mushers would scratch, while female fans were betting that she and Medley would make it all the way to Nome.

Lolly Medley remembers that it wasn't just the fans who were opinionated about the subject. Several male competitors chose to scratch rather than continue to race and place lower than the two women. Shields became the first woman to finish the Iditarod when she overtook Medley just outside of Nome. The women came in twenty-third and twenty-fourth, and only two men finished behind them.

Since that first year, women have become an annual presence on the trail. From 1974 through the completion of the 1984 race, twenty-two different women successfully finished the Iditarod. Many milestones were achieved: in 1978, Susan Butcher became the first woman to finish in the top twenty (in her rookie run); in 1979, Butcher finished in the top ten; and in 1980, she broke into the top five. By the beginning of the 1985 race, she had come in second twice. It seemed just a matter of time before Susan Butcher would become the first woman to win the Iditarod.

During this entire twelve-year period, only ten articles about the Iditarod appeared in major magazines, and two of those (in *National Geographic* and *Reader's Digest*) were written by Susan Butcher before she had ever won the race. Although he was briefly mentioned, Rick Swenson, who had accumulated four victories by 1982, was not featured in a single magazine story.

Susan Butcher gears up for battle.

*Libby Riddles left the men behind when she set out into the teeth of a wicked
coastal storm. Asked in the finish chute how she felt about her victory,
Riddles replied, "What I feel is, if I died right now, it'd be okay."*
© *Jeff Schultz/Alaska Stock Images*

1985 - 1990: Women Dominate The Iditarod

In 1985, Susan Butcher was running her best team to date and
many people expected her to win. That possibility evaporated when
her dog team was attacked by a moose. Near the end of the race,
another steely and wily woman, Libby Riddles, set out from Shaktoolik into the teeth of a storm, seizing victory for herself. The Iditarod
would never be the same again. The Anchorage headline blazed
"LIBBY DID IT" in 1½" letters.

More articles in major periodicals were written about Riddles' win
than had been published in the preceding twelve years. *Sports Illustrated* ran a fourteen-page story entitled, "Valiant Lady." A model-like
photo of blonde, blue-eyed Riddles faced *Vogue's* coverage, "Libby Riddles: Racing to Victory. A Woman Challenges the Elements and Wins."

In the meantime, Susan Butcher rebuilt her team in preparation for
the 1986 race. Shortly after she had first come to Alaska, Butcher spent

several years learning dog mushing from Joe Redington, Sr. Following a 1979 ascent of Denali by dog team with Redington, Butcher relocated to the Eureka area, northwest of Fairbanks. She established her new dog lot within a few miles of Rick Swenson and the two became close friends.

Early in the 1986 race, a sweeper knocked Butcher off of the sled and her friend Swenson carried her with him until they found the wayward team. Butcher won her first Iditarod that year, setting a new record time for the northern (or any) race route. Commenting on her reception after this victory, Butcher explained that male mushers did not mind her competing as long as she was not a real threat. Once Butcher began winning, however, some resentment was openly displayed.

Adding fuel to the fire, feminist Iditarod T-shirts sold briskly, proclaiming slogans such as **Alaska: Where Men Are Men and Women Win the Iditarod** and **A Woman's Place is First to Nome**.

A seven-page write-up in the February 1987 issue of *Women's Sports & Fitness* billed the upcoming Iditarod as "Arctic Dreams: Susan Butcher and Libby Riddles Face Each Other—and 60 Men—in the Coldest Race on Earth." In the story, Butcher defused this battle-of-

Following the 1985 victory of Libby Riddles, and Susan Butcher's 1986 championship, feminist Iditarod T-shirts sold briskly.

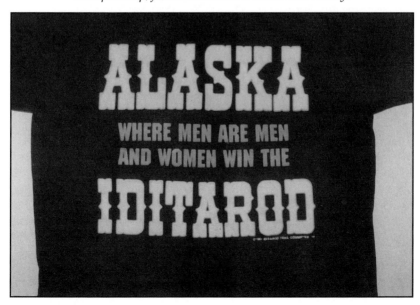

This male chauvinist answer to earlier feminist T-shirts was produced by Alaska Serigraphics to celebrate Rick Swenson's fifth victory in 1991.

the-women-champions hype by clarifying that her goal was never to be the first female champion or the best woman musher. She simply wanted to be the top Iditarod racer. Butcher also pointed out that playing up the Riddles/Butcher duel overlooked the fact that Rick Swenson, having won four victories, was rightfully acknowledged to be the reigning champion.

Acrimonious remarks were made by Rick Swenson near the end of the 1987 race. One writer observed that while some of Swenson's utterances were inexcusable, others were merely misjudgments, made in response to harassment by reporters at a time when he was operating without sleep and facing the prospect that his yearly income was about to be halved by finishing second. Butcher won the 1987 race and set a new speed record for the southern (or any) course.

Despite a continuing barrage of bitter remarks, Butcher won an unprecedented third consecutive victory in 1988, bettering her 1986 record for the northern race route.

Once again, the national media fanned the flames. The title of *Outside* magazine's July 1988 Iditarod coverage is representative—"Butcher's

Doggone Dynasty: Seventy-below windchills, a crippled sled, and a few good men are no match, again, for the Iditarod champion."

Prior to the 1989 Iditarod, *Alaska* magazine sent half of their subscribers (chosen at random) a March issue with Susan Butcher featured on the cover and profiled on the last page ("Susan Butcher: Sugar 'N Spice?"). They mailed the other half a cover portraying Rick Swenson with a final-page piece called "Rick Swenson: Shooting from the Lip." Swenson may have earned himself that caption, but it is ironic that the first full-page article about the four-time champion that appeared in a major magazine was negative.

Following four straight years of victories by females, men rejoiced in 1989 when Joe Runyan claimed the championship, leaving the women in his wake. *Sports Illustrated* ran a five-page postrace article

Commenting on her relationship with Rick Swenson, Susan Butcher said, "Rick has been an old long-time friend in spite of what the press says. We've had a close relationship for years." Swenson reiterated this: "The whole thing with Susan is just built up in the media. We've been friends for a very long time. I have only respect for Susan." Swenson must trust Butcher — he let her trim his mustache during the 1992 Iditarod.
© *Jeff Schultz/Alaska Stock Images*

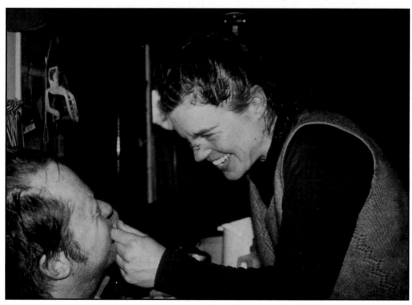

Humanitarian Award winner Rick Swenson is famous for his outstanding dog care, as well as for his unequaled racing record.

that proclaimed, "Man's Best Friends: When Joe Runyan and his dogs won the Iditarod, males wept with joy."

The following year, in the 1990 Iditarod, a moose ran through Rick Swenson's team just past McGrath, forcing him to drop his two main leaders. A subdued Swenson remarked that it was the only time in fifteen years of running the Iditarod that he felt helpless. Despite dropping her legendary lead dog Granite, Butcher set a new record, winning the 1990 race (her fourth victory) in 11 days, 1 hour, 53 minutes, and 23 seconds. Joe Runyan came in second, and Rick Swenson finished seventh.

From 1985 - 1990, women won five of six Iditarods. More than fifty major magazine articles cover these six years alone, compared to ten during the previous twelve years. Susan Butcher was interviewed by Johnny Carson, David Letterman, Joan Rivers and *20/20*. She also met and was photographed with President Reagan and President Bush. In 1988, PBS aired a one-hour documentary about her entitled *The Susan Butcher Story.* A year later, The National Geographic Society devoted a quarter of its hour-long special *Those Wonderful Dogs* to Butcher. The stage was set for the biggest battle yet: who would become the first five-time champion of the Iditarod?

1991: The Fight For Number Five

The cover of the March 1, 1991, *Weekly Reader* introduced school-children nationwide to Susan Butcher; *Outside's* March issue contained nine pages about the defending champion; and the February 11 *Sports Illustrated* issue included an eleven-page preview, "The Dogged Pursuit of Excellence: Susan Butcher is mushing toward a record fifth win in the Iditarod race." A one-quarter page bulletin in *Dog World* announced, "Swenson attempts fifth Iditarod win." Butcher was expected to win: she had been victorious four of the last five years, while Swenson had not won an Iditarod since 1982.

Early in the 1991 race, Swenson was already in trouble. Leaving Rohn, he lost the trail in the Farewell Burn area. By the time Swenson was back on track, he had a four-hour handicap. Coming off his twenty-four-hour layover in McGrath, he trailed Butcher by six hours.

Then Mother Nature gave Swenson a gift: deep, fresh snow clogged the trail from Ophir to Iditarod. This slowed down the race leaders and allowed Swenson to catch up.

Eleven checkpoints later, however, a weary Swenson chided the press for trying to pretend that the race was still a showdown between him and Butcher. At the end of his mandatory layover in White Mountain, Swenson would leave more than an hour behind Butcher. All that remained was a seventy-seven-mile sprint through Safety to Nome. Swenson insisted that the only way he could catch Butcher would be if she went the wrong way. His words soon proved to be prophetic in an eerie episode on the trail.

Not long after Swenson left White Mountain in pursuit of Butcher, the weather deteriorated. The temperature plunged to -30° F and a howling wind blew the swirling snow horizontally. Swenson took pains to ensure that his dogs were all fit, and then pressed on, even though visibility was so poor that he could often see no farther than his wheel dogs.

Two hours later, a surprised Swenson came upon Susan Butcher taking a nap in the trail. Euphoric, Swenson took the lead, only to have his headlamp burn out a few minutes later. As he struggled to change the tiny bulb in the -90° F windchill, Butcher appeared. Working by the beam of her headlamp, Swenson was able to finish replacing the bulb. In the Iditarod, even the keenest rivalry is set aside when survival is at stake.

The Iditarod's two four-time champions set out together in search of a sheltered spot. Suddenly, they became separated. Swenson felt certain that Butcher had somehow gotten ahead, and he forged on to find her.

Butcher, meanwhile, headed for a light that turned out to be Joe Runyan's headlamp. After briefly discussing trail conditions, she and Runyan decided to return to White Mountain. Butcher later commented that she could second-guess this decision the rest of her life, but at that moment she felt that her team was not mentally prepared to travel another fifty-five miles.

Swenson stopped when visibility decreased to the point that he couldn't see his own feet. Noting that his dogs seemed ready to go on, and figuring that he could walk to Nome if he had to, Swenson fastened together several spare necklines, hooked them to his lead dogs to form a leash, and led his team one step at a time toward victory.

Ten hours after leaving White Mountain, Swenson stopped at a shelter cabin that lay nestled at the bottom of Topkok Hill. He fed his dogs a hot meal, dried his gear, and plopped a bag of shrimp in garlic sauce with fettucine into the water he was boiling for his dogs' next dinner. After several hours of rest, Swenson and his team left for Safety, the last checkpoint before Nome.

Despite a -50° F windchill and the lateness of the hour, a crowd of over 500 ardent fans waited at the finish line to welcome the conquering hero home. At 1:34 A.M. on Friday, March 15, 1991, Rick Swenson pulled under the burled arch, pumped his fist in the air, and was proclaimed the first five-time champion of the Iditarod.

In postrace interviews, Swenson reflected that he had worked harder for this one victory than for all of his other four championships put together. He commented that he would enjoy not having to hear about how he let those women beat him again. He also speculated that perhaps now that she had four wins to her name, Butcher was getting a bit soft. Radiating with pleasure, Swenson threw down the gauntlet, announcing that Butcher would have to win *six* Iditarods now in order to be the top dog.

Later, however, Swenson told Butcher that he felt as though he had stolen the race from her. He explained to the media one more time that he and Butcher were long-time friends and that he had nothing but respect for her. Butcher indicated that as an old friend, she couldn't be happier for Swenson. In an emotional moment, Butcher did admit that she and her husband David would have liked to have garnered a fifth win, hung up the harnesses, and had some children.

Sports Illustrated followed up its eleven-page prerace article about Butcher with a one-paragraph description of Swenson's victory. Rick Swenson's unprecedented fifth win was not covered in a single article in a major magazine.

An Alaskan entrepreneur produced a male chauvinist T-shirt emblazoned **"Key Moments in Mushing History: Brains vs. Brawn."** The drawing on it is dated "March 14, 1991—Iditarod Trail" and shows Rick Swenson talking to Susan Butcher near White Mountain. Swenson gestures ahead, and instructs Butcher, "Wait here, I'll be right back."

Since the 1991 race, the battle of the sexes has settled down to a slow simmer. In the succeeding years, Butcher and Swenson have placed respectively 2nd and 4th (1992), 4th and 9th (1993), and 10th and 4th (1994). At the conclusion of the 1994 Iditarod, Susan Butcher announced her retirement from the race. Following his tenth-place finish in 1995 (Swenson's lowest finish since his rookie run in 1976), Rick Swenson proclaimed that he will not run the Iditarod again before the year 2000.

Until another woman renews the war, it looks like feminist fans will have to wait for Butcher's comeback bid. 89-year-old Norman Vaughan has proved that older mushers can compete. That gives Susan Butcher about fifty years to topple top dog Rick Swenson from his five-time pedestal!

HUMANE TREATMENT OF IDITAROD DOGS

In recent years, some people have expressed concern that sled-dog racing may not be safe for the animals. Proposals for addressing this issue range from working with the Iditarod Trail Committee to continually improve race rules to banning sled-dog racing altogether. The question of whether it is humane to expose sled dogs to risk is a matter of active debate among mushers and animal-rights activists.

The quintessential question seems to be, "If sled dogs were capable of making the choice, like their human partners, would they choose to run the Iditarod despite the risks?" Undertaking risks as part of a sport is *not* the issue; no one is lobbying against auto racing or mountaineering, which claim many human lives each year. Those who seek to stop sled-dog racing argue that the dogs are forced to endanger their lives because someone else has made the decision for them to compete in a potentially dangerous activity.

No one has to force a sled dog to race, however—that's what they most enjoy doing. In fact, it's difficult to prevent a husky from running. When Susan Butcher parked her dog team for a rest break in McGrath during the 1993 race, she announced that she was dropping

Humanitarian Award winner DeeDee Jonrowe with her leader Bird Dog.

several dogs. One had a slightly sore shoulder and she didn't want to risk aggravating it. When the dropped-dog caretaker, himself a previous Iditarod competitor, came to escort this dog from the team to the Dodge Lodge shelter (a tent provided by Dodge Trucks for the observation and care of dogs no longer competing in the race), the animal refused to go. No doubt tired and sore, Butcher's dog obstinately resisted being led away from his beloved job. The caretaker had to pick up the canine and carry him away to the comfort of enforced rest.

Another consideration is that, unlike horse and greyhound racing, the musher is doing the same thing as the animals. Granted, the drivers don't run as much as the dogs. Competitive mushers *do* run up the hills, pedal on the flats, and hang off or scramble behind to increase drag on the downhills. The humans experience the same weather conditions as the animals, too, often sleeping outside in their sleds to be near their teams. At rest stops, the dogs sleep while the driver prepares hot food for them; during a four-hour break, the team sleeps most of the four hours, while the musher gets less than one hour of rest.

PRIDE cofounder Jeff King with his lead dog Jake.

After the dogs have eaten a carefully prepared meal which may include boneless lambchops (or perhaps beef or chicken), rice, salmon, and vitamin supplements, the driver may wash down trail mix with a cup of coffee. The dogs' diet is the priority. Whatever energy the musher has left goes into the preparation of his or her own food.

At each checkpoint, a veterinarian examines the dogs. Sick or injured human racers must often fend for themselves, hopefully locating a villager, fellow competitor, volunteer, or spectator who is qualified to help. The ITC does not provide medical doctors at each checkpoint.

Regarding the comparison to greyhound and horse racing, one more note is in order. The absence of pari-mutuel betting in the sport of sled-dog racing greatly reduces the incentive for corruption. There is not the same lure of huge gains to be made by the practice of drug abuse.

Finally, sled dogs have an important safety valve: they can lie down and refuse to run. This is commonly called a "lie-down strike." Like the proverbial horse being led to water, the dogs ultimately are the ones in control. If you've ever tried to feed a finicky toddler, you know how mushers feel when their dogs cease to cooperate.

As mentioned in the "Welfare of the Animals" chapter, every pre-caution is taken to ensure that Iditarod dogs are safe and happy. In addition, Iditarod rules prohibit the mistreatment of animals and specify harsh penalties—ranging from disqualification to lifetime banishment from the race—for any infraction.

Iditarod mushers care deeply about the welfare of their animals. Many competitors have committed their entire lifestyle to dog mushing, and often their spouse, parents, and more than one full-time handler are equally devoted. These mushers have a major investment in maintaining the integrity of the Iditarod. Humanitarian Award winner DeeDee Jonrowe speaks for the mushing community when she notes that dogs deserve the best care possible from when they are an intellectual concept (during breeding plans) until their retirement.

STANDINGS AND
STATISTICS

Maybe my priorities are out of order, but finishing my first Iditarod was more gratifying than receiving my M.D., running a marathon, or even clipping a brain aneurysm.

Cliff Roberson
Neurosurgeon, Seattle, Washington

24

Placement of All Starters, 1973 to 1996

This chapter consists primarily of charts presenting information about how various Iditarod entrants have placed. The first table gives The Top Fifty Iditarod Mushers Ranked by their Average Finish, a who's who of the Iditarod; these competitors have successfully finished at least three races. The second table also looks at drivers who have completed the race three times or more, listing Iditarod Mushers with the Most Top Ten Finishes. Final Standings are also presented for each year's race, indicating each entrant's place, name, finish time, and prize money, and showing those mushers who scratched from the race or who were disqualified or withdrawn.

Before getting into these charts, here are some special stats:

- The fastest winning time (up to and including the 1996 Iditarod) is held by Doug Swingley, who finished the 1995 race in 9 days, 2 hours, 42 minutes, and 19 seconds.
- The slowest winning time is held by Carl Huntington, who finished the 1974 Iditarod in 20 days, 15 hours, 1 minute, and 7 seconds. This winning finish time would have earned Huntington a

Red Lantern (the award given to the last-place finisher) in ten subsequent Iditarods (1981, 1984, 1986, 1987, 1988, 1989, 1992, 1993, 1994, and 1995).

- The fastest Red Lantern winner is Andy Sterns, who completed the 1996 race in 15 days, 23 hours, 48 minutes, and 22 seconds. Sterns' Red Lantern time would have *won* six previous Iditarods (in 1973, 1974, 1976, 1977, 1982, and 1985).
- The slowest Red Lantern winner is John Schultz, who finished the 1973 (inaugural) Iditarod in 32 days, 5 hours, 9 minutes, and 1 second (more than a month after starting). To put this in perspective, Doug Swingley, running his 1995 record pace, could have traversed the entire trail three and one-half times before Schultz got to Nome.
- The largest margin of time between the champion and the Red Lantern is more than twelve days, the difference between Dick Wilmarth's win and John Schultz's finish in 1973.
- The largest margin of victory between the champion and the second-place finisher is twenty hours, set by Carl Huntington in 1974.
- Norman Vaughan, who has finished four Iditarods (1978 at age seventy-two, 1980 at age seventy-four, 1983 at age seventy-seven, and 1990 at age eighty-four), has never received the Red Lantern Award.
- In 1994, Martin Buser's teams finished first *and* last: Buser won, and his nephew Mark Chapoton, driving a group of Buser's young dogs, was the last one to cross the finish line.
- Susan Butcher's 1993 fourth-place time of 10 days, 22 hours, 2 minutes, and 40 seconds was faster than any of her four previous record-setting championship times.
- Ron Aldrich is the only musher who finished the 1973 Iditarod who is still competing in the race. Aldrich's forty-fifth-place finish time in the 1994 race (15 days, 9 hours, 00 minutes, and 00 seconds) would have been good enough to win four of the previous five races that he completed (1973, 1974, 1976, and 1979, but not 1978). If the Top Fifty Iditarod Mushers chart were extended a few places, Aldrich would be the fifty-seventh musher on that Iditarod who's who list.
- The largest number of teams to scratch in a single year is twenty-five in 1980.
- The largest field of competitors to start the race is seventy-six in 1992. The greatest number of teams to finish is sixty-three, also in 1992.

- The most mushers to finish on the same day is twenty, all of whom crossed under the burled arch within fourteen hours of each other in 1976.
- The most mushers to finish in the same hour is seventeen, which happened after a bad coastal storm let up in 1993.
- In 1995, Doug Swingley became the first musher from the Lower 48 to win the Iditarod.
- Terry Adkins ran twenty of the first twenty-two Iditarods; Rick Swenson has finished twenty times.
- The first (and only) father/son champions are Dick Mackey (1978) and Rick Mackey (1983).
- The first musher to win the halfway award and the race is Dean Osmar (1984); the only other mushers to have done so are Jeff King (in 1993) and Doug Swingley (in 1995).
- The first husband and wife to finish the race in the same year were Jacques and Claire Philip of France in 1985; in 1986, Bill Hall and Pat Danly became the first American couple to do so.
- The most women to finish in the top twenty is five in 1993 and 1994.
- The only Triple Crown Champion (winner of the Iditarod, Yukon Quest, and Alpirod long-distance sled-dog races) is Joe Runyan. Jeff King has won two of the three—the Iditarod and the Yukon Quest. All of the champions of the Yukon Quest have also competed in the Iditarod.
- Only three mushers have completed the Iditarod and the Yukon Quest in the same year—Sonny Lindner, Charlie Boulding, and Bob Holder.
- Only one Iditarod champion has also won the Fur Rendezvous World Championship sprint race—Carl Huntington.
- Ten-time Fur Rendezvous World Championship winner and eight-time Open North American sprint champion George Attla finished the Iditarod in fourth place in 1973 and won a shortened (fifty-mile) version of the Iditarod in 1969.
- Sprint champion Roxy Wright-Champaine has won the Open North American Championship title three times. She has won the Fur Rendezvous World Championship eight times in the women's division and three times since women have competed in the Open Division. In addition, she is an Alpirod champion and finished the Iditarod in 1983 (she was Roxy Woods then).
- Eleven-time Iditarod finisher Bill Cotter won the Yukon Quest in 1987, and has also competed in the Fur Rendezvous World Championship and the Open North American sprint races.

- Rick Swenson has the most wins (five), the most top-five finishes (fifteen), the most top-ten finishes (twenty), the most completed races (twenty), the most consecutive races (twenty), has never finished out of the top ten, has never scratched, and is the youngest champion in the history of the Iditarod (he was twenty-six when he first won in 1977).
- Susan Butcher has an unmatched string of successes: from 1986 through 1993, she finished first, first, first, second, first, third, second, and fourth, for an average finish of 1.875. Not even Rick Swenson can match those numbers. Butcher also holds the record for the most consecutive victories—three—and for the greatest amount of prize money earned ($378,299 compared to Rick Swenson's total of $356,898).

THE TOP FIFTY IDITAROD MUSHERS
RANKED BY THEIR AVERAGE FINISH*

1.	Rick Swenson	4.00
2.	Susan Butcher	4.75
3.	Doug Swingley	5.20
4.	Joe Runyan	5.86
5.	Tim Osmar	7.27
6.	Jerry Riley	7.57
7.	Herbert Nayokpuk	7.60
8.	Warner Vent	8.00
9.	Joe May	8.00
10.	Don Honea	8.25
11.	Jeff King	8.29
12.	Martin Buser	8.46
13.	Rick Mackey	9.63
14.	Dick Mackey	10.14
15.	Marc Boily	10.33
16.	Sonny Lindner	10.43
17.	Lavon Barve	10.55
18.	Robert Schlentner	10.67
19.	Emmitt Peters	10.75
20.	Roger Nordlum	10.75
21.	John Cooper	11.00
22.	Alan Perry	11.33
23.	Guy Blankenship	11.50
24.	Rudy Demoski	11.50
25.	Howard Albert	11.50
26.	Larry "Cowboy" Smith	11.60
27.	Ernie Baumgartner	12.00
28.	Vern Halter	12.11
29.	DeeDee Jonrowe	12.29
30.	Robin Jacobson	12.40
31.	Joe Garnie	12.67
32.	Bill Cotter	12.82
33.	David Monson	13.00
34.	Tom Mercer	13.00
35.	Eep Anderson	14.00
36.	Jerry Austin	14.44
37.	Ramy Brooks	14.67
38.	Kate Persons	14.75
39.	Duane (Dewey) Halverson	15.33
40.	Charlie Boulding	15.50
41.	Matt Desalernos	15.50
42.	Jacques Philip	15.50
43.	Joe Redington, Sr.	15.57
44.	Ken Chase	15.90
45.	Victor Katongan	16.25
46.	Rod Perry	16.67
47.	Harry Sutherland	16.83
48.	Libby Riddles	17.60
49.	Bruce Lee	17.75
50.	Terry Adkins	18.28

* As of 1996, 544 mushers have competed in the Iditarod. The top 50 were selected in order of best average finish and include only those entrants who have completed the Iditarod at least 3 times. Average finish statistics have been rounded off, and in case of a tie, the competitor with the greatest number of finishes has been listed first.

IDITAROD MUSHERS WITH THE
MOST TOP TEN FINISHES*

1.	Rick Swenson	20
2.	Susan Butcher	15
3.	Rick Mackey	11
4.	Martin Buser	10
5.	Tim Osmar	9
6.	DeeDee Jonrowe	9
7.	Herbert Nayokpuk	8
8.	Lavon Barve	7
9.	Emmitt Peters	7
10.	Joe Redington, Sr.	7
11.	Dick Mackey	6
12.	Jerry Austin	6
13.	Doug Swingley	5
14.	Joe Runyan	5
15.	Jeff King	5
16.	Jerry Riley	4
17.	Sonny Lindner	4
18.	John Cooper	4
19.	Vern Halter	4
20.	Joe Garnie	4
21.	Bill Cotter	4
22.	Eep Anderson	4
23.	Duane (Dewey) Halverson	4
24.	Warner Vent	3
25.	Don Honea	3
26.	Larry "Cowboy" Smith	3
27.	Charlie Boulding	3
28.	Ken Chase	3
29.	Terry Adkins	3
30.	Joe May	2
31.	Robert Schlentner	2
32.	Roger Nordlum	2
33.	Guy Blankenship	2
34.	Rudy Demoski	2
35.	Howard Albert	2
36.	Ernie Baumgartner	2
37.	Robin Jacobson	2
38.	Matt Desalernos	2
39.	Ron Aldrich	2

* Mushers must have completed the Iditarod at least 3 times. In case of a tie, competitors are listed in order
  of their average finish record. (Based on 1973 - 1996 finishes.)

IDITAROD FINAL STANDINGS
1973

Place	*Musher*	*Days*	*Hours*	*Minutes*	*Seconds*	*Prize*
1	Dick Wilmarth	20	00	49	41	$12,000
2	Bobby Vent	20	14	08	46	8,000
3	Dan Seavey	20	14	35	16	6,000
4	George Attla	21	08	47	53	4,000
5	Herbert Nayokpuk	21	11	00	19	3,000
6	Isaac Okleasik	21	18	21	25	2,500
7	Dick Mackey	22	04	03	49	2,000
8	John Komak	22	04	36	34	1,800
9	John Coffin	23	06	43	29	1,600
10	Ron Aldrich	24	09	58	36	1,400
11	Bill Arpino	24	12	12	00	1,000
12	Jamie "Bud" Smyth	26	11	25	35	950
13	Ken Chase	26	11	45	35	900
14	Ron Oviak	26	15	54	01	850
15	Victor Katongan	28	23	41	04	800
16	Robert & Owen Ivan	29	11	34	25	750
17	Rod Perry	30	01	39	21	700
18	Tom Mercer	31	?	35	45	650
19	Terry Miller	31	04	20	07	600
20	Howard Farley	31	11	59	11	500
21	Bruce Mitchell	31	12	05	06	0
22	John Schultz	32	05	09	01	0

Scratched

1	Dr. Hal Bartko
2	John Schultheis
3	Darrell Reynolds
4	Barry McAlpine
5	Slim Randles
6	Raymie Redington
7	John Luster
8	Alex Tatum
9	C. Killigrock
10	David Olson
11	Herbert Foster
12	Ford Reeves & Mike Schrieber

Note: Casey Culusnik of Fairbanks, one of the mushers in the double team with John Schultz, also scratched. 1973 was the only year that double teams were allowed.

IDITAROD FINAL STANDINGS
1974

Place	Musher	Days	Hours	Minutes	Seconds	Prize
1	Carl Huntington	20	15	01	07	$12,000
2	Warner Vent	21	11	18	42	3,255
3	Herbert Nayokpuk	21	18	28	42	2,449
4	Rudy Demoski	21	21	32	02	1,627
5	Dan Seavey	22	11	43	55	1,224
6	Ken Chase	23	01	03	50	1,023
7	Raymie Redington	23	01	55	01	821
8	Ron Aldrich	23	03	01	10	728
9	Joee Redington, Jr.	23	03	25	19	651
10	Dick Mackey	23	05	21	20	573
11	Joe Redington, Sr.	23	10	15	57	465
12	Tom Mercer	24	08	18	22	387
13	Jamie "Bud" Smyth	24	09	52	23	372
14	Rod Perry	26	18	34	30	341
15	David Olson	27	04	17	29	325
16	Reuben Seetot	27	04	29	22	310
17	Robert Ivan	27	07	02	49	279
18	Victor Katongan	27	09	35	26	248
19	Terry Adkins	27	13	28	08	232
20	Tim White	27	17	35	00	196
21	Desi Kamerer	27	23	53	30	0
22	Clifton Jackson	28	05	09	06	0
23	Mary Shields	28	18	56	30	0
24	Lolly Medley	28	19	25	30	0
25	Joel Kottke	29	06	34	49	0
26	Red Olson	29	06	36	19	0

Scratched

1	Dr. Steve Murphy (prior to race)	16	Warren Coffin
2	Carl Topkok	17	Tom Johnson
3	Richard Korb	18	Isaac Okleasik
4	John Ace		
5	Bernie Willis		
6	Ward Olanna		
7	John Luster		
8	Don Rosevear		
9	John Coffin		
10	Wilbur Sampson		
11	George Attla		
12	John Schultheis		
13	Ralph "Babe" Anderson		
14	Jerry Riley		
15	Bill Vaudrin		

IDITAROD FINAL STANDINGS
1975

Place	Musher	Days	Hours	Minutes	Seconds	Prize
1	Emmitt Peters	14	14	43	15	$15,000
2	Jerry Riley	14	15	?	39	10,000
3	Joee Redington	14	15	?	02	7,500
4	Herbert Nayokpuk	14	20	29	07	5,000
5	Joe Redington, Sr.	15	15	23	43	3,000
6	Henry Beatus	15	16	20	36	2,500
7	Dick Mackey	16	09	41	30	2,000
8	Ken Chase	16	09	43	25	1,500
9	Rudy Demoski	16	14	10	17	750
10	Eep Anderson	16	15	06	09	350
11	Alan Perry	17	06	01	33	350
12	Ray Jackson	17	09	48	34	350
13	Rick Mackey	18	05	55	39	350
14	Victor Katongan	18	07	38	15	350
15	Ralph Lee	19	06	55	18	350
16	Robert Schlentner	19	07	08	15	0
17	Bill Cotter	19	07	27	27	0
18	Chris Camping	19	08	12	35	0
19	Bill Vaudrin	19	17	01	07	0
20	Darrell Reynolds	20	07	14	17	0
21	Richard Burnham	22	13	17	17	0
22	Jim Kershner	22	13	17	37	0
23	John Ace	22	15	15	00	0
24	Mike Sherman	23	00	55	55	0
25	Steve Fee	29	08	37	13	0

Scratched

1	Col. Norman Vaughan
2	Edward Bosco
3	Hans Algottsen
4	Sandy Hamilton
5	Michael T. Holland
6	Ginger Burcham
7	Bobby Vent
8	Guy Blankenship
9	Terry McMullin
10	Lavon Barve
11	Carl Huntington
12	Walt Palmer
13	Charlie Fitka
14	Doug Bartko
15	Franklin Paniptchuk
16	John Komak

IDITAROD FINAL STANDINGS
1976

Place	Musher	Days	Hours	Minutes	Seconds	Prize
1	Jerry Riley	18	22	58	17	$7,200
2	Warner Vent	19	03	42	00	4,200
3	Harry Sutherland	19	04	02	52	3,600
4	Jamie "Bud" Smyth	19	04	38	19	2,400
5	Emmitt Peters	19	05	10	12	1,800
6	Ralph Mann	19	06	35	34	1,500
7	William "Sonny" Nelson	19	06	36	07	1,200
8	Dick Mackey	19	06	43	06	1,080
9	Tom Mercer	19	07	00	31	960
10	Rick Swenson	19	07	57	27	840
11	Joe May	19	08	08	29	600
12	Don Honea	19	08	34	38	570
13	Alan Perry	19	10	53	05	540
14	Ray Jackson	19	10	56	33	510
15	Ken Chase	19	10	58	37	480
16	Billy Demoski	19	11	07	52	450
17	Terry Adkins	19	11	17	04	420
18	Rudy Demoski	19	13	27	07	390
19	Jack Hooker	19	13	33	33	360
20	Ford Reeves	19	14	26	36	300
21	Ralph "Babe" Anderson	19	18	02	28	0
22	Lavon Barve	20	03	31	58	0
23	Jerry Austin	20	04	20	25	0
24	Ron Aldrich	20	07	46	31	0
25	Richard Burnham	20	08	06	06	0
26	Charlie Fitka	20	14	10	58	0
27	Steve Jones	20	14	11	31	0
28	Clarence Towarak	20	15	55	25	0
29	Alex Sheldon	20	16	45	31	0
30	William Solomon	21	13	35	25	0
31	Allan Marple	21	13	44	48	0
32	Peter Nelson	22	05	45	50	0
33	Jon Van Zyle	26	08	42	42	0
34	Dennis Corrington	26	08	42	51	0

Scratched

1	Joe Redington, Sr.	8	Lee Chamberlain
2	Col. Norman Vaughan	9	Oran Knox
3	Dr. Richard Hanks	10	Mel Fudge
4	Trent Long	11	Bruce Mitchell
5	Robert Schlentner	12	Phillip Foxie
6	Peter Kakaruk	13	Steve Fee
7	John Giannone		

IDITAROD FINAL STANDINGS
1977

Place	Musher	Days	Hours	Minutes	Seconds	Prize
1	Rick Swenson	16	16	27	13	$9,600
2	Jerry Riley	16	16	32	05	5,600
3	Warner Vent	16	16	44	39	4,900
4	Emmitt Peters	16	19	57	02	3,200
5	Joe Redington, Sr.	17	01	26	30	2,400
6	Dick Mackey	17	01	35	15	2,000
7	Don Honea	17	03	34	34	1,600
8	Robert Schlentner	17	03	44	59	1,440
9	Ralph "Babe" Anderson	17	?	51	57	1,280
10	Jack Hooker	17	09	05	56	1,020
11	Ken Chase	17	11	18	28	800
12	Alex Sheldon	17	11	51	18	760
13	Pete McManus	17	12	17	41	720
14	Terry Adkins	17	14	41	42	680
15	Al Crane	17	16	25	10	640
16	Howard Albert	17	17	24	31	600
17	William "Sonny" Nelson	17	18	17	33	560
18	Roger Nordlum	17	19	25	24	520
19	Rod Perry	17	23	18	18	480
20	Richard Burnham	18	07	18	30	400
21	Stein Havard	18	15	23	15	0
22	Bill Cotter	18	15	53	46	0
23	Rick Mackey	18	16	22	25	0
24	Sandy Hamilton	19	02	16	29	0
25	Bob Chlupach	19	02	28	06	0
26	Charlie Harrington	19	10	51	23	0
27	Eep Anderson	20	08	21	33	0
28	Jim Smarz	20	08	32	16	0
29	Duane (Dewey) Halverson	21	04	45	47	0
30	Peter Kakaruk	21	06	00	03	0
31	Randy DeKuiper	21	08	35	47	0
32	Dale Swartzentruber	21	15	30	50	0
33	Jerry Mercer	21	15	31	03	0
34	Varona Thompson	21	18	00	00	0
35	Jim Tofflemire	22	04	53	20	0
36	Vasily Zamitkyn	22	09	06	06	0

Scratched

1	Don Montgomery	8	Franklin Paniptchuk
2	Tom Mathias	9	John Ace
3	Ray Jackson	10	Dinah Knight
4	Rudy Demoski	11	Jerry Austin
5	Rick McConnell	12	John Hancock
6	Bob Watson	13	William Solomon
7	Ron Gould		

IDITAROD FINAL STANDINGS
1978

Place	Musher	Days	Hours	Minutes	Seconds	Prize
1	Dick Mackey	14	18	52	24	$12,000
2	Rick Swenson	14	18	52	25	8,000
3	Emmitt Peters	14	19	28	32	6,000
4	Ken Chase	15	00	02	00	4,000
5	Joe Redington, Sr.	15	03	14	58	3,000
6	Eep Anderson	15	03	?	51	2,500
7	Howard Albert	15	03	40	59	2,000
8	Robert Schlentner	15	05	57	54	1,800
9	Jerry Austin	15	06	33	16	1,600
10	Alan Perry	15	10	13	25	1,400
11	Sonny Lindner	15	12	03	03	1,000
12	Ron Aldrich	15	12	17	11	950
13	Pete McManus	16	01	26	53	900
14	Bob Chlupach	16	03	44	54	850
15	Ron Tucker	16	04	29	43	800
16	Terry Adkins	16	05	11	25	750
17	Harry Sutherland	16	05	53	27	700
18	Richard Burnham	16	07	10	34	650
19	Susan Butcher	16	15	40	30	600
20	Varona Thompson	16	16	40	30	500
21	Joe Garnie	17	02	01	54	0
22	Jerry Mercer	17	02	01	57	0
23	Charlie Fitka	17	16	28	38	0
24	Ernie Baumgartner	18	05	09	53	0
25	Jack Goodwin	18	06	04	00	0
26	Rick McConnell	18	07	37	34	0
27	William Solomon	18	09	28	01	0
28	James Brandon	18	12	12	12	0
29	Shelley Vandiver	19	15	07	08	0
30	John Wood	19	15	07	27	0
31	Ray Gordon	19	15	14	52	0
32	Gary Campen	21	02	25	04	0
33	Col. Norman Vaughan	22	03	29	41	0
34	Andrew Foxie	22	03	29	44	0

Scratched
1 Roger Roberts
2 Duke Bertke
3 Mike Demarco
4 Bill Rose
5 Ralph "Babe" Anderson

Note: William "Sonny" Nelson of Ekwok, who had paid his entry fee and was ready for the 1978 Iditarod, was killed in a plane crash coming into Anchorage for the race. The pilot and all of Nelson's dogs except two were also killed. His dog handler and helper James Brandon ran the race in his memory. Al Crane of Nome drew the Number One bib number for Nelson.

IDITAROD FINAL STANDINGS
1979

Place	Musher	Days	Hours	Minutes	Seconds	Prize
1	Rick Swenson	15	10	37	47	$12,000
2	Emmitt Peters	15	11	19	07	8,000
3	Sonny Lindner	15	14	17	32	6,000
4	Jerry Riley	15	19	29	44	4,000
5	Joe May	16	01	09	15	3,000
6	Don Honea	16	02	21	41	2,500
7	Howard Albert	16	07	26	40	2,000
8	Rick Mackey	16	11	00	01	1,800
9	Susan Butcher	16	11	15	32	1,600
10	Joe Redington, Sr.	16	11	34	01	1,400
11	Gary Hokkanen	16	16	57	05	1,000
12	Terry Adkins	16	19	45	16	950
13	Dick Peterson	17	03	37	37	900
14	Ken Chase	17	04	43	07	850
15	Ernie Baumgartner	17	04	47	48	800
16	Melvin Adkins	17	04	54	23	750
17	Bob Chlupach	17	06	23	19	700
18	Victor Katongan	17	07	35	06	650
19	Keith Jones	17	09	16	08	600
20	Patty Friend	17	09	47	16	500
21	Brian Blandford	17	16	04	54	0
22	John Wood	18	02	20	35	0
23	Ron Aldrich	18	08	10	31	0
24	Eep Anderson	18	11	33	33	0
25	Myron Angstman	18	19	22	32	0
26	Walter Kaso	18	22	23	40	0
27	Jim Rowe	18	22	29	43	0
28	Steve Vollertsen	19	01	25	40	0
29	Rick McConnell	19	06	57	57	0
30	Rome Gilman	19	13	01	43	0
31	Jamie "Bud" Smyth	20	00	42	14	0
32	Bill Rose	20	01	02	38	0
33	Steve Adkins	20	01	31	48	0
34	Cliff Sisson	20	04	36	53	0
35	Ron Brinker	20	04	37	09	0
36	Del Allison	20	08	23	23	0
37	John Barron	20	09	26	06	0
38	Karl Clauson	21	12	08	29	0
39	Jerry LaVoie	22	08	23	44	0
40	Gayle Nienhueser	22	09	14	53	0
41	Richard Burmeister	22	12	57	37	0
42	Jon Van Zyle	22	13	50	50	0
43	Jim Lanier	24	06	44	18	0
44	Ron Gould	24	07	25	50	0

IDITAROD FINAL STANDINGS
1979
(Continued)

Place	Musher	Days	Hours	Minutes	Seconds	Prize
45	Don Montgomery	24	07	27	11	0
46	Prentice "Harry" Harris	24	07	37	09	0
47	Gene Leonard	24	09	02	22	0

Scratched

1	Mark Couch	5	Terry McMullin
2	Kelly Wages	6	Herbert Nayokpuk
3	Lee Gardino	7	Clarence Towarak
4	Isaac Okleasik	8	Joe Garnie

IDITAROD FINAL STANDINGS
1980

Place	Musher	Days	Hours	Minutes	Seconds	Prize
1	Joe May	14	07	11	51	$12,000
2	Herbert Nayokpuk	14	20	32	12	8,000
3	Ernie Baumgartner	15	09	09	59	6,000
4	Rick Swenson	15	10	12	29	4,000
5	Susan Butcher	15	10	17	06	3,000
6	Roger Nordlum	15	10	34	14	2,500
7	Jerry Austin	15	13	57	13	2,000
8	Walter Kaso	15	15	42	32	1,800
9	Emmitt Peters	15	16	14	07	1,600
10	Donna Gentry	15	16	39	06	1,400
11	Marc Boily	15	17	03	46	1,000
12	Joe Garnie	15	17	55	24	950
13	Larry "Cowboy" Smith	15	18	01	37	900
14	Bruce Johnson	15	18	22	07	850
15	Rudy Demoski	16	09	35	56	800
16	David Olson	16	09	52	51	750
17	Terry Adkins	16	10	56	16	700
18	Libby Riddles	16	13	58	34	650
19	Harold Ahmasuk	16	14	44	11	600
20	Henry Johnson	16	15	28	27	500
21	William Bartlett	16	16	12	46	0
22	Martin Buser	17	06	50	05	0
23	Jack Goodwin	17	07	07	16	0
24	DeeDee Jonrowe	17	07	59	24	0
25	Ken Chase	17	08	32	14	0
26	Bruce Denton	17	13	29	01	0
27	Clarence Shockley	17	13	29	29	0
28	John Cooper	17	14	18	06	0
29	Michael Harrington	17	14	29	36	0
30	Marjorie Ann Moore	20	07	01	17	0
31	Eric Poole	20	09	14	20	0
32	Douglas Sherrer	20	09	38	22	0
33	Ron Cortte	22	03	07	28	0
34	John Gartiez	22	18	05	50	0
35	Col. Norman Vaughan	24	09	19	25	0
36	Barbara Moore	24	09	25	45	0

IDITAROD FINAL STANDINGS
1980
(Continued)

Scratched

1	Bill Boyko	14	Lee Gardino
2	Jan Masek	15	Don Honea
3	Ed Craver	16	Ralph "Babe" Anderson
4	Eugene Russel Ivey	17	Don Eckles
5	Larry Cogdill	18	Frank Sampson
6	Robert E. Neidig	19	Warner Vent
7	John Eckles	20	Sonny Lindner
8	Steven R. Conaster	21	Joe Redington, Sr.
9	Duke Bertke	22	Dick Mackey
10	Varona Thompson	23	Alton Walluk
11	Fred Jackson	24	Bruce Woods
12	John Barron	25	Jerry Riley
13	Dick Peterson		

IDITAROD FINAL STANDINGS
1981

Place	Musher	Days	Hours	Minutes	Seconds	Prize
1	Rick Swenson	12	08	45	02	$24,000
2	Sonny Lindner	12	09	33	22	16,000
3	Roger Nordlum	12	09	42	13	12,000
4	Larry "Cowboy" Smith	12	10	22	46	8,000
5	Susan Butcher	12	12	45	24	6,000
6	Eep Anderson	12	14	08	37	5,000
7	Herbert Nayokpuk	12	22	17	45	4,000
8	Clarence Towarak	13	01	48	04	3,600
9	Rick Mackey	13	03	58	07	3,200
10	Terry Adkins	13	07	32	04	2,800
11	Duane (Dewey) Halverson	13	13	55	19	2,000
12	Emmitt Peters	13	14	14	49	1,900
13	Jerry Austin	13	14	40	38	1,800
14	Joe Redington, Sr.	13	15	19	02	1,700
15	Harry Sutherland	13	18	02	07	1,600
16	Joe Garnie	13	18	17	35	1,500
17	Gary Attla	13	22	01	37	1,400
18	Donna Gentry	13	22	20	20	1,300
19	Martin Buser	14	02	47	23	1,200
20	Libby Riddles	14	06	27	43	1,000
21	David Monson	14	14	44	04	0
22	Bruce Denton	14	22	05	13	0
23	John Barron	14	23	57	00	0
24	Gene Leonard	15	00	32	14	0
25	Bob Martin	15	00	45	09	0
26	Neil Eklund	15	03	44	00	0
27	Mark Freshwaters	15	03	45	37	0
28	Jeff King	15	07	02	47	0
29	Steve Flodin	16	01	52	14	0
30	Gary Whittemore	16	04	13	06	0
31	DeeDee Jonrowe	16	05	05	43	0
32	Sue Firmin	16	05	05	56	0
33	Mike Storto	16	11	37	57	0
34	Dan Zobrist	17	03	28	43	0
35	Dennis Boyer	17	16	28	00	0
36	Jan Masek	18	03	44	44	0
37	Burt Bomhoff	18	05	22	58	0
38	Jim Strong	18	06	30	30	0

IDITAROD FINAL STANDINGS
1981
(Continued)

Scratched

1	Ken Chase (prior to race)	9	Jamie "Bud" Smyth
2	Frank Sampson	10	Ted English
3	Harold Ahmasuk	11	Wes McIntyre
4	Robert Ivan	12	Willie French
5	William Webb	13	Clifton Jackson
6	Ernie Baumgartner	14	Bill Thompson
7	Gordon Castanza	15	Jerry Riley
8	Douglas Sherrer	16	Myron Angstman

IDITAROD FINAL STANDINGS
1982

Place	Musher	Days	Hours	Minutes	Seconds	Prize
1	Rick Swenson	16	04	40	10	$24,000
2	Susan Butcher	16	04	43	53	16,000
3	Jerry Austin	16	04	52	11	12,000
4	Emmitt Peters	16	05	06	42	8,000
5	David Monson	16	05	13	24	6,000
6	Ernie Baumgartner	16	05	17	03	5,000
7	Bob Chlupach	16	05	26	46	4,000
8	Don Honea	16	06	41	00	3,600
9	Stan Zuray	16	06	44	00	3,200
10	Bruce Denton	16	13	11	22	2,800
11	Rick Mackey	16	13	30	47	2,000
12	Herbert Nayokpuk	16	14	08	21	1,900
13	Dean Osmar	16	14	54	54	1,800
14	Terry Adkins	16	15	37	47	1,700
15	Joe May	16	15	43	23	1,600
16	Marc Boily	16	17	54	55	1,500
17	Joe Redington, Sr.	17	08	25	45	1,400
18	Ed Foran	17	09	09	29	1,300
19	Guy Blankenship	17	09	13	22	1,200
20	John Stam	17	09	18	18	1,000
21	Alex Sheldon	17	09	24	46	0
22	Mitch Seavey	17	10	27	00	0
23	Glenn Findlay	17	11	57	53	0
24	John Wood	17	12	39	46	0
25	Ralph "Babe" Anderson	17	21	12	02	0
26	Jim Strong	18	17	15	36	0
27	Ron Cortte	18	17	17	59	0
28	Larry "Cowboy" Smith	18	23	09	23	0
29	Dean Painter	20	03	05	06	0
30	Ken Chase	20	04	01	45	0
31	Steve Gaber	20	04	23	32	0
32	Rose Albert	20	04	54	53	0
33	Jan Masek	20	10	13	24	0
34	Chris Deverill	20	12	45	00	0
35	Leroy Shank	21	12	43	31	0
36	Steve Flodin	21	13	00	00	0
37	Frank I. Brown	21	14	54	59	0
38	Mark "Bigfoot" Rosser	21	16	05	27	0
39	Bill Yankee	21	22	02	45	0
40	James Cole	22	05	53	42	0
41	Richard Burmeister	22	06	29	00	0
42	Rick Tarpey	22	07	18	30	0
43	Eric Buetow	22	14	48	28	0

IDITAROD FINAL STANDINGS
1982
(Continued)

Place	Musher	Days	Hours	Minutes	Seconds	Prize
44	Rome Gilman	24	00	23	47	0
45	Jack Studer	24	14	54	54	0
46	Ralph Bradley	26	13	59	59	0

Scratched

1	Michael Harrington	5	Smokey Moff
2	Col. Norman Vaughan	6	Bill Rose
3	Steve Haver	7	Gary Whittemore
4	Sue Firmin	8	John Barron

IDITAROD FINAL STANDINGS
1983

Place	Musher	Days	Hours	Minutes	Seconds	Prize
1	Rick Mackey	12	14	10	44	$24,000
2	Eep Anderson	12	15	50	36	16,000
3	Larry "Cowboy" Smith	12	20	19	56	12,000
4	Herbert Nayokpuk	12	22	04	28	8,000
5	Rick Swenson	13	02	49	46	6,000
6	Lavon Barve	13	03	00	49	5,000
7	Duane (Dewey) Halverson	13	04	42	00	4,000
8	Sonny Lindner	13	05	28	20	3,600
9	Susan Butcher	13	10	25	32	3,200
10	Roger Legaard	13	11	33	45	2,800
11	Joe Runyan	13	12	39	34	2,000
12	Guy Blankenship	13	12	54	59	1,900
13	David Monson	13	14	08	54	1,800
14	Sue Firmin	13	17	28	52	1,700
15	DeeDee Jonrowe	13	18	10	25	1,600
16	Howard Albert	13	22	11	39	1,500
17	Bruce Denton	14	00	37	07	1,400
18	David Olson	14	03	35	29	1,300
19	Emmitt Peters	14	03	36	20	1,200
20	John Barron	14	05	44	30	1,000
21	Neil Eklund	14	10	32	03	0
22	Burt Bomhoff	14	12	23	20	0
23	Roxy Woods	14	15	56	16	0
24	Walter Kaso	15	05	00	53	0
25	Eric Buetow	15	08	06	39	0
26	Jim Strong	15	10	07	54	0
27	Ken Hamm	15	10	15	15	0
28	Vern Halter	15	10	40	17	0
29	Shannon Poole	15	13	10	56	0
30	William Hayes	15	15	15	15	0
31	Walter Williams	15	23	17	34	0
32	Christine O'Gar	16	00	19	05	0
33	Ted English	16	00	37	29	0
34	Jamie "Bud" Smyth	16	09	34	00	0
35	Ron Brennan	17	00	42	57	0
36	Wes McIntyre	17	10	49	39	0
37	Ken Johnson	17	11	12	06	0
38	Steve Reiger	17	11	13	01	0
39	Connie Frerichs	17	11	16	26	0
40	Ray Dronenburg	17	12	31	51	0
41	Gary Paulsen	17	12	38	38	0
42	Ed Forstner	18	06	52	16	0
43	Mark Nordman	18	17	54	34	0
44	Dick Barnum	18	23	59	59	0

IDITAROD FINAL STANDINGS
1983
(Continued)

Place	Musher	Days	Hours	Minutes	Seconds	Prize
45	David Wolfe	19	04	28	40	0
46	Leroy Shank	19	15	07	54	0
47	Robert Gould	20	00	42	29	0
48	Fritz Kirsch	20	01	34	24	0
49	Steve Haver	20	12	55	56	0
50	Ron Gould	20	13	12	05	0
51	Pam Flowers	20	13	12	54	0
52	Col. Norman Vaughan	21	02	21	16	0
53	Norm McAlpine	21	02	44	22	0
54	Scott Cameron	21	04	36	41	0

Scratched

1	Terry Adkins
2	Russell Ivey
3	Gene Leonard
4	Beverly Jerue
5	William Cowart
6	Alex Sheldon
7	Bob Bright
8	Saul Paniptchuk
9	Ken Chase
10	Clifton Cadzow

Disqualified

1	Les Atherton
2	Dr. Hal Bartko
3	Doug Bartko
4	Jan Masek

IDITAROD FINAL STANDINGS
1984

Place	Musher	Days	Hours	Minutes	Seconds	Prize
1	Dean Osmar	12	15	07	33	$24,000
2	Susan Butcher	12	16	41	42	16,000
3	Joe Garnie	12	17	18	48	12,000
4	Marc Boily	13	04	52	51	8,000
5	Jerry Austin	13	05	59	53	6,000
6	Rick Swenson	13	07	04	21	5,000
7	Joe Redington, Sr.	13	08	43	11	4,000
8	Terry Adkins	13	13	54	43	3,600
9	John Cooper	14	00	22	24	3,200
10	Larry "Cowboy" Smith	14	01	57	44	2,800
11	Vern Halter	14	03	55	19	2,000
12	Burt Bomhoff	14	07	49	18	1,900
13	Rusty Miller	14	08	44	17	1,800
14	Mark Freshwaters	14	10	31	10	1,700
15	Bob Chlupach	14	10	31	12	1,600
16	Ed Foran	14	11	27	41	1,500
17	Emmitt Peters	14	15	08	00	1,400
18	Rick Armstrong	14	16	55	30	1,300
19	Ray Gordon	14	18	43	32	1,200
20	John Barron	14	22	54	34	1,000
21	Jim Strong	15	07	16	07	0
22	Bob Toll	15	09	23	23	0
23	Eep Anderson	15	11	00	54	0
24	Gordon Castanza	15	11	05	55	0
25	Ron Cortte	15	13	18	38	0
26	Jerry Raychel	15	13	57	29	0
27	Diana Dronenburg	15	15	29	49	0
28	Sue Firmin	15	19	09	15	0
29	Rick Mackey	15	19	09	23	0
30	DeeDee Jonrowe	15	19	18	13	0
31	David Olson	15	19	30	00	0
32	Gary Whittemore	15	20	44	14	0
33	Eric Buetow	16	00	56	29	0
34	Frank Bettine	16	08	03	07	0
35	Kari Skogen	16	08	03	19	0
36	Calvin Lauwers	16	12	?	00	0
37	Dan Cowan	16	12	35	02	0
38	Francine Bennis	16	13	40	03	0
39	Rick Adkinson	17	03	23	19	0
40	Jim Lanier	17	05	49	22	0
41	David Sheer	17	08	53	05	0
42	Steve Peek	17	10	58	55	0
43	Fred Agree	19	07	41	07	0
44	Ed Borden	19	09	43	17	0
45	Bill Mackey	19	09	43	33	0

IDITAROD FINAL STANDINGS
1984
(Continued)

Scratched

1	Ted English
2	James Cole
3	Jan Masek
4	Dave Aisenbrey
5	Gene Leonard
6	Ray Dronenburg
7	Gordon Brinker
8	Connie Frerichs
9	Don Honea
10	Lolly Medley
11	Larry Dogdill
12	Brian Johnson
13	Miki Collins
14	Steve Gaber
15	Bill Thompson
16	Melvin Adkins
17	Bob Sunder
18	Darrell Reynolds
19	Vern Cherneski
20	Ron Brennan

Disqualified

1	Guy Blankenship
2	Armen Khatchikian

IDITAROD FINAL STANDINGS
1985

Place	Musher	Days	Hours	Minutes	Seconds	Prize
1	Libby Riddles	18	00	20	17	$50,000
2	Duane (Dewey) Halverson	18	02	45	36	30,000
3	John Cooper	18	06	59	33	20,000
4	Rick Swenson	18	07	29	24	15,000
5	Rick Mackey	18	14	44	54	13,000
6	Vern Halter	18	14	55	26	11,000
7	Guy Blankenship	18	16	16	39	9,500
8	Herbert Nayokpuk	18	17	20	00	8,000
9	Sonny Lindner	18	18	33	33	6,500
10	Lavon Barve	18	19	25	04	5,500
11	Tim Moerlein	18	21	10	56	4,500
12	Emmitt Peters	18	23	21	22	4,000
13	Tim Osmar	18	23	43	43	3,750
14	Jerry Austin	19	03	32	43	3,500
15	Terry Adkins	19	22	51	49	3,250
16	Roger Nordlum	19	23	51	15	3,000
17	Glenn Findlay	20	01	34	33	2,750
18	John Barron	20	03	21	22	2,500
19	Raymie Redington	20	03	38	19	2,250
20	Burt Bomhoff	20	03	59	17	2,000
21	Jacques Philip	20	05	00	21	0
22	Bob Bright	21	02	34	27	0
23	Peter Fromm	21	02	34	33	0
24	Steve Flodin	21	05	08	04	0
25	Warner Vent	21	05	31	54	0
26	Ron Robbins	21	05	40	25	0
27	Kazuo Kojima	21	06	12	12	0
28	Nathan Underwood	21	06	54	00	0
29	Betsy McGuire	21	07	07	15	0
30	Kevin Saiki	21	08	04	09	0
31	Earl Norris	21	09	38	00	0
32	Kevin Fulton	21	09	39	00	0
33	John Coble	21	10	13	00	0
34	Alan Cheshire	21	10	21	00	0
35	Victor Jorge	21	10	25	00	0
36	Fred Agree	21	11	25	36	0
37	Claire Philip	21	11	35	37	0
38	John Ace	21	21	01	01	0
39	Rick Armstrong	21	21	01	02	0
40	Monique Bene	22	03	45	45	0

IDITAROD FINAL STANDINGS
1985
(Continued)

Scratched

1	Dave Aisenbrey	13	Dennis Towarak
2	Terry Hinsley	14	Ernie Baumgartner
3	Susan Butcher	15	Rudy Demoski
4	Ted English	16	Col. Norman Vaughan
5	Jan Masek	17	Armen Khatchikian
6	Joe Redington, Sr.	18	Scott Cameron
7	Fred Jackson	19	Chuck Shaeffer
8	Victor Katongan		
9	Gary Paulsen		Disqualified
10	Ray Dronenburg		
11	Joseph Maileile, Sr.	1	Bobby Lee
12	Terry McMullin	2	Wes McIntyre

IDITAROD FINAL STANDINGS
1986

Place	Musher	Days	Hours	Minutes	Seconds	Prize
1	Susan Butcher	11	15	06	00	$50,000
2	Joe Garnie	11	16	01	11	30,000
3	Rick Swenson	11	23	59	43	20,000
4	Joe Runyan	12	02	11	31	15,000
5	Duane (Dewey) Halverson	12	02	27	51	13,000
6	John Cooper	12	03	28	03	11,000
7	Lavon Barve	12	04	17	55	9,500
8	Jerry Austin	12	10	15	01	8,000
9	Terry Adkins	13	00	22	29	6,500
10	Rune Hesthammer	13	04	20	00	5,500
11	John Barron	13	04	27	45	4,500
12	Guy Blankenship	13	07	12	29	4,000
13	Tim Moerlein	13	07	40	31	3,750
14	Bob Chlupach	13	10	32	13	3,500
15	Jerry Riley	13	14	36	49	3,250
16	Vern Halter	13	15	29	29	3,000
17	Gary Whittemore	13	20	37	23	2,750
18	Ted English	13	23	01	26	2,500
19	Nina Hotvedt	14	06	20	41	2,250
20	Rick Atkinson	14	06	21	21	2,000
21	Rusty Miller	14	11	04	54	0
22	Peter Sapin	14	11	17	42	0
23	Frank Torres	14	16	43	15	0
24	Paul Johnson	15	00	08	06	0
25	Martin Buser	15	00	53	56	0
26	John Wood	15	04	29	42	0
27	Dan MacEachen	15	05	09	14	0
28	Jerry Raychel	15	07	09	14	0
29	Raymie Redington	15	07	12	24	0
30	Mike Pemberton	15	07	44	37	0
31	Dave Olesen	15	09	44	15	0
32	Steve Bush	15	09	55	31	0
33	Kari Skogen	15	10	52	49	0
34	Gordon Brinker	15	15	20	31	0
35	Bobby Lee	16	10	34	03	0
36	Ron Robbins	16	15	03	19	0
37	Dave Scheer	16	15	03	58	0
38	Gordy Hubbard	16	16	44	44	0
39	Matt Desalernos	16	19	22	59	0
40	Alan Cheshire	16	21	09	57	0
41	Ray Lang	16	22	39	02	0
42	Roger Roberts	16	22	53	02	0
43	Allen Miller	17	05	41	37	0
44	Armen Khatchikian	17	08	12	29	0

IDITAROD FINAL STANDINGS
1986
(Continued)

Place	Musher	Days	Hours	Minutes	Seconds	Prize
45	Don McQuown	17	15	59	49	0
46	Mike Lawless	18	01	20	52	0
47	Mark Jackson	18	11	01	34	0
48	Joe LeFaive	18	18	07	24	0
49	Peter Thomann	18	18	07	34	0
50	Pat Danly	19	00	38	21	0
51	Bill Hall	19	00	38	48	0
52	Bill Davidson	19	00	55	55	0
53	Scott Cameron	19	19	51	27	0
54	Stan Ferguson	19	21	42	58	0
55	Mike Peterson	20	13	42	21	0

Scratched

1	Abel Akpik
2	John Nels Anderson
3	Frank Bettine
4	Roger Bliss
5	Ron Brennan
6	Joe Carpenter
7	William Cowart
8	Jim Darling
9	Ray Dronenburg
10	Don Honea
11	Fred Jackson
12	Rick Mackey
13	Jan Masek
14	Earl Norris
15	Joe Redington, Sr.
16	Douglas Sheldon
17	John Stam
18	Col. Norman Vaughan

IDITAROD FINAL STANDINGS
1987

Place	Musher	Days	Hours	Minutes	Seconds	Prize
1	Susan Butcher	11	02	05	13	$50,000
2	Rick Swenson	11	06	25	43	30,000
3	Duane (Dewey) Halverson	11	08	27	51	20,000
4	Tim Osmar	11	11	11	27	15,000
5	Jerry Austin	11	12	16	05	13,000
6	Joe Runyan	11	13	13	48	11,000
7	Lavon Barve	11	20	15	22	9,500
8	Ted English	11	?	12	03	8,000
9	John Cooper	12	00	14	14	6,500
10	Martin Buser	12	02	26	28	5,500
11	Joe Garnie	12	03	24	24	4,500
12	Guy Blankenship	12	05	11	10	4,000
13	Jerry Riley	12	06	59	00	3,750
14	Diana Dronenburg	12	09	13	18	3,500
15	Steve Adkins	12	09	30	30	3,250
16	Matt Desalernos	12	09	31	40	3,000
17	Harry Sutherland	12	11	25	11	2,750
18	Robin Jacobson	12	14	35	30	2,500
19	Bruce Johnson	12	17	15	00	2,250
20	Jacques Philip	12	18	27	53	2,000
21	Sue Firmin	13	02	57	11	0
22	DeeDee Jonrowe	13	02	58	15	0
23	Terry Adkins	13	04	06	21	0
24	Gary Whittemore	13	04	56	24	0
25	Herbert Nayokpuk	13	10	27	47	0
26	Claire Philip	13	10	33	33	0
27	Gary Guy	15	04	35	14	0
28	Dave Olesen	15	04	46	13	0
29	Dan MacEachen	15	08	33	15	0
30	Kazuo Kojima	15	08	53	17	0
31	Bruce Barton	15	09	24	22	0
32	Dick Mackey	15	13	28	22	0
33	Joe Redington, Sr.	15	14	13	12	0
34	Dennis J. Lozano	15	15	29	28	0
35	John Nels Anderson	15	18	06	46	0
36	John Coble	15	18	14	50	0
37	Michael V. Owens	15	18	39	49	0
38	Roger Roberts	17	10	32	42	0
39	Pat Danly	17	11	02	22	0
40	Bill Chisholm	17	11	16	28	0
41	Henry Horner	17	11	28	10	0
42	Caleb Slemons	17	12	33	39	0
43	Mike Lawless	17	13	30	00	0
44	Roy Wade	17	15	21	51	0

IDITAROD FINAL STANDINGS
1987
(Continued)

Place	Musher	Days	Hours	Minutes	Seconds	Prize
45	John T. Gourley	18	04	51	49	0
46	Don McQuown	18	12	34	35	0
47	Matt Ace	18	12	45	38	0
48	Brian Johnson	18	23	32	23	0
49	Andre Monnier	18	23	35	30	0
50	Rhodi Karella	19	09	01	01	0

Scratched

1	Peter Thomann
2	Rick Mackey
3	Raymie Redington
4	John Barron
5	Burt Bomhoff
6	Gordy Hubbard
7	Libby Riddles
8	Gordon Brinker
9	Joe LeFaive
10	Dave Aisenbrey

Withdrew

1	Carolyn Muegge
2	Tony Burch
3	Col. Norman Vaughan

IDITAROD FINAL STANDINGS
1988

Place	Musher	Days	Hours	Minutes	Seconds	Prize
1	Susan Butcher	11	11	41	40	30,000
2	Rick Swenson	12	02	10	09	21,000
3	Martin Buser	12	04	21	46	16,500
4	Joe Garnie	12	09	21	39	13,200
5	Joe Redington, Sr.	13	03	25	28	9,000
6	Herbert Nayokpuk	13	03	26	44	7,200
7	Rick Mackey	13	14	43	29	6,900
8	Lavon Barve	13	15	22	42	6,000
9	DeeDee Jonrowe	13	16	29	06	5,400
10	Robin Jacobson	13	17	19	48	4,800
11	Jerry Austin	13	19	06	03	4,500
12	Jan Masek	13	22	18	03	4,200
13	Lucy Nordlum	13	23	47	31	3,900
14	Jacques Philip	14	00	02	43	3,600
15	Bill Cotter	14	01	33	18	3,300
16	Tim Osmar	14	01	49	16	3,000
17	Dan MacEachen	14	02	46	11	2,700
18	John Patten	14	03	57	06	2,400
19	Harry Sutherland	14	04	16	56	2,100
20	Matt Desalernos	14	05	01	36	1,800
21	Bill Hall	14	05	49	07	0
22	Darwin McLeod	14	06	01	06	0
23	Horst Maas	14	07	11	11	0
24	Ted English	14	08	52	23	0
25	Jerry Raychel	14	09	17	09	0
26	John Barron	14	09	54	24	0
27	Duane (Dewey) Halverson	14	11	19	55	0
28	Peter Thomann	14	12	38	45	0
29	Conrad Saussele	14	21	24	20	0
30	Burt Bomhoff	14	21	46	25	0
31	Frank Teasley	15	06	42	51	0
32	Peryll Kyzer	15	12	30	48	0
33	Ken Chase	15	12	54	20	0
34	Ralph "Babe" Anderson	15	13	06	49	0
35	Ian MacKenzie	17	06	45	45	0
36	Mike Tvenge	17	08	01	59	0
37	Mark Merrill	18	01	29	14	0
38	John Suter	18	01	50	50	0
39	John T. Gourley	18	06	52	30	0
40	Jennifer Gourley	18	06	54	12	0
41	Peter Kelly	18	07	06	41	0
42	Tim Mowry	18	07	21	41	0
43	Matt Ace	18	07	34	06	0
44	Gordon Brinker	18	07	44	07	0
45	Lesley Anne Monk	19	13	22	55	0

IDITAROD FINAL STANDINGS
1988
(Continued)

Scratched
1   Tim Moerlein
2   Terry Adkins
3   Joe Runyan
4   Brian Carver
5   Ray Dronenburg
6   Col. Norman Vaughan

Disqualified

1   Stan Ferguson

IDITAROD FINAL STANDINGS
1989

Place	Musher	Days	Hours	Minutes	Seconds	Prize
1	Joe Runyan	11	05	24	34	$50,000
2	Susan Butcher	11	06	28	50	35,000
3	Rick Swenson	11	08	50	50	27,000
4	DeeDee Jonrowe	11	13	47	16	20,000
5	Lavon Barve	11	16	46	53	15,000
6	Martin Buser	12	02	06	05	12,000
7	Guy Blankenship	12	02	22	24	11,000
8	Rick Mackey	12	02	25	00	10,000
9	Joe Redington, Sr.	12	02	57	16	9,000
10	Tim Osmar	12	03	33	03	8,000
11	Jacques Philip	12	04	40	46	7,500
12	Matt Desalernos	12	05	33	38	7,000
13	Bob Chlupach	12	06	17	41	6,500
14	John Barron	12	08	10	08	6,000
15	Joe Garnie	12	08	33	28	5,500
16	Libby Riddles	12	08	34	44	5,000
17	Jerry Riley	12	13	35	21	4,500
18	Bill Cotter	12	15	22	59	4,000
19	Frank Teasley	12	16	54	19	3,500
20	Terry Adkins	13	07	13	57	3,000
21	Richard Self	13	09	56	57	0
22	Jerry Austin	13	09	57	56	0
23	Mitch Brazin	13	10	05	54	0
24	Diana Dronenburg	13	10	34	40	0
25	Jamie Nelson	13	11	26	35	0
26	Linwood Fiedler	13	13	37	37	0
27	Tim Mowry	13	21	19	09	0
28	Bill Cavaney	14	01	30	38	0
29	Karin Schmidt	14	09	24	12	0
30	Bernie Willis	14	10	06	06	0
31	Pat Danly	14	10	16	10	0
32	Kathy Halverson	14	10	43	32	0
33	Kazuo Kojima	14	13	45	07	0
34	Frank Winkler	14	22	35	34	0
35	Conner Thomas	14	22	51	20	0
36	John Suter	14	22	54	44	0
37	Duane Lamberts	16	01	04	04	0
38	Bob Hoyte	17	11	19	19	0

Scratched

1	Kevin Saiki	7	Mike Ross
2	Carolyn Muegge-Vaughan	8	Dave Aisenbrey
3	Joe LeFaive	9	Col. Norman Vaughan
4	Michael Madden	10	Roger Roberts
5	Bill Chisholm	11	Jan Masek
6	Gary Whittemore		

IDITAROD FINAL STANDINGS
1990

Place	Musher	Days	Hours	Minutes	Seconds	Prize
1	Susan Butcher	11	01	53	23	$50,000
2	Joe Runyan	11	04	21	12	35,000
3	Lavon Barve	11	07	15	04	27,000
4	Tim Osmar	11	14	40	53	20,000
5	DeeDee Jonrowe	11	14	41	31	15,000
6	Robin Jacobson	11	16	32	02	12,000
7	Rick Swenson	11	16	55	45	11,000
8	Linwood Fiedler	12	01	19	16	10,000
9	Joe Garnie	12	02	05	12	9,000
10	Martin Buser	12	02	33	44	8,000
11	Bill Cotter	13	03	54	28	7,500
12	Rick Mackey	13	08	19	46	7,000
13	Michael Madden	13	08	41	06	6,500
14	Jacques Philip	13	08	42	50	6,000
15	Sonny Russell	13	09	07	26	5,500
16	John Barron	13	09	07	41	5,000
17	Matt Desalernos	13	09	09	39	4,500
18	John T. Gourley	13	09	11	22	4,000
19	Jerry Austin	13	09	17	52	3,500
20	Bill Chisholm	13	09	19	19	3,000
21	Dan MacEachen	14	09	37	31	1,000
22	Norm Stoppenbrink	14	09	56	31	1,000
23	Michael V. Owens	14	11	29	23	1,000
24	Terry Adkins	14	12	44	04	1,000
25	Joe Redington, Sr.	14	12	59	13	1,000
26	Mitch Brazin	14	13	54	13	1,000
27	Kevin Saiki	14	14	12	44	1,000
28	Diana Dronenburg	14	22	23	27	1,000
29	Bob Chlupach	14	23	11	08	1,000
30	Harry Sutherland	15	02	13	03	1,000
31	Don McEwen	15	05	34	02	1,000
32	Raymie Redington	15	05	37	16	1,000
33	Frank Winkler	15	08	07	25	1,000
34	Bill Hall	15	09	10	56	1,000
35	Beverly Masek	15	14	13	21	1,000
36	Malcolm Vance	15	14	13	22	1,000
37	Roy Wade	15	17	05	29	1,000
38	Roy Monk	15	18	15	29	1,000
39	Dave Breuer	15	18	22	31	1,000
40	Duane Lamberts	15	20	50	09	1,000
41	Emmitt Peters	15	21	11	39	1,000
42	Bob Hickel	15	22	27	19	1,000
43	Macgill Adams	15	22	53	12	1,000
44	Lynda Plettner	16	00	29	39	1,000

IDITAROD FINAL STANDINGS
1990 (continued)

Place	Musher	Days	Hours	Minutes	Seconds	Prize
45	John Suter	16	00	41	00	1,000
46	Larry Harris	16	00	46	33	1,000
47	Greg Tibbetts	16	00	49	04	1,000
48	Bryan Moline	16	01	18	18	1,000
49	Jim Wood	16	01	47	28	1,000
50	Bert Hanson	16	04	06	55	1,000
51	Peter Kelly	16	09	06	12	1,000
52	Pecos Humphreys	16	09	19	01	1,000
53	Bill Davidson	17	02	16	58	1,000
54	Lorren Weaver	18	02	30	00	1,000
55	Lars Ekstrand	18	02	30	?	1,000
56	Larry Munoz	18	12	38	14	1,000
57	John Ace	18	15	41	08	1,000
58	Paul Byrd	18	16	39	09	1,000
59	Terry Hinesley	18	16	59	19	1,000
60	Col. Norman Vaughan	21	10	26	06	1,000
61	Steve Haver	21	10	26	26	1,000

Scratched

1	Guy Blankenship
2	Pascal Nicoud
3	Joe LeFaive
4	Chuck Shaeffer
5	Tim Mundy
6	Mike Ross
7	Lesley Anne Monk

Disqualified

1	Frank Teasley
2	Jerry Riley

IDITAROD FINAL STANDINGS
1991

Place	Musher	Days	Hours	Minutes	Seconds	Prize
1	Rick Swenson	12	16	34	39	$50,000
2	Martin Buser	12	18	41	49	39,500
3	Susan Butcher	12	21	59	03	32,000
4	Tim Osmar	12	22	33	33	24,500
5	Joe Runyan	12	22	36	30	19,000
6	Frank Teasley	13	12	27	57	15,000
7	DeeDee Jonrowe	13	13	44	10	14,000
8	Matt Desalernos	13	13	44	35	13,000
9	Rick Mackey	13	13	54	39	12,000
10	Bill Cotter	13	13	57	28	11,000
11	Kate Persons	13	14	20	59	9,500
12	Jeff King	13	14	24	40	9,000
13	Jacques Philip	13	15	07	39	8,500
14	Jerry Austin	13	17	10	51	8,000
15	Michael Madden	13	20	06	26	7,500
16	Ketil Reitan	13	21	54	12	6,500
17	Lavon Barve	13	22	20	14	6,000
18	Peryll Kyzer	14	16	26	26	5,500
19	Terry Adkins	14	16	46	51	5,000
20	Bill Jack	14	19	38	14	4,500
21	Beverly Masek	15	09	03	51	1,000
22	Laird Barron	15	10	07	15	1,000
23	Joe Garnie	15	11	53	33	1,000
24	Rick Armstrong	15	12	24	07	1,000
25	Linwood Fiedler	15	23	45	15	1,000
26	Burt Bomhoff	16	08	48	36	1,000
27	Dan MacEachen	16	09	08	46	1,000
28	Dave Olesen	16	10	01	52	1,000
29	Raymie Redington	16	10	02	23	1,000
30	Dave Allen	16	10	25	26	1,000
31	Joe Redington, Sr.	16	11	56	56	1,000
32	Jerry Raychel	16	17	51	17	1,000
33	Mark Nordman	16	17	55	38	1,000
34	Malcolm Vance	17	09	30	00	1,000
35	Macgill Adams	17	10	10	13	1,000
36	Nikoli Ettyne	17	10	53	00	1,000
37	Alexander Reznyuk	17	11	54	12	1,000
38	Tony Shoogukwruk	17	12	34	11	1,000
39	Rollin Westrum	17	13	44	00	1,000
40	Brian Stafford	17	15	35	48	1,000
41	John Suter	17	18	23	31	1,000
42	Roger Roberts	17	22	08	00	1,000
43	Larry Munoz	17	22	59	52	1,000
44	Jim Cantor	18	00	02	00	1,000

IDITAROD FINAL STANDINGS
1991 (continued)

Place	Musher	Days	Hours	Minutes	Seconds	Prize
45	Terry Seaman	18	00	08	35	1,000
46	Kazuo Kojima	18	00	29	28	1,000
47	Rich Bosela	18	00	50	45	1,000
48	Pat Danly	18	02	23	36	1,000
49	Dave Breuer	18	04	49	29	1,000
50	Chris Converse	18	05	09	50	1,000
51	Sepp Herrman	21	05	59	26	1,000
52	Lynda Plettner	21	21	04	06	1,000
53	Jon Terhune	22	00	11	04	1,000
54	Gunnar Johnson	22	00	57	48	1,000
55	Urtha Lenharr	22	01	05	09	1,000
56	Tom Daily	22	01	06	50	1,000
57	Mark Williams	22	01	06	58	1,000
58	Catherine Mormile	22	01	18	28	1,000
59	Don Mormile	22	01	35	16	1,000
60	Brian O'Donoghue	22	05	55	55	1,000

Scratched

1	Dave Aisenbrey
2	John Nels Anderson
3	Roy Monk
4	Gary Moore
5	John Ace
6	Sonny Russell
7	Robin Jacobson
8	Steve Fossett
9	Alan Garth
10	Bill Peele
11	Barry Lee
12	Ken Chase
13	John Barron
14	Gary Whittemore

Disqualified

1	Joe Carpenter

IDITAROD FINAL STANDINGS
1992

Place	Musher	Days	Hours	Minutes	Seconds	Prize
1	Martin Buser	10	19	17	15	$51,600
2	Susan Butcher	11	05	36	03	41,280
3	Tim Osmar	11	05	49	39	36,120
4	Rick Swenson	11	07	51	49	30,960
5	DeeDee Jonrowe	11	09	05	00	25,800
6	Jeff King	11	10	40	35	20,640
7	Vern Halter	11	13	08	40	18,576
8	Rick Mackey	11	13	20	23	17,544
9	Doug Swingley	11	13	47	00	16,512
10	Ketil Reitan	11	14	38	00	15,480
11	Matt Desalernos	11	15	15	12	14,448
12	Bruce Lee	11	15	38	40	13,416
13	Claire Philip	11	15	43	20	12,384
14	Ed Iten	11	16	01	43	11,868
15	Bill Cotter	11	17	00	00	11,352
16	Kate Persons	11	20	14	42	10,836
17	Lavon Barve	11	21	38	03	10,320
18	John Barron	11	23	53	21	9,804
19	Dan MacEachen	12	04	05	53	9,288
20	Joe Garnie	12	05	46	50	8,772
21	Kathy Swenson	12	05	53	50	0
22	Sonny Lindner	12	08	06	08	0
23	Beverly Masek	12	13	20	55	0
24	Jerry Austin	12	13	26	53*	0
25	Linwood Fiedler	12	21	59	50	0
26	Dave Olesen	12	22	15	30	0
27	Bill Jack	13	00	21	22	0
28	Frank Teasley	13	03	03	58	0
29	Rick Armstrong	13	03	41	59	0
30	Terry Adkins	13	07	55	25	0
31	Bob Chlupach	13	08	41	45	0
32	Burt Bomhoff	13	10	23	25	0
33	Bill Hall	13	14	07	10	0
34	Gary Whittemore	13	17	15	18	0
35	Tomas Israelson	13	20	17	00	0
36	Kathy Tucker	14	00	55	30	0
37	Susan Cantor	14	01	42	42	0
38	Roy Monk	14	02	09	06	0
39	Lynda Plettner	14	02	46	54	0
40	Norm Stoppenbrink	14	02	49	52	0
41	Joe Redington, Sr.	14	03	00	00	0
42	Raymie Redington	14	04	12	13	0
43	Charlie Boulding	14	04	12	35	0
44	Mike Williams	14	08	46	47	0

IDITAROD FINAL STANDINGS
1992 (continued)

Place	Musher	Days	Hours	Minutes	Seconds	Prize
45	John Nels Anderson	14	09	07	45	0
46	Kim Teasley	14	11	42	47	0
47	Steve Fossett	14	11	58	18	0
48	Jon Terhune	14	12	24	10	0
49	Bob Holder	14	13	34	12	0
50	Jim Oehlschlaeger	14	14	40	30	0
51	Cliff Roberson	14	14	56	40	0
52	Pete Johnson	14	15	01	40	0
53	Steve Christon	14	17	38	15	0
54	Skin Wysocki	15	02	58	20	0
55	Mellen Shea	15	13	45	15	0
56	Bill Bass	15	13	48	00	0
57	Bob Hickel	15	14	12	45	0
58	Debbie Corral	15	14	36	40	0
59	James Reiter	18	12	03	15	0
60	Loren Weaver	18	12	12	27	0
61	Jim Davis	18	13	03	45	0
62	John Peterson	18	13	04	58	0
63	Vern Cherneski	18	13	05	02	0

Scratched

1	Tim Mundy
2	Catherine Mormile
3	Carolyn Muegge-Vaughan
4	Col. Norman Vaughan
5	William Orazietti
6	Robin Jacobson
7	Pascal Nicoud
8	Emmitt Peters
9	Sonny Russell
10	Joe Runyan
11	Eep Anderson
12	Krista Maciolek
13	Bob Ernisse

IDITAROD FINAL STANDINGS
1993

Place	*Musher*	*Days*	*Hours*	*Minutes*	*Seconds*	*Prize*
1	Jeff King	10	15	38	15	$50,000
2	DeeDee Jonrowe	10	16	10	50	43,000
3	Rick Mackey	10	18	07	55	37,000
4	Susan Butcher	10	22	02	40	32,000
5	Tim Osmar	10	22	07	00	27,000
6	Martin Buser	11	00	47	39	22,000
7	Matt Desalernos	11	05	47	03	19,000
8	Doug Swingley	11	06	38	28	18,000
9	Rick Swenson	11	08	14	45	17,000
10	Bruce Lee	11	12	00	35	16,000
11	Vern Halter	11	13	04	15	15,000
12	Joe Runyan	11	13	06	12	14,000
13	Claire Philip	11	13	15	45	13,000
14	Kathy Swenson	11	15	10	30	12,500
15	John Barron	11	15	59	03	12,000
16	Joe Garnie	11	18	42	20	11,500
17	Linwood Fiedler	11	21	02	50	11,000
18	Sonny Lindner	11	23	49	40	10,500
19	Bill Cotter	11	23	49	50	10,000
20	Kate Persons	11	23	50	20	9,500
21	Dan MacEachen	12	08	02	21	0
22	Dave Olesen	14	17	52	35	0
23	Jerry Austin	14	17	52	40	0
24	Laird Barron	14	17	53	38	0
25	Kathy Tucker	14	17	53	56	0
26	Diana Dronenburg	14	17	54	00	0
27	Frank Teasley	14	17	54	04	0
28	Lynda Plettner	14	17	54	50	0
29	Terry Adkins	14	17	55	00	0
30	Duane (Dewey) Halverson	14	17	55	30	0
31	Mike Williams	14	17	55	41	0
32	Mark Nordman	14	17	56	02	0
33	Bob Holder	14	17	56	12	0
34	Jason Barron	14	17	56	20	0
35	Keizo Funatsu	14	17	56	30	0
36	Ketil Reitan	14	17	57	42	0
37	Pecos Humphreys	14	17	58	50	0
38	Peryll Kyzer	14	17	59	02	0
39	Jim Oehlschlaeger	16	13	56	45	0
40	Skin Wysocki	16	13	57	05	0
41	Jerry Louden	16	13	57	45	0
42	Pat Danly	17	01	06	04	0
43	Stan Smith	17	06	21	44	0
44	Jack Goode	17	06	23	13	0

IDITAROD FINAL STANDINGS
1993 (continued)

Place	Musher	Days	Hours	Minutes	Seconds	Prize
45	Roger Haertel	17	06	23	44	0
46	Paul Rupple	17	08	39	20	0
47	Joe Carpenter	17	08	53	33	0
48	Mark Chapoton	17	08	54	17	0
49	Kirsten Bey	17	08	59	59	0
50	Bert Hanson	17	09	12	55	0
51	Harry Caldwell	17	17	27	07	0
52	John Peterson	17	22	23	23	0
53	Spencer Thew	17	22	38	38	0
54	Lloyd Gilbertson	18	04	49	19	0

Finisher

1   Beverly Masek

Scratched

1   Julius Burgert
2   Norman Lee
3   Terry Hinesly
4   Val Aron
5   David Aisenbrey
6   Gary Moore
7   Gary Whittemore
8   Robin Jacobson
9   Rick Townsend
10 Robert Morgan
11 Lavon Barve
12 John Shandelmeier

Disqualified

1   Dave Branholm

IDITAROD FINAL STANDINGS
1994

Place	Musher	Days	Hours	Minutes	Seconds	Prize
1	Martin Buser	10	13	02	39	$50,000
2	Rick Mackey	10	18	18	14	39,500
3	Jeff King	10	21	46	09	32,000
4	Rick Swenson	10	22	19	41	25,820
5	Bill Cotter	10	22	39	39	21,516
6	Doug Swingley	11	00	00	31	17,213
7	Charlie Boulding	11	01	38	06	14,201
8	Tim Osmar	11	03	38	56	13,340
9	DeeDee Jonrowe	11	04	25	15	12,480
10	Susan Butcher	11	06	07	20	11,619
11	Matt Desalernos	11	08	53	34	10,758
12	Kate Persons	11	08	57	29	9,898
13	Vern Halter	11	11	34	13	9,037
14	Peryll Kyzer	11	11	48	02	8,607
15	Robin Jacobson	11	13	54	00	8,176
16	Dave Olesen	11	15	39	15	7,746
17	Ramy Brooks	11	15	41	30	7,316
18	Linwood Fiedler	11	15	57	30	6,885
19	Diana Dronenburg	11	17	21	40	6,455
20	Kenth Fjellborg	11	17	28	10	6,025
21	Ramey Smyth	12	06	46	10	0
22	Jerry Austin	12	07	17	07	0
23	Ketil Reitan	12	07	48	10	0
24	Bruce Lee	12	07	51	11	0
25	Laird Barron	12	09	53	46	0
26	Frank Teasley	12	09	54	35	0
27	Stan Smith	12	12	42	42	0
28	Mike Williams	12	13	13	25	0
29	Lynda Plettner	12	19	54	30	0
30	Bill Hall	13	05	55	29	0
31	Bob Holder	13	06	06	39	0
32	Gus Guenther	13	06	20	55	0
33	Terry Adkins	13	06	34	44	0
34	Jack Berry	13	08	09	00	0
35	Krista Maciolek	13	08	58	03	0
36	Robert Somers	13	16	22	00	0
37	Aaron Burmeister	14	10	33	22	0
38	Cliff Roberson	14	10	56	32	0
39	Simon Kinneen	14	16	50	45	0
40	Bob Morgan	15	03	53	29	0
41	Steve Adkins	15	04	33	22	0
42	Dave Branholm	15	05	55	00	0
43	Bob Ernisse	15	06	39	57	0
44	Harry Caldwell	15	07	25	10	0

IDITAROD FINAL STANDINGS
1994 (continued)

Place	Musher	Days	Hours	Minutes	Seconds	Prize
45	Ron Aldrich	15	09	00	00	0
46	Jon Terhune	15	19	16	00	0
47	Kazuo Kojima	15	20	11	04	0
48	Roger Bliss	16	04	04	04	0
49	Bruce Moroney	16	10	52	53	0
50	Mark Chapoton	16	16	17	35	0

Scratched

1	Rick Townsend
2	Chris Converse
3	Jamie Nelson
4	Mark Nordman
5	Lloyd Gilbertson
6	Lisa Moore
7	Beth Baker

Withdrew

1	Catherine Mormile

IDITAROD FINAL STANDINGS
1995

Place	Musher	Days	Hours	Minutes	Seconds	Prize
1	Doug Swingley	9	02	42	19	$52,500
2	Martin Buser	9	08	47	44	38,080
3	Bill Cotter	9	10	52	23	30,940
4	DeeDee Jonrowe	9	11	24	07	26,775
5	Charlie Boulding	9	14	58	00	23,205
6	Rick Mackey	9	15	52	00	21,212
7	Jeff King	9	18	52	10	19,828
8	Vern Halter	9	20	05	30	18,445
9	Tim Osmar	9	21	25	08	17,062
10	Rick Swenson	9	22	32	00	15,678
11	Peryll Kyzer	10	01	55	40	13,150
12	John Barron	10	04	12	40	11,127
13	Linwood Fiedler	10	08	27	00	9,609
14	Matt Desalernos	10	11	14	10	8,598
15	David Sawatsky	10	12	58	03	8,092
16	Ramy Brooks	10	14	08	00	7,854
17	Jerry Austin	10	22	56	00	7,497
18	Dave Olesen	10	23	51	51	7,140
19	Ramey Smyth	11	00	07	07	6,783
20	Mitch Seavey	11	00	07	31	6,426
21	John Gourley	11	00	33	59	0
22	Mark Wildermuth	11	05	14	38	0
23	David Milne	11	08	07	34	0
24	Randy Adkins	12	05	07	05	0
25	Harry Caldwell	12	17	07	00	0
26	Jack Berry	12	17	43	00	0
27	Art Church	12	23	00	29	0
28	Cliff Roberson	13	00	27	19	0
29	Dave Branholm	13	00	42	00	0
30	Robert Salazar	13	01	07	00	0
31	Bob Holder	13	01	36	00	0
32	Kazuo Kojima	13	02	13	00	0
33	Libby Riddles	13	02	15	00	0
34	David Dalton	13	03	20	00	0
35	Don Lyrek	13	05	56	00	0
36	Nicolas Pattaroni	13	06	32	00	0
37	Pat Danly	13	08	14	00	0
38	Paula Gmerek	13	08	54	27	0
39	Rollin Westrum	13	09	42	00	0
40	Robert Bundtzen	13	09	55	09	0
41	Wayne Curtis	13	19	59	03	0
42	Jon Terhune	13	20	05	36	0
43	Nikolai Ettyne	14	15	45	00	0
44	Kjell Risung	14	16	05	00	0

IDITAROD FINAL STANDINGS
1995 (continued)

Place	Musher	Days	Hours	Minutes	Seconds	Prize
45	Susan Whiton	14	22	54	54	0
46	Max Hall	15	05	13	39	0
47	Larry Williams	16	23	23	26	0
48	Ben Jacobson	17	06	02	05	0

Finisher

1   Tim Triumph

Scratched

1   Lorren Weaver
2   Don Bowers
3   Pecos Humphreys
4   Barrie Raper
5   Kathleen Swenson
6   Robert Somers
7   Diana (Dronenburg) Moroney
8   Andy Sterns

Withdrew

1   Keizo Funatsu

IDITAROD FINAL STANDINGS
1996

Place	Musher	Days	Hours	Minutes	Seconds	Prize
1	Jeff King	9	05	43	13	$50,000
2	Doug Swingley	9	08	31	59	32,000
3	Martin Buser	9	17	58	15	26,000
4	Tim Osmar	9	18	31	30	22,500
5	DeeDee Jonrowe	9	20	18	03	19,500
6	Bill Cotter	9	21	53	50	17,825
7	Charlie Boulding	9	22	00	00	16,663
8	David Sawatzky	9	22	29	13	15,500
9	Vern Halter	10	00	59	12	14,338
10	Peryll Kyzer	10	01	29	53	13,175
11	Ramy Brooks	10	02	56	18	11,050
12	David Scheer	10	04	00	03	9,350
13	Robin Jacobson	10	04	41	53	8,075
14	Lavon Barve	10	05	54	43	7,225
15	Mitch Seavey	10	06	27	59	6,800
16	John Barron	10	06	35	31	6,600
17	Linwood Fiedler	10	07	25	18	6,300
18	Cim Smyth	10	08	00	00	6,000
19	Roger Dahl	10	08	28	00	5,700
20	Sven Engholm	10	14	06	00	5,400
21	Jerry Austin	10	16	38	40	0
22	Johnny Baker	10	23	26	36	0
23	Tomas Israelsson	11	07	52	58	0
24	Duane (Dewey) Halverson	11	07	55	48	0
25	Bruce Lee	11	07	57	30	0
26	Paul Gebhardt	11	08	08	49	0
27	Diana Moroney	11	08	10	21	0
28	Andy Willis	11	12	11	52	0
29	Dave Olesen	11	14	13	50	0
30	Nicolas Pattaroni	12	07	04	19	0
31	Conner Thomas	12	08	27	11	0
32	Steve Adkins	12	09	15	50	0
33	Kazuo Kojima	12	09	26	41	0
34	Michael Nosko	12	11	56	20	0
35	Harry Caldwell	12	13	14	18	0
36	Mike Webber	13	04	43	25	0
37	Jim Davis	13	05	15	51	0
38	Randy Romenesko	13	05	24	15	0
39	Susan Whiton	13	05	29	40	0
40	Lori Townsend	13	05	36	48	0
41	Bill Gallea	13	07	53	37	0
42	Mark Nordman	13	11	31	26	0
43	Aaron Burmeister	14	04	48	00	0
44	Rob Carss	14	05	07	00	0

IDITAROD FINAL STANDINGS
1996 (continued)

Place	Musher	Days	Hours	Minutes	Seconds	Prize
45	Armen Khatchikian	14	06	14	00	0
46	Dave Branholm	14	06	37	00	0
47	Lisa Moore	15	14	15	38	0
48	Don Bowers	15	14	16	04	0
49	Andy Sterns	15	23	48	22	0

Scratched
1 Bill Hall
2 Roy Monk
3 Rich Bosela
4 Stan Zuray
5 Jack Berry
6 Kjell Risung
7 Mark Black

Withdrew
1 Rick Swenson
2 Ralph Ray
3 Linda Joy
4 Bob Bright

I have been first into almost every checkpoint along that race trail, except Nome. But I keep thinking . . . maybe next year. That is the Iditarod Spirit.

Joe Redington, Sr.
Father of the Iditarod and
fourteen-time Iditarod finisher

Iditarod Award Winners
1973 to 1996

The Iditarod champion receives the fattest cut of the race purse (about $50,000), a brand-new Dodge truck (since 1991), and a winner's trophy (a perpetual version of which is on display at ITC headquarters). Although the prize money is displayed in one-dollar bills, so far each victor has opted to accept a check instead. All other mushers who complete the race receive an Official Iditarod Finisher's belt buckle (given once—the first year you finish) and a large Official Iditarod Finisher's patch. In addition to these prizes, many other special awards are presented. A description of these awards and a listing of their recipients follows.

HONORARY MUSHERS

Each year, the Iditarod Trail Committee's board of directors selects a well-known dog driver or a person who has contributed to the sport of sled-dog racing and to the Iditarod to be the honorary "number-one" musher(s). The #1 starting bib is symbolically reserved for those so honored. A brief biography is read at the start and printed in the annual race program. To date, the honorary mushers have been:

1973 - 1979	Leonhard Seppala
1980	"Wild Bill" Shannon
1981	Edgar Kalland
1982	Bill McCarty
1983	Charlie Evans & Edgar Nollner
1984	Pete McManus & Howard Albert
1985	William A. Egan
1986	Fred Machetanz
1987	Eva Brunell "Short" Seeley
1988	Marvin "Muktuk" Marston
1989	Otis "Del" Carter & John Auliye
1990	Victor Katongan & Henry Ivanoff
1991	Roland Lombard
1992	Herbie Nayokpuk
1993	Pete Curran & Leroy Swenson
1994	Dick Tozier & Michael Merkling, Jr.
1995	John Komak
1996	Bill Vaudrin

National Bank of Alaska (NBA) Nome branch manager Mitch Erickson displays the $50,000 winner's check. NBA donates this, and sponsors the Red Lantern Award, the Gold Coast Award, and both banquets.

A perpetual victors' trophy is on display at the Iditarod Trail Committee headquarters in Wasilla.

SPIRIT OF IDITAROD AWARD

This award began in 1989 and is presented to someone who exemplifies the ideals of the Iditarod and whose actions and philosophy help preserve the Iditarod spirit for future generations. In the tradition of the 1925 serum run, those ideals are courage, perseverance, compassion, and reverence for the Alaskan wilderness. From mushers to volunteers, anyone connected with the race may win this award. The winner is announced at the prerace banquet and receives a cut-crystal trophy. A perpetual trophy is also on display at ITC headquarters. Recipients to date are:

1989	Norman Vaughan
1990	Dorothy G. Page
1991	Joe Redington, Sr.
1992	Herbie Nayokpuk
1993	Jim Brown
1994	David Monson

(1995–1996 award lapsed)

LEONHARD SEPPALA HUMANITARIAN AWARD

Alaska Airlines presents this award to the musher who has demonstrated outstanding care of his or her team throughout the race, while remaining competitive. The Iditarod veterinary staff selects the winner, who receives a lead-crystal cup, transportation home for the musher and team, and two round-trip tickets to any Alaska Airlines' destination. The award is presented at the finishers' banquet in Nome, and a perpetual trophy is on display at ITC headquarters. This award is highly coveted by mushers, as evinced by 1992 recipient Rick Swenson, who remarked upon accepting it, "I only wish my father could have been here to see me receive this award. [Leroy Swenson died three days before the 1992 race began.] This trophy would have meant more to him than any of my five winner's trophies." Begun in 1982, this honor has been conferred upon the following competitors:

1982	Jerry Austin
1983	Rick Mackey
1984	Burt Bomhoff
1985	Libby Riddles
1986	Rick Adkinson
1987	Dave Olesen
1988	Martin Buser
1989	Frank Teasley
1990	Linwood Fiedler
1991	DeeDee Jonrowe
1992	Rick Swenson
1993	Martin Buser
1994	Bill Cotter
1995	Martin Buser
1996	David Sawatzky

Every musher who completes the race is awarded a large Official Iditarod Finisher's patch.

FIRST MUSHER TO THE YUKON AWARD

The Regal Alaskan Hotel prepares a seven-course gourmet meal (complete with linen tablecloths, candelabra, and fine wine) for the first musher to reach the Yukon River (at Anvik in odd years and at Ruby in even years). Often the winning driver shares the feast with the next competitor to arrive. An "after-dinner mint" of $3,500 accompanies the meal, as does a gold-pan trophy. The recipient and a guest are also offered the chance to repeat the meal in a more leisurely style at the Regal Alaskan Hotel in Anchorage. A perpetual plaque hangs at ITC headquarters. Diners include:

1983	Larry "Cowboy" Smith
1984	Dean Osmar
(1985 - 1986 award lapsed)	
1987	Jerry Austin
1988	Joe Redington, Sr.
1989	Rick Swenson

1990	Susan Butcher
1991	Jeff King
1992	Joe Runyan
1993	Jeff King
1994	Rick Mackey
1995	Doug Swingley
1996	Martin Buser

DOROTHY G. PAGE HALFWAY AWARD

General Communications, Inc. (GCI) awards the first musher to reach the race's midpoint (Iditarod in odd years and Cripple in even years) $3,000 and a commemorative trophy, given to the driver upon arrival at the checkpoint and then formally presented at the Nome banquet. A perpetual trophy is on display at ITC headquarters. This award was first given in 1980 by Alascom, which poured $3,000 in specially minted silver ingots into a silver trophy held by the winning musher. Assuming the sponsorship in 1994, GCI now weighs out three thousand dollars worth of gold nuggets, mined locally in the Iditarod area, in an antique scale. Only three competitors have overcome the famous "halfway jinx" by receiving this award and going on to win the race: Dean Osmar in 1984, Jeff King in 1993, and Doug Swingley in 1995. Mushers to reach the race's midpoint first include:

1980	Herbie Nayokpuk
1981	Larry "Cowboy" Smith
1982	Emmitt Peters
1983	Eep Anderson
1984	Dean Osmar
1985	Burt Bomhoff
1986	Jerry Austin
1987	Dewey Halverson
1988	Joe Redington, Sr.
1989	Susan Butcher
1990	Lavon Barve
1991	Susan Butcher & DeeDee Jonrowe
1992	Doug Swingley
1993	Jeff King
1994	Dave Olesen
1995	Doug Swingley
1996	Martin Buser

JOE REDINGTON, SR. AWARD

Tesoro Alaska began this award in 1994. The winner is drawn from a collection of all of the mushers' names and receives either 2,500 gallons of Tesoro gasoline or a check for $2,500 (winner's choice). Weather permitting, the drawing is held at Joe Redington, Sr.'s hometown of Knik, or alternately, at the restart. As a consolation prize, each musher whose name was not drawn receives twenty-five gallons of fuel. The check or gift certificate is formally presented at the finishers' banquet in Nome. Names drawn so far have been:

1994	Jerry Austin
1995	Matt Desalernos
1996	Steve Adkins

A perpetual plaque of the First to the Yukon Award hangs at ITC headquarters. A seven-course gourmet meal with a $3,500 "after-dinner mint" is presented by the Regal Alaskan Hotel to the first musher to arrive at the Yukon River (Anvik in odd years and Ruby in even years), in addition to a gold-pan trophy.

GOLD COAST AWARD

The National Bank of Alaska recognizes the first musher to reach the Bering Sea coast at Unalakleet by the presentation of $2,500 in real Alaskan gold nuggets and a trophy. First sponsored in 1984 and 1985 by Burt Bomhoff, Jeff Hankerd, and Johnny Ellison, the Gold Coast Award lapsed for some time until its sponsorship was renewed by the National Bank of Alaska (which also provides the winner's purse and the Red Lantern and funds both banquets). The award is formally given at the finishers' banquet, and a perpetual trophy is on display at ITC headquarters. Mushers who have arrived first at Unalakleet include:

1984	Dewey Halverson
1985	Martin Buser
(1986 - 1992 award lapsed)	
1993	Rick Mackey
1994	Martin Buser
1995	Doug Swingley
1996	Jeff King

ROOKIE OF THE YEAR AWARD

Jerry and Clara Austin present the top-finishing rookie with $1,500 and a trophy at the awards banquet in Nome each year. In selecting the recipient, a rookie is defined as someone who is racing his or her first Iditarod. Although this award was not begun until 1979, the highest finishing rookie from each earlier race is also listed here:

1973	Dick Wilmarth	1st place
1974	Carl Huntington	1st place
1975	Emmitt Peters	1st place
1976	Harry Sutherland	3rd place
1977	Pete McManus	13th place
1978	Sonny Lindner	11th place
1979	Gary Hokkanen	11th place
1980	Donna Gentry	10th place
1981	Gary Attla	17th place
1982	Stan Zuray	9th place
1983	Roger Legaard	10th place
1984	Rusty Miller	13th place

1985	Tim Moerlein	11th place
1986	Rune Hesthammer	10th place
1987	Robin Jacobson	18th place
1988	Lucy Nordlum	13th place
1989	Richard Self	21st place
1990	Sonny Russell	15th place
1991	Kate Persons	11th place
1992	Doug Swingley	9th place
1993	Jason Barron &	34th place
	Keizo Funatsu	35th place
1994	Ramy Brooks	17th place
1995	David Sawatsky	15th place
1996	Cim Smyth	18th place

Rick Mackey was the first musher into Unalakleet in 1993. In recognition of this, National Bank of Alaska awarded Mackey $2,500 in real gold nuggets and a trophy.

STERLING ACHIEVEMENT AWARD

Alaska Commercial Company (AC) honors a musher who has demonstrated outstanding performance and commitment and who has finished significantly higher than in a previous race or races. The musher who receives the Sterling Achievement Award (selected by his or her peers) is given a $500 AC gift certificate and a plaque, which are presented at the Nome banquet. The most improved mushers since the award began in 1987 are:

1987	Ted English	18th in 1986, and 8th in 1987
(1988 award lapsed)		NA
1989	Tim Mowry	42nd in 1988, and 27th in 1989
1990	Mike Madden	scratched due to severe illness in 1989, and 13th in 1990
1991	Frank Teasley	31st in 1988, 19th in 1989, and 6th in 1991

The Gold Coast Award, consisting of $2,500 in real gold nuggets, is presented to the first musher to reach the Bering Sea coast at Unalakleet.

1992	Claire Philip	37th in 1985, 26th in 1987, and 13th in 1992
1993	Bob Holder	49th in 1992, and 33rd in 1993
1994	Charlie Boulding	43rd in 1992, and 7th in 1994
1995	Harry Caldwell	51st in 1993, 44th in 1994, and 25th in 1995
1996	David Sheer	41st in 1984, and 12th in 1996

FASTEST TIME FROM SAFETY TO NOME AWARD

The Nome Kennel Club has sponsored this award since 1975. The top-twenty finisher who sets the fastest pace from Safety to Nome wins $500, which is presented to him or her at the postrace banquet. Unfortunately, records for this award are not complete, as indicated below by "NA," meaning "not available." Record holders are:

1975	NA	
1976	Ken Chase	4:28:37
1977	NA	
1978	* Peter McManus	4:13:00
1979	* Rick Swenson	2:49:47
1980	* Rick Swenson	2:22:00
1981	Rick Mackey	2:19:07
1982	* Rick Swenson	2:55:00
1983	NA	
1984	John Cooper	1:59:24
1985	* Rick Swenson	2:05:00
1986	Jerry Riley	NA
1987	* Rick Swenson	2:20:00
1988	Rick Mackey	2:22:29
1989	Rick Mackey	2:33:00
1990	Susan Butcher	2:17:00
1991	Rick Mackey	2:24:00
1992	Vern Halter	2:30:40
1993	Jeff King	2:22:00
1994	Vern Halter	2:36:13
1995	Ramey Smyth	2:00:07
1996	Cim Smyth	2:01:00

* Provided by Nome's KNOM radio

Each competitor who completes the Iditarod receives an Official Iditarod Finisher's belt buckle that is awarded once — the first year a musher finishes.

SPORTSMANSHIP AWARD

Iditarod mushers select one or more of their compatriots who have exhibited outstanding sportsmanship to receive this award. A trophy is presented to the winner(s) at the finishers' banquet, and a perpetual version is displayed at ITC headquarters. Begun in 1977, this honor has been conferred upon the following Iditarod drivers:

1977   Ken Chase
1978   James Brandon
1979   Sonny Lindner
1980   Marc Boily
1981   DeeDee Jonrowe
1982   Dean Osmar
1983   Rick Swenson
1984   Dave Olson

1985	Terry Adkins
	Alan Cheshire
1986	Dave Olesen
1987	Jerry Austin
1988	Ted English
1989	Linwood Fiedler
	Jamie Nelson
	Kathy Halverson
	Mitch Brazin
	Bernie Willis
	Jerry Austin
1990	Joe Redington, Sr.
1991	Terry Adkins
1992	Bob Hickel
1993	Jerry Austin
	Dave Olesen
1994	Beth Baker
	Jamie Nelson
1995	Cliff Roberson
1996	Dewey Halverson

MOST INSPIRATIONAL MUSHER AWARD

At the banquet in Nome, the Iditarod Official Finishers' Club awards a plaque to the musher(s) voted by fellow competitors to have best exemplified courage and perseverance in the face of trail adversities. Mushers selected since 1986 have been:

1986	Terry Adkins
1987	Norman Vaughan
1988	Joe Redington, Sr. & Herbie Nayokpuk
1989	Joe Redington, Sr.
1990	Lavon Barve
1991	Lavon Barve & Joe Garnie
1992	Mike Williams
1993	DeeDee Jonrowe
1994	Dave Olesen & Bruce Lee
1995	Peryll Kyzer
1996	Rick Swenson

GOLDEN PACE AWARD

Beginning in 1995, the first musher to arrive at the Kuskokwim River village of McGrath will receive a gold-nugget watch from the Alaska Commercial Company. The recipients of this award are:

1995	Bill Cotter
1996	Martin Buser

GOLDEN HARNESS AWARD

Wasilla musher and harness-maker Lolly Medley (one of the first two women to finish the Iditarod in 1974) handcrafts a golden harness, which is presented to the most outstanding lead dog(s) at the finishers' banquet. Made of gold-colored material, the harness is functional but has special detailing and the name of the award and the year sewn onto it. Initiated in 1976, this award is also determined by the mushers themselves, and regrettably, the records are incomplete. Dogs that have received a golden harness are:

1976	NA	NA	NA
1977	Pilot	Ken Chase	11th place
1978	Nugget & Blackie	Babe Anderson	scratched
1979	Digger	Emmitt Peters	2nd place
1980	Trooper	Herbie Nayokpuk	2nd place
1981	Silver	Larry "Cowboy" Smith	4th place
1982	Brandy	Ernie Baumgartner	6th place
1983	NA	NA	NA
1984	Bullet & Red	Dean Osmar	1st place
1985	Dugan & Axle	Libby Riddles	1st place
1986	Sister	Joe Garnie	2nd place
1987	Blackie	Herbie Nayokpuk	25th place
1988	Granite	Susan Butcher	1st place
1989	Ferlin	Joe Runyan	1st place
1990	Tip	Lavon Barve	3rd place
1991	Major & Goose	Rick Swenson	1st place
1992	Dusty	Joe Garnie	20th place
1993	Kitty & Herbie	Jeff King	1st place
1994	D-2 & Dave	Martin Buser	1st place
1995	Vic	Doug Swingley	1st place
1996	Blondie	Martin Buser	3rd place

RED LANTERN AWARD

The tradition of awarding a red lantern to the last-place finisher in a sled-dog race apparently began at the 1953 Fur Rendezvous race, when Tom Wharton bought a lantern as a joke for Ken O'Hara, explaining that he "was so far behind, he needed to light his way home." Over the years, however, the red lantern has come to symbolize tenacity and endurance.

The National Bank of Alaska presents the Red Lantern to the race's final finisher at the second banquet in Nome, which is held once all competitors have safely crossed under the burled arch. Lantern bearers have been:

Year	Name	Time
1973	John Schultz	32:05:09:01
1974	Red Olson	29:06:36:19
1975	Steve Fee	29:08:37:13
1976	Dennis Corrington	26:08:42:51
1977	Vasily Zamitkyn	22:09:06:06
1978	Andrew Foxie	22:03:29:44
1979	Gene Leonard	24:09:02:22
1980	Barbara Moore	24:09:25:45
1981	Jim Strong	18:06:30:30
1982	Ralph Bradley	26:13:59:59
1983	Scott Cameron	21:04:36:41
1984	Bill Mackey	19:09:43:33
1985	Monique Bene	22:03:45:45
1986	Mike Peterson	20:13:42:21
1987	Rhodi Karella	19:09:01:01
1988	Lesley Monk	19:13:22:55
1989	Bob Hoyte	17:11:19:19
1990	Steve Haver	21:10:26:26
1991	Brian O'Donoghue	22:05:55:55
1992	Vern Cherneski	18:13:05:02
1993	Lloyd Gilbertson	18:04:49:19
1994	Mark Chapoton	16:16:17:35
1995	Ben Jacobson	17:06:02:05
1996	Andy Sterns	15:23:48:22

DISCONTINUED AWARDS

Fastest Time, Anchorage to Eagle River

The Eagle River Veterans of Foreign Wars Post #9785 sponsored this award from 1985 through 1992 (the years during which mushers' times to Eagle River were recorded). The winner received $1,249 (the entry fee at that time), and in addition to setting the fastest time from Anchorage to Eagle River, also had to finish the race. Fastest times were set by:

1985	Raymie Redington	NA
1986	John Cooper	NA
1987	Martin Buser	2:15
1988	Martin Buser	2:06
1989	Martin Buser	2:00
1990	Martin Buser	2:19
1991	Martin Buser	2:18
1992	Dan MacEachen	2:43

Arctic Sports Medicine/Human Performance Award

The Health Science Department of the University of Alaska in Anchorage gave this award from 1988 through 1992 to the musher(s) who demonstrated the strongest athletic performance and endurance under the stress of arctic and subarctic conditions. Mushers who received this plaque were:

1988	Susan Butcher & Joe Redington, Sr.
1989	DeeDee Jonrowe & Joe Runyan
1990	Robin Jacobson
1991	Lavon Barve & Rick Swenson
1992	Martin Buser

MORE
MUSH

It's nationwide. It's international.
It almost feels intergalactic.

Burt Bomhoff
Iditarod finisher and
former Iditarod Trail Committee President

26

Iditarod
Trail Committee
Hotlines and Catalog

RACE HOTLINES

If you can't be there in person, the next best way to follow the Iditarod is by calling a race hotline daily. Because volunteers field calls from around the world, you may get a busy signal, but be patient and persevere. To increase your chances of getting through, here are three numbers to try:

Iditarod Headquarters at the Regal Alaskan Hotel in Anchorage
   1-907-248-MUSH (6874)

Iditarod Headquarters in Nome
   1-907-443-MUSH (6874)

Iditarod Headquarters in Fairbanks
   1-907-451-8055

A Checkpoint Tally Sheet is printed in this chapter. Feel free to photocopy this chart and use it to record information each time you call for current standings. Hotline operators will tell you, if asked, the

CHECKPOINT TALLY SHEET

Name of Checkpoint _____

Miles to next checkpoint _____

Total miles from Anchorage completed _____

First mushers in to this checkpoint:

	Musher's Name	Date	Checkpoint	Time In	Time Out	# dogs
1st						
2nd						
3rd						
4th						
5th						
___	(your favorite musher)					
___	(your favorite musher)					

Weather: _____
_____

Interesting anecdotes: _____
_____
_____
_____

IDITAROD HOTLINES

Anchorage	Nome	Fairbanks
1−907−248−MUSH (6874)	1−907−443−MUSH (6874)	1−907−451−8055

appropriate checkpoint(s), the number of miles to the next checkpoint, and the total miles that competitors have completed since leaving Anchorage. They will also read you the placement of the top mushers (or a specific musher or mushers of particular interest to you), including the date and time that they checked in and out of the most recent checkpoint, and the number of dogs that they are running. Don't hesitate to ask about the weather or to inquire if anything interesting is happening. Race volunteers are usually curious to know where you are calling from, so don't be surprised to be asked.

These hotline numbers will be a long-distance charge on your phone bill unless you live in or are visiting one of the cities where the Iditarod headquarters is located. For those who have contracted a serious case of Iditarod fever, however, the opportunity to keep up with the race makes the cost of the calls worthwhile.

ITC CATALOG

One of the surest ways to strike up interesting conversations is to wear Iditarod-related items. You'd be surprised how many people, from farmers to restaurant managers to co-workers, are closet Iditarod fans. It's easy to proclaim your partisanship—just call:

1-800-545-MUSH (6874)

You can order right away, or you can ask for a catalog and peruse it at your leisure. The ITC hasn't overlooked much. You can start with T-shirts and sweatshirts, which come in a yearly design or a variety of other Iditarod and Alaskan themes. Adult and children's sizes are available. Feeling dog tired? Put on your Iditarod nightshirt and matching dog-paw socks, and curl up for a well-deserved snooze. Going out? Better grab your Iditarod jacket and cap (several choices of each) and don't forget to sew a patch or clip a collectible pin on them. Driving? You'll need your Iditarod key ring. Is the family pooch begging to go with you again? Tie a racing bandanna on that pup and allow him to enjoy delusions of grandeur. Of course, the well-equipped vehicle displays an Iditarod license plate holder, while your driveway is embellished by a yellow road sign that cautions: "Dog Team Crossing."

Headed for the office? Leave the T-shirts at home and opt for the tie tack instead. You can decorate your personal space with an Iditarod letter opener, notepaper, and calculator.

Jeff King's dog Booster surveys his domain.

You know those difficult people on your gift list—they either already have it or it costs too much? Problem solved. They undoubtedly don't have a land deed showing that they own a piece of the Iditarod Trail. Another one-of-a-kind gift is a cachet (a commemorative envelope stamped in Anchorage and backstamped in Nome) carried by a favorite musher over the entire length of the trail. Neither of these is shown or listed in recent catalogs, but both are available.

Need a stocking-stuffer or an Easter basket goodie? Kids love the plush sled dogs, Iditarod yo-yos, rubber stamps, and also three-ring-notebook pencil holders complete with Iditarod-emblazoned pens, pencils, rulers, and puppy-shaped erasers.

Ready to relax in the comfort of your own home? Lie back in your favorite recliner with an Iditarod throw tucked over you. Have a hot drink in a race mug. Take a mini-vacation to Alaska via an exciting Iditarod video. Dying to perk up the decor? Consider a poster, ornament, magnet or additions to your library. A beautiful Jeff Schultz calendar will help keep your schedule straight.

All this and more is in the Iditarod Trail Committee catalog, and if you become an ITC member, you'll get a 10 percent discount on every purchase. So what are you waiting for? Shop 'til you drop . . . the ITC is a not-for-profit organization, and Iditarod merchandise helps finance the Last Great Race!

To receive a membership application, catalog, or additional information, you can write to the following address:

Iditarod Trail Committee
P.O. Box 870800
Wasilla, AK 99687-0800

Iditarod fan James Hood demonstrates how a well-dressed
race watcher is attired.

It's not the destination,
it's the experience.

Bruce Hamler
Iditasport competitor

27

There's More
To Mushing . . .

Now that you know more about the Iditarod, perhaps you would enjoy attending a local sled-dog race or would even like to participate in some type of dog-related sport. It is important to remember that there is more to mushing than the Iditarod. This chapter briefly describes a variety of options for those who want to experience the thrill of recreational or competitive dog mushing firsthand, and lists sources for additional information.

OTHER DOG-RELATED
COMPETITIONS AND ACTIVITIES

Long-Distance Races - Any sled-dog race of more than 300 miles is considered to be long distance.

Mid-Distance Races - A race of 100 - 300 miles is in the mid-distance range.

Sprint Races - Often run in several heats, sprint races have classes for teams of one dog up to a class for an unlimited number of dogs.

Gig Racing - Sled dogs race pulling a cart or wheeled rig (gig) in seasons or locations where there is inadequate snowfall for sleds.

383

Skijoring - A dog or dogs pull a skier in competition or for recreation. This is one of the fastest growing fields of dog mushing because it only requires one dog to get started.

Pulka Racing - A dog or dogs pull a sleek, low-profile sled (pulka). The musher skis behind, attached to the pulka by a long bungee cord. Extremely popular in Northern Europe, this sport is spreading quickly elsewhere.

Weight Pulls - A dog (of almost any medium-to-large breed) pulls a loaded sled forward a set distance, competing against other dogs of a similar size. Dogs are called to come by their handlers and are in no way forced to pull or allowed to over-exert themselves.

Lead-Dog Contests - These test gee/haw skills by requiring dogs to negotiate a set course successfully.

Stampede/Scramble Races - Mushers start a race lying in their sleeping bags, then have to pack their sled, harness the team, and go.

Freight Races - Dogs pull large freight sleds, loaded as they might have been in earlier times, in an effort to preserve the skills of larger, slower, working sled dogs.

Miscellaneous - Dogs also pull people in wheelchairs as companion helpers, kids on skateboards or rollerblades (with proper safety equipment!), and can be hooked to bicycles (again, safety gear is necessary). Many a musher started out with the family Fido pulling an old red wagon or a traditional wooden sled. With sensible supervision, dogs enjoy pulling just about anything that rolls or glides.

FOR MORE INFORMATION . . .

If you'd like to know more about any of these types of competitive or recreational dog mushing, you can write to the following organizations, requesting additional information:

Mushing magazine
P.O. Box 149
Ester, AK 99725 USA
(Publishes a sled-dog event calendar and a sled-dog club directory)

Team and Trail: The Musher's Monthly Newspaper Since 1963
Box 128
Center Harbor, NH 03226-0128

International Sled Dog Racing Association, Inc. (ISDRA)
P.O. Box 446
Nordman, ID 83848
(Publishes *Info* magazine and many informative booklets)

Mush with PRIDE (Providing Responsible Information on a Dog's Environment)
P.O. Box 84915
Fairbanks, AK 99708
(Publishes *Sled Dog Care Guidelines*)

John Patten enjoys twelve inches of fresh snow, blue skies, and perfect mushing weather as he takes a training run on the Beargrease Trail in northern Minnesota. Patten is one of the founders of the Beargrease and is the 1985 champion.

Arpiq [the Eskimo name given to Alastair Scott] knew this journey was ruining him. He doubted whether he could enjoy travelling—the actual going—ever again if it had to be by means other than dogs. They heard things he could never hear and sensed things far beyond his atrophied powers of perception. For these reasons they became an extension of his awareness and led him to probe a relationship with his surroundings on a level he could not rationalise. They touched something primitive and biologically distant in him. Call it instinct if you will, it remained dim and undefined. They linked him to the subconscious land.

Alastair Scott
Scottish adventurer/author
summarizing his mushing expedition across Alaska

Selected Bibliography

BOOKS OF GENERAL INTEREST TO FANS AND TEACHERS

Elliot, Nan. *I'd Swap My Old Skidoo For You: A Portrait of Characters on the Last Frontier.* Issaquah, Washington: Sammamish Press, 1989.

Emert, Phyllis Raybin. *Sled Dogs.* Mankato, MN: Crestwood House, 1985.

Freedman, Lew. *Iditarod Classics: Tales of the Trail Told by the Men and Women Who Race Across Alaska.* Fairbanks/Seattle: Epicenter Press, 1992.

Freedman, Lew. *Iditarod Dreams: A Year in the life of Alaskan sled dog racer DeeDee Jonrowe.* Fairbanks/Seattle: Epicenter Press, 1995.

Heacox, Kim. *Iditarod Spirit.* Portland, OR: Graphic Arts Center Publishing Co., 1991.

Henry, Sue. *Murder on the Iditarod Trail.* New York: The Atlantic Monthly Press, 1991.

Huntington, James as told to Lawrence Elliott. *On the Edge of Nowhere.* New York: Crown Publishers, Inc., 1966.

Jans, Nick. *The Last Light Breaking.* Seattle: Alaska Northwest Books, 1993.

Jones, Tim. *The Last Great Race.* Seattle: Madrona Publishers, 1982. Paperback reprint, Harrisburg, PA: Stackpole Books, 1988.

Lopez, Barry. *Arctic Dreams: Imagination and Desire in a Northern Landscape.* New York: Charles Scribner's Sons, 1986.

Morey, Walt. *Kävik: the wolf dog*. New York: EP Dutton, 1968.

Nielsen, Nicki J. *The Iditarod: Women on the Trail*. Anchorage, AK: Wolfdog Publications, 1986.

Paulsen, Gary. *Dogsong*. New York: Bradbury Press, 1985.

Paulsen, Gary. *Woodsong*. New York: Bradbury Press, 1990.

Rennick, Penny, ed. *Dogs of the North*. Anchorage, AK: The Alaska Geographic Society, Vol. 14, No. 1, 1987.

Riddles, Libby and Tim Jones. *Race Across Alaska: First woman to win the Iditarod tells her story*. Harrisburg, PA: Stackpole Books, 1988.

Scott, Alastair. *Tracks Across Alaska: A Sled Dog Journey*. New York: The Atlantic Monthly Press, 1990.

Sherwonit, Bill (a photo essay of Jeff Schultz's Iditarod images). *Iditarod: The Great Race to Nome*. Anchorage/Seattle: Alaska Northwest Books, 1991.

Shields, Mary. *Sled Dog Trails*. Anchorage, AK: Alaska Northwest Publishing Company, 1984.

Specht, Robert. *Tisha: The Story of a Young Teacher in the Alaskan Wilderness*. New York: St. Martin's Press, 1976.

Stuck, Hudson. *Ten Thousand Miles With a Dog Sled*. New York: Charles Scribner's Sons, 1914. Reprinted by the University of Nebraska Press, 1988.

Ungermann, Kenneth A. *The Race to Nome: The story of the heroic Alaskan dog teams that rushed diphtheria serum to stricken Nome in 1925*. New York: Harper & Row, 1963. Paperback reprint, Sunnyvale, CA: Press North America, 1993.

Van Zyle, Jon. *Best of Alaska: The Art of Jon Van Zyle*. Fairbanks/Seattle: Epicenter Press, 1990.

Vaughan, Norman with Cecil B. Murphy. *My Life of Adventure*. Mechanicsburg, PA: Stackpole Books, 1995.

Wallis, Velma. *Two Old Women*. Fairbanks/Seattle: Epicenter Press, 1993.

CHILDREN'S BOOKS (Adults will love them too!)

Calvert, Patricia. *The Hour of the Wolf*. New York: Charles Scribner's Sons, 1983.

Carlstrom, Nancy White. *Northern Lullaby*. New York: Philomel Books, 1992.

Gardiner, John Reynolds. *Stone Fox*. New York: Thomas Y. Crowell, 1980.

George, Jean Craighead. *Julie of the Wolves*. New York: Harper & Row, 1972.

Gill, Shelley. *Kiana's Iditarod*. Homer, AK: Paws IV Publishing Company, 1984.

Gill, Shelley. *North Country Christmas*. 1993.

Joosse, Barbara M. *Mama, Do You Love Me?* San Francisco: Chronicle Books, 1991.

Kreeger, Charlene and Shannon Cartwright. *Alaska ABC Book*. 1978.

Machetanz, Frederick. *On Arctic Ice*. New York: Charles Scribner's Sons, 1940. (a sequel to *Panuck: Eskimo Sled Dog*)

Machetanz, Frederick. *Panuck: Eskimo Sled Dog*. New York: Charles Scribner's Sons, 1939.

O'Dell, Scott. *Black Star, Bright Dawn*. Boston: Houghton Mifflin, 1988.

Paulsen, Gary. *Dogteam*. New York: Delacorte Press, 1993.

Riddles, Libby with Shelley Gill. *Danger: The Dog Yard Cat*. Homer, AK: Paws IV Publishing, 1989.

Seibert, Patricia. *Mush! Across Alaska in the World's Longest Sled-Dog Race*. Brookfield, CT: The Millbrook Press, 1992.

Shields, Mary. *Can Dogs Talk?* (Vol. 1 *The Alaskan Happy Dog Trilogy*) Fairbanks, AK: Pyrola Publishing, 1991.

Shields, Mary. *Loving a Happy Dog*. (Vol. 2 *The Alaskan Happy Dog Trilogy*) Fairbanks, AK: Pyrola Publishing, 1992.

Shields, Mary. *Secret Messages: Training a Happy Sled Dog*. (Vol. 3 *The Alaskan Happy Dog Trilogy*) Fairbanks, AK: Pyrola Publishing, 1993.

HOW-TO BOOKS (Some of the information will be outdated!)

Attla, George with Bella Levorsen. *Everything I Know about Training and Racing Sled Dogs*. Rome, NY: Arner Publications, Inc., 1974.

Collins, Miki and Julie. *Dog Driver: A Guide for the Serious Musher*. Loveland, CO: Alpine Publications, 1991.

Flanders, Nöel K. *The Joy of Running Sled Dogs: A Step-by-Step Guide*. Loveland, CO: Alpine Publications, 1989.

Levorsen, Bella, ed. *Mush! A Beginner's Manual of Sled Dog Training*. Westmoreland, NY: Arner Publications, Inc., 1976.

Swenson, Rick with Steve Chamberlain. *The Secrets of Long Distance Training and Racing.* Wasilla, AK: L&B Color Printing, 1987.

Vaudrin, Bill. *Racing Alaskan Sled Dogs.* Anchorage, AK: Alaska Northwest Publishing Company, 1976.

Welch, Jim. *The Speed Mushing Manual: How to Train Racing Sled Dogs.* Eagle River, AK: Sirius Publishing, 1989.

MISCELLANEOUS BOOKS

Anderson, LaVere. *Balto: Sled Dog of Alaska.* Champaign, IL: Garrard Publishing Company, 1976.

Casey, Brigid and Wendy Haugh. *Sled Dogs.* New York: Dodd, Mead & Company, 1983.

Cellura, Dominique. (translated by Kaye Guerin Mann) *Travelers of the Cold: Sled Dogs of the Far North.* Anchorage, AK: Alaska Northwest Books, 1990.

Cooper, Michael. *Racing Sled Dogs: An Original North American Sport.* New York: Clarion Books, 1988.

Coppinger, Lorna with the ISDRA. *The World of Sled Dogs: From Siberia to Sport Racing.* New York: Howell Book House, 1977.

Hedin, Robert and Gary Holthaus, eds. *Alaska: Reflections on Land and Spirit.* Tucson: University of Arizona Press, 1989.

Olesen, Dave. *Cold Nights, Fast Trails: Reflections of a Modern Dog Musher.* Minocqua, WI: NorthWord Press, Inc., 1989.

Reit, Seymour. *Race Against Death: A True Story of the Far North.* New York: Dodd, Mead & Company, 1976.

Ring, Elizabeth. *Sled Dogs: Arctic Athletes.* Brookfield, CT: The Millbrook Press, 1994.

MAGAZINE ARTICLES

"1991 KNOM IDITAROD DIARY©." *Team & Trail* June, July, August 1991.

Alaska, particularly March 1990, 1991, 1992, 1993, 1994, and 1995 — Iditarod Issues.

Beargrease Hike! 1989 Race Issue, April 1989, October 1989, Mid-December 1989, 1991 Race Issue.

Bridgman, Joe. "Riddles Solves the Problem." *Women's Sports* June 1985: 19-20.

Brody, Liz. "A Shaggy-Dog Story from Alaska." *Shape* February 1994: 110-113.

Burian, Peter. *Outdoor Photographer* February 1993.

Butcher, Susan. "Thousand-Mile Race to Nome: A Woman's Icy Struggle." *National Geographic* March 1983: 411-422.

Clifton, Merritt. "Dogs on Ice: Is It Exploitation?" *The Animals' Agenda* January/February 1990: 47-49.

Current Biography Yearbook 1991. Entry for Susan Butcher: 96-99.

Derr, Mark. "The Perilous Iditarod." *The Atlantic Monthly* March 1995: 119-123.

"Dog Sled Race Concludes." *Facts on File* 11 August 1994: 576.

"Dog Star." *Time* 26 March 1990: 75.

Doherty, Jim. "A Legend Still Lives as Sled Dogs Race Across the Snows." *Smithsonian* March 1983: 89-97.

Elements: Journal of Outdoor Experience Autumn/Winter 1992 (Iditarod-related issue).

Fisher, Eugene. "Weather Ops: Here's the background you'll need to walk away from an arctic shoot with amazing results." *Outdoor Photographer* February 1995: 44-46 and 78.

"For the Record." *Sports Illustrated* 25 March 1991: 86.

"For the Record." *Sports Illustrated* 23 March 1992: 90.

"Happy Trails to Sue." *Sports Illustrated* 30 March 1987: 12.

Horan, Kevin. "Dogging It Through the Wilderness." *National Wildlife* February/March 1986: 40-45.

"Huskies Hounded." *The Economist* 5 March 1994: 104.

"The Ice Queen." *Newsweek* 26 March 1990: 45.

Iditarod Runner Iditarod Trail Committee 1991 Annual to 1995 (6 issues per year).

Info by ISDRA (International Sled Dog Racing Association) March 1991, April 1991, June/July 1991.

"An Intensive Drive." *Women's Sports & Fitness* March 1989: 66-67.

"It's Smooth Sailing for Susan." *Country Woman* January/February 1992: 48.

Jones, Robert F. "Man's Best Friends." *Sports Illustrated* 27 March 1989: 40-47.

Krakauer, Jon. "Butcher's Doggone Dynasty." *Outside* July 1988: 78-82 and 98-100.

Lawrence, Katherine. "Man's Best Friend Has Pull Where It Counts." *Macleans* 2 March 1981: 12-14.

Leerhsen, Charles. "For the Love of Mushing." *Newsweek* 21 March 1983: 79.

"Manly Mush." *Macleans* 25 March 1991: 27.

"Master Psychologist." *Sports Illustrated* 21 March 1994: 11.

McCoy, Kathleen. "Arctic Dreams." *Women's Sports & Fitness* February 1987: 22-27 and 72.

Mueller, Larry. "Arctic Adventures." *Outdoor Life* January 1991: 16-17.

Mueller, Larry. "Making Time." *Outdoor Life* February 1991: 18-23.

Munson, Russell. "Iditarod's Air Force Mushes On." *Flying* July 1992: 61-69.

"Mush Man." *U. S. News & World Report* 27 March 1989: 14.

"Mush Mother." *U. S. News & World Report* 28 March 1988: 11.

"Musher." *The New Yorker* 5 October 1987: 34-35.

Mushing September/October 1991, May/June 1992, and November/December 1992 to 1995. (6 issues per year)

"No Place Like Nome." *Sports Illustrated* 1 April 1985: 28-29.

Paulsen, Gary. "Dogspirit." *Lands' End* March 1991: 92-93. (Catalog)

Peterson, B. "Moose." *Popular Photography* February 1993: 10-11 and 63.

Phillips, Rob. "Grueling Iditasport Tests Spirit, Endurance." *Compass Readings* February 1991: 98-102.

Phinizy, Coles. "Pull North to Nome." *Sports Illustrated* 19 January 1976: 64-72.

Posey, Sam. "Runyan Racing 20DT: Unless you're the lead dog, the scenery never changes." *Road & Track* April 1992: 94-99.

"Racing Across Alaska." *National Geographic World* January 1981: 29-35.

Reed, Susan. "Racing Across a Lonely Frontier." *People Weekly* 16 April 1984: 28-35.

Riddles, Libby with Anita Verschoth. "Valiant Lady." *Sports Illustrated* 17 February 1986: 91-104.

Scott, Mary. "Coldwear Fabrics Guide." *Outdoor Photographer* November 1994: 68-70 and 96.

Skow, John. "Here's One Musher Who Is No Lazy Susan." *Sports Illustrated* 15 February 1988: 8-9.

Skow, John. "On, Hermit! On, Sluggo!" *Outside* March 1991: 58-64 & 128-130.

Souders, Paul. "Hot Shots on Cold Days: An Alaskan Primer on Staying Warm and Shooting Well." *Petersen's Photographic* February 1994: 28-31 and 124.

Steptoe, Sonja. "The Dogged Pursuit of Excellence." *Sports Illustrated* 11 February 1991: 190-204.

Strand, Mark. "Libby Riddles: Racing to Victory. A Woman Challenges the Elements and Wins." *Vogue* December 1985: 332-333.

Sturgis, Kent. "Butcher Wants to Be No. 1." *The Sporting News* 13 March 1989: 46.

Sullivan, Robert. "Dogged Pursuit." *Sports Illustrated* 16 March 1987: 9-10.

"Swenson attempts fifth Iditarod win." *Dog World* March 1991: 53.

"Swingley Wins Iditarod." *Facts on File* 6 April 1995: 259.

Trausch, Susan. "Call of the Wild." *The Boston Globe Magazine* 18 October 1987: 22-50.

"Turning Men Into Mush." *Sports Illustrated* 20 March 1989: 13-16.

Ward, Alex. "A Classic Race: Man and Dog vs. Alaska." *New York Times Magazine* 24 February 1985: 31-32.

Warden, John W. "Shooting Below Zero: How to Turn Freezing Temperatures into Hot Images." *Petersen's Photographic* December 1992: 56-58.

Wills, David K. "For the Love of Man." *HSUS News* Summer 1991 Volume 36 Number 3: 10-12.

"Woman Mushes Way to Iditarod Victory." *Sporting News* 1 April 1985: 6.

"You Call This A Vacation?" *Women's Sports & Fitness* July 1987: 50.

NEWSPAPERS

Albom, Mitch. *Detroit Free Press*, March 1991 series of twelve columns.

Anchorage Daily News, March 1992, and March 1993 to 1995 (daily subscription).

Dodd, Mike. "Surgeon hitches his desire for action to a sled team." *USA Today*, March 3, 1995, p. 3C.

Kaplan, Lissa. "Call of the Wild warms his heart: Swenson faces Iditarod defense." *Dayton Daily News*, Feb. 28, 1992, pp. D1 & 4.

The Nome Nugget, March 11, 1993.

Rosen, Yereth. "High-Tech Mushing on the Iditarod Trail." *The Christian Science Monitor*, March 26, 1993, p. 14.

Rowell, Galen. "Mush! A rookie takes a spin behind a team of sled dogs." *The Columbus Dispatch*, Sept. 4, 1994, pp. G1 & 2.

Wasilla Frontiersman Iditarod Special Edition 1991, 1992, 1993 and also March 20, 1991.

VIDEOS

Videos Produced by KTUU, Anchorage, Channel 2:

Iditarod 1987 - The Iditarod Race: 1,049 Miles Across Alaska! SkyRiver Films, 1987.

Trail to Gold! The Iditarod History and the 1988 Journey, Alaska Video Publishing, Inc., 1988.

Iditarod 1989 and Iditarod - The Greatest Race on Earth, Alaska Video Publishing, Inc., 1989.

Born to Run and Iditarod XVIII: An Alaskan Odyssey 1990, Alaska Video Publishing, Inc., 1990.

Gold and Glory: Iditarod XIX, 1991, Alaska Video Publishing, Inc., 1991.

The Long Run: Iditarod XX, 1992, Alaska Video Publishing, Inc., 1992.

The Distant Place: Iditarod XXI, 1993, SkyRiver Films, 1993.

Passage to Nome: Iditarod XXII, 1994, SkyRiver Films, 1994.

Other Iditarod-related Videos

Beyond Courage: The Dogs of the Iditarod, an Iditarod Trail Committee Production, 1993.

Season of the Sled Dog, (about Mary Shields), Pyrola Publishing, 1988.

The Susan Butcher Story: Alaska's Great Race, Pal Productions, 1988.

Those Wonderful Dogs, The National Geographic Society, 1988.

ABC's *Wide World of Sports* coverage 1991, 1992, and 1993.

MISCELLANEOUS SOURCES

1995 Iditarod Trail Sled Dog Race Musher's/Veterinarian's Handbook, Iditarod Trail Committee, 1995.

Cold Weather Wisdom: Your Guide to Winter Warmth and Northern Outfitters Clothing, Northern Outfitters™.

The Dogsledder's Resource Guide, Ester, AK: Marketing Association for Sled Dog Publications, 1993.

Iditarod Sled Dog Race 1992 Limited Edition Collector Cards, 110 Cards, Orlando, FL: Motor Art, Inc., 1992.

1991 Iditarod Trail International Sled Dog Race, Iams Company poster.

Iditarod Trail Map and Guide: Past to Present. Anchorage, AK: The Maps Place, 1991.

Iditarod Trail Sled Dog Race Press Packet 1993, Iditarod Trail Committee, 1993.

International Directory of Companies and Clubs & Sled Dog Events Calendar 1994-95. The International Council for Sleddog Sports (ICSS) and Mushing Magazine.

Schultz, Jeff. Yearly calendars, 1990-1995.

Sled Dog Care Guidelines, Mush with PRIDE (Providing Responsible Information on a Dog's Environment), 1993.

Sled Dog Racing: The World's Fastest Growing Winter Sport. ISDRA (International Sled Dog Racing Association, Inc.).

Swenson, Rick. *Pawprint News*, March 1, 1993.

Van Zyle, Jon. Calendar, 1990 and 1991.

The days have all run together. Faces, names, places blend. The fact is Iditarod is much more than a race. It is the knitting together of a dozen or so communities strung along a vast landscape of wild reaches. It is a chance to meet and share the trail with hundreds of people. You don't lock doors or worry about your possessions. You just go, and it is as if your soul breathes in the country with some deep, primordial longing.

Shannon Lowry
Managing Editor, Alaska magazine

Permissions
Acknowledgments

The author gratefully acknowledges permission to reprint quotations from the following sources:

"Hobo" Jim Varsos, "Iditarod Trail" song, ©Hobo Jim Music. Reprinted courtesy of Jim Varsos.

p. 2 Sam Posey, ABC *Wide World of Sports*, 1992. Reprinted courtesy of Sam Posey.

p. 4 Gary Paulsen, "Dogspirit" from *Lands' End*, March 1991. Reprinted courtesy of Gary Paulsen.

p. 6 Rick Armstrong from "1992 Iditarod Race Lineup" in the *1992 Iditarod Race Program*. Reprinted courtesy of *Alaska* magazine.

p. 18 Dick Mackey from Lew Freedman's *Iditarod Classics: Tales of the Trail Told by the Men and Women Who Race Across Alaska*, Epicenter Press, 1992. Reprinted courtesy of Epicenter Press.

p. 24 Martin Buser, from the *Iditarod Runner*, February 1994. Published by the Iditarod Trail Committee.

p. 42 Frank Gerjevic from "Spirit of adventure survives Iditarod hype" in the *Anchorage Daily News*, March 7, 1993. Reprinted courtesy of the *Anchorage Daily News*.

p. 50 Erin Gerrin from Tim Jones' *The Last Great Race*, Madrona Publishers, 1982. Reprinted by Stackpole Books, 1988. Used by permission of Stackpole Books.

p. 60 Ron Dalby, "Trail Boss" from *Alaska* magazine, March 1990. Reprinted courtesy of *Alaska* magazine.

p. 62 Myron Gavin from Lew Freedman's *Iditarod Classics: Tales of the Trail Told by the Men and Women Who Race Across Alaska*, Epicenter Press, 1992. Reprinted courtesy of Epicenter Press.

p. 70 Alaska Airlines advertisement from the *Iditarod Runner*, September/October 1991. Reprinted courtesy of Alaska Airlines.

p. 80 Gary Paulsen, "Dogspirit" from *Lands' End*, March 1991. Reprinted courtesy of Gary Paulsen.

p. 86 Tony Dawson from *Alaska* magazine, March 1991. Reprinted courtesy of *Alaska* magazine.

p. 98 Galen Rowell from "Mush!" in *The Columbus Dispatch*, September 4, 1994. Reprinted courtesy of Galen Rowell through the Universal Press Syndicate.

p. 98 Jack Niggemyer, from an interview with the author.

p. 113 Alastair Scott from *Tracks Across Alaska: A Sled Dog Journey*, The Atlantic Monthly Press, ©1990 by Alastair Scott. Used by permission of Grove/Atlantic, Inc.

p. 122 Stan Smith, from the *Iditarod Runner*, February 1994. Published by the Iditarod Trail Committee.

p. 134 Rick Swenson: The following excerpts are reprinted courtesy of SPORTS ILLUS-TRATED from the March 27, 1989 issue. Copyright ©1989, Time Inc. "Man's Best Friends" by Robert F. Jones. All Rights Reserved.

p. 146 Libby Riddles and Tim Jones from *Race Across Alaska: First woman to win the Iditarod tells her story*, Stackpole Books, 1988. Used by permission of Stackpole Books.

p. 148 Bruce Hamler from Rob Phillips' "Grueling Iditasport Tests Spirit, Endurance" in Northwest Airlines' *Compass Readings*, February 1991. Reprinted courtesy of Rob Phillips.

pp. 151 - 152 Nicki J. Nielsen from *The Iditarod: Women on the Trail*, Wolfdog Publications, 1986. Reprinted courtesy of Nicki J. Nielsen.

p. 156 from *Alaska* magazine, July 1986. Reprinted courtesy of *Alaska* magazine.

p. 163 Joan Brockelsby, "The sun, the snow, and your eyes" from *Mushing* magazine, September/October 1991. Reprinted with permission from *Mushing* magazine, P.O. Box 149, Ester, AK 99725 USA, phone/fax 907-479-0454.

p. 165 from *Alaska* magazine, July 1987. Reprinted courtesy of *Alaska* magazine.

p. 168 Bert Hanson, from the *Iditarod Runner*, 1991 Annual. Published by the Iditarod Trail Committee.

p. 173 from "Sled Dog Racing: The World's Fastest Growing Winter Sport," a pamphlet published by ISDRA, the International Sled Dog Racing Association, Inc. Reprinted courtesy of ISDRA.

pp. 178 - 179 Patti Harper from *Alaska* magazine, March 1990. Reprinted courtesy of *Alaska* magazine.

p. 184 Bill Vaudrin from Ron Wendt's "Not old-time mushing, but darn close," in the *Wasilla Frontiersman*, 1991 Iditarod Special Section. Reprinted courtesy of the *Wasilla Frontiersman*.

p. 216 Sam Posey from ABC's *Wide World of Sports*, 1993. Reprinted courtesy of Sam Posey.

pp. 222 - 223 Dave Olesen from *Cold Nights, Fast Trails: Reflections of a Modern Dog Musher*, NorthWord Press, Inc., 1989. Reprinted courtesy of NorthWord Press, Inc.

p. 226 Mary Shields from her video *Season of the Sled Dog*, Pyrola Publishing, 1988. Reprinted courtesy of Mary Shields, Pyrola Publishing, P.O. Box 80961, Fairbanks, AK 99708.

pp. 229 - 230 Alastair Scott from *Tracks Across Alaska: A Sled Dog Journey*, The Atlantic Monthly Press, ©1990 by Alastair Scott. Used by permission of Grove/Atlantic, Inc.

pp. 231 - 232 Susan Butcher, "Thousand-Mile Race to Nome: A Woman's Icy Struggle" from *National Geographic*, March 1983. Reprinted courtesy of *National Geographic*.

pp. 234 - 235 and 236 Libby Riddles and Tim Jones from *Race Across Alaska: First woman to win the Iditarod tells her story*, Stackpole Books, 1988. Used by permission of Stackpole Books.

p. 238 Terry Adkins from the video *Passage to Nome: Iditarod XXII, 1994*, SkyRiver Films, 1994. Reprinted courtesy of Tim Woolston and Greg Lytle, Producers, KTUU-TV, Channel 2 Broadcasting, Anchorage, Alaska.

p. 247 Joe Garnie from Lew Freedman's *Iditarod Classics: Tales of the Trail Told by the Men and Women Who Race Across Alaska*, Epicenter Press, 1992. Reprinted courtesy of Epicenter Press.

p. 250 Kathy Halverson from Lew Freedman's *Iditarod Classics: Tales of the Trail Told by the Men and Women Who Race Across Alaska*, Epicenter Press, 1992. Reprinted courtesy of Epicenter Press.

p. 254 Miki and Julie Collins from *Dog Driver*, Alpine Publications, 1991. Reprinted courtesy of Alpine Publications.

pp. 265 - 266 Jim Welch from *The Speed Mushing Manual*, Sirius Publishing, 1989. Reprinted courtesy of Sirius Publishing, Box 770404, Eagle River, AK 99577.

p. 267 Dick Mackey from Lew Freedman's *Iditarod Classics: Tales of the Trail Told by the Men and Women Who Race Across Alaska*, Epicenter Press, 1992. Reprinted courtesy of Epicenter Press.

p. 268 Gary Paulsen from an interview by Northern Minnesota Correspondent Larry Oakes which appeared in the October 1989 *Beargrease Hike!* Reprinted courtesy of the Minneapolis *Star Tribune*.

pp. 270 - 271 Susan Butcher from *The Susan Butcher Story* video, Pal Productions, 1988. Reprinted courtesy of Pal Productions.

pp. 271 and 410 Jon Van Zyle from Lew Freedman's *Iditarod Classics: Tales of the Trail Told by the Men and Women Who Race Across Alaska*, Epicenter Press, 1992. Reprinted courtesy of Epicenter Press.

p. 274 Ramey Smyth, from the *Iditarod Runner*, September 1993. Published by the Iditarod Trail Committee.

p. 280 John Barron, from the *Iditarod Runner*, 1991 Annual. Published by the Iditarod Trail Committee.

p. 288 Peter Goodman, "Second start the real one" from the *Anchorage Daily News*, March 7, 1994. Reprinted courtesy of the *Anchorage Daily News*.

p. 289 Martin Buser in Bill Sherwonit's "A Chat with the Champ" from the *1995 Iditarod Race Program*. Reprinted courtesy of *Alaska* magazine.

p. 290 Catherine Stadem from *Alaska* magazine, March 1994. Reprinted courtesy of *Alaska* magazine.

p. 292 Nan Elliot, "Struggling for Safety" from the *Anchorage Daily News*, March 25, 1995. Reprinted courtesy of the *Anchorage Daily News*.

p. 293 Lew Freedman, "Nome offers chance to work on chip shot" from the *Anchorage Daily News*, March 21, 1994. Reprinted courtesy of the *Anchorage Daily News*.

p. 296 Alan D. Hyde, from an interview with the author.

p. 312 Cliff Roberson from "1994 Iditarod Race Lineup" in the *1994 Iditarod Race Program*. Reprinted courtesy of *Alaska* magazine.

p. 358 Joe Redington, Sr. from Kim Heacox's *Iditarod Spirit*, Graphic Arts Center Publishing, 1991. Reprinted courtesy of Graphic Arts Center Publishing.

p. 376 Burt Bomhoff from Yereth Rosen's "High-tech Mushing on the Iditarod trail" in the *Christian Science Monitor*, March 26, 1993. Reprinted courtesy of Yereth Rosen.

p. 382 Bruce Hamler from Rob Phillips' "Grueling Iditasport Tests Spirit, Endurance" in Northwest Airlines' *Compass Readings*, February 1991. Reprinted courtesy of Rob Phillips.

p. 386 Alastair Scott from *Tracks Across Alaska: A Sled Dog Journey*, The Atlantic Monthly Press, ©1990 by Alastair Scott. Used by permission of Grove/Atlantic, Inc.

p. 396 Shannon Lowry from "No Roads lead to Rohn," *Alaska* magazine, March 1990. Reprinted courtesy of *Alaska* magazine.

Index

Photos are indicated by **boldface** type.

401

Running the Iditarod completely changed my life.
It made me aware I could do anything if I put my mind
to it.

Jon Van Zyle
Iditarod finisher and
official Iditarod artist

About the Author

Although Alaska is a favorite travel destination, Mary H. Hood has always lived in the Midwest: in Indiana, Minnesota, and Ohio. Along with her brother and sister, she grew up with a Collie Shepherd, Scottish Terrier, and Labrador Retriever; Mary now shares her home with a German Shepherd named Sheena. While Sheena does not pull a sled, she is a faithful companion for Mary's two young boys, guards their property, and would rather play than eat.

While Mary lived in Minnesota, she was fortunate to attend and photograph the 500-mile Beargrease Sled Dog Marathon, which ignited her already established interest in dog mushing. When she returned home, she began visiting her local library to acquire more information about mushing. She quickly became frustrated with the lack of consolidated material about the Iditarod. Her obsession with collecting this scattered information led to the creation of *A Fan's Guide to the Iditarod*. Mary's research was key to the foundation of the book, but her own experiences as photographer, race volunteer, and interviewer of countless race competitors, villagers, sponsors, volunteers, and experts in the field of dog mushing allow her to combine the facts of the Iditarod "story" with all of the emotion associated with this grueling, exhilarating race.

Unconventional sporting events are not a new interest for Mary. In junior high and high school, she acted as crew for her father on a Hobie Cat 16 racing catamaran. She and her parents enjoyed traveling the Midwest racing circuit and also relished recreational sailing in the

Author Mary H. Hood holding two of Chief Veterinarian Karin Schmidt's purebred Siberian Huskies.
Photo by Paul Rupple.

Atlantic, the Pacific, and the Great Lakes.

To fulfill her high school foreign language requirement, Mary chose to study Latin. She immediately became involved in the National Catapult Contest and began building Zephyrus, a full-size, operational counterweight catapult. Zephyrus holds the world record for hurling a 40-pound rock 798 feet and a 100-pound boulder 579 feet. Mary's exploits were featured in a *Sports Illustrated* article, on the front page of *The New York Times'* second section, and garnered her an appearance on "To Tell the Truth" as the "real Mary Hyde."

High school Latin was so much fun that Mary decided to earn a double major in Classics and English at Earlham College, where she graduated Phi Beta Kappa. For the next six years, Mary taught junior high and high school Latin and English, bringing Latin to life for her students through chariot races around the Indianapolis 500 Motor Speedway racetrack, toga parties, and excursions to local theatrical productions.

Between the birth of their two sons, Mary and her husband (college sweetheart) Stephen designed a brick ranch home, and Mary spent many hours overseeing and photographing all aspects of its construction.

A stay-at-home Mom, Mary now works on writing and photography whenever she can. Her hobbies include baking, reading, landscaping her five-acre lot, watching PBS's *Mystery*, traveling with her family, playing with her sons and dog, and following the Iditarod year round. She hopes you enjoy reading her book. She welcomes comments and suggestions and may be reached through Alpine Publications.

CHUKCHI SEA

Kotzebue

ARCTIC

Cape South Wales

Teller

Candle

27 26 25

Nome

24 22

18a 17a 16a

23 21

20 19 15a

1a 14a

17a 13

Norton Sound

16a 12

Yukon River

15a 11 10

14a

9

Bethel

Kuskokwim River

BERING SEA

Mt. Redoubt ▲

Dillingham

King Salmon

Kodi

ALEUTIAN ISLANDS

THE IDIT